1a, 1b

¡Avancemos!

Lesson Plans

McDougal Littell

A DIVISION OF HOUGHTON MIFFLIN COMPANY

Evanston, Illinois • Boston • Dallas

ISBN-13: 978-0-618-75325-3
ISBN-10: 0-618-75325-7   1 2 3 4 5 6 7 8 9 – MDO – 10 09 08 07 06
Internet: www.mcdougallittell.com

Contents

Lesson Plan Overview

1. Introduction to lesson plans

It is natural for teachers to take time adjusting to a new textbook program, especially to set an appropriate pace. To help you teach successfully right from the start, the *¡Avancemos!* program provides a wealth of tools and resources.

In this book, you will find detailed lesson plans for the different sections of each *¡Avancemos!* unit. These lesson plans offer strategies for presenting material on a section-by-section basis and are designed to show the variety of teaching options available. In general, each lesson plan includes the sections to be taught in one traditional 50-minute class period.

2. Using the lesson plans

As you will see from the Sample Lesson Plan Pacing Guides on pp. ix–x, the suggested pacing cycle for each *¡Avancemos!* lesson is nine days for traditional schedules and five days for block schedules. It is very important to be flexible in order to achieve an appropriate pace of instruction and still teach the required material in a timely fashion. The lesson plans contained in this book offer a wealth of options for teaching and practicing the material, managing the classroom, assessing, and reteaching. You may want to consider all the options within each lesson plan and choose the most appropriate ones according to your particular classroom needs and schedules.

Lesson plan structure

- **Objectives** The main objectives for each textbook section are included here for your use during lesson planning.

- **Course Objectives** The Sunshine State Standards for each lesson are succinctly listed for your convenience.

- **Focus and Motivate** Each lesson plan provides a suggestion for how to grab your students' attention at the beginning of the·lesson.

- **Teach** The main points that you need to cover in each lesson are clearly laid out in an easy-to-follow checklist.

- **Practice and Apply** This list contains suggestions of the activities to assign in class so that your students practice the material you present in each lesson.

- **Assess and Reteach** *¡Avancemos!* provides a variety of ways to assess that your students have understood the material and you can choose the best method for your classes from the options provided.

- **Optional Resources** The wealth of resources available within the *¡Avancemos!* program are listed here with page references for all related material. You will find this useful as you vary and enrich each lesson to suit the needs of your classroom.

- **Technology Tools** *¡Avancemos!* is supported by a robust technology package that offers tools for you as well as many ways to provide your students with additional practice.

3. Adjusting to middle school

Schedules and curricula for middle school foreign language classes vary widely across school systems. You may find it necessary to adjust the suggested pacing guide depending on whether your classes meet every day or every other day, for the entire school year or for half the year, or some other variation.

Some schools offer half-year programs, in which students study two different languages, each for half of the school year. Others offer exploratory programs in which students study more than two languages for less than half the year each. Regardless of any curriculum variation, you will find the *¡Avancemos!* program easily adaptable to your situation.

Special elements have been added to make *¡Avancemos!* more approachable for middle school students. The Juegos y diversiones page, which offers fun and exciting games to help students review key vocabulary and grammar concepts, gives students the chance to learn in an active way. Many practice activities have also been added to give students more opportunities to master the material by interacting with their classmates.

If you refer to the Sample Lesson Plan Pacing Guides on pp. ix–x, you will see that the Juegos y diversiones page is suggested to be taught on the same day as Todo junto. These two elements are also included in the same lesson plan. However, these games can be used at any point at the end of the lesson for review. You may find that it works best, for example, on the same day as the Lectura or Lectura cultural, or with the Repaso de la lección.

4. Traditional scheduling

Traditional scheduling refers to classes of 45–50 minutes in duration that meet every school day for an entire school year. Teachers will find these lesson plans well suited for their schedule, as each lesson plan details the material to be taught in a 45–50 minute class.

The eight plans for Lesson 1 correspond to the first eight days of the teaching cycle as depicted on the 50-Minute Sample Lesson Plan Pacing Guide on p. ix. The ninth day of the cycle is designated for the Lesson 1 Test and does not require a lesson plan.

Lesson 2 of each unit contains two more sections than Lesson 1: Comparación cultural and Repaso inclusivo. As a result, the lesson plans do not correspond exactly to the Pacing Guide. The first six lesson plans correspond to the first six days of the Lesson 2 cycle (days 10–15 in the Pacing Guide on p. ix). The next day of the Pacing Guide calls for the completion of the Lectura cultural and the Repaso de la lección. The lesson plan for the Lectura cultural includes the Proyectos culturales, which are omitted from the Pacing Guide. The Repaso de la lección has a distinct lesson plan. These three sections are all optional, and can be used at your discretion. The Repaso de la lección does offer students excellent opportunities for review. The final lesson plan contains the Comparación cultural and Repaso inclusivo, which are both on the final day of the Pacing Guide, following the assessment day.

Please note that the lesson plan for the Repaso de la lección lists the Lesson 2 Test under Assess and Reteach while the lesson plan for the Comparación cultural and Repaso inclusivo lists the Unit Test. It is not necessary to give both tests. If you decide to give the Lesson 2 Test and not the

Unit Test, you can follow the suggested sequence in the Pacing Guide. If you decide to give the Unit Test instead, then students would benefit from completing some or all of the Repaso inclusivo. In that case, we recommend switching days 17 and 18 of the Pacing Guide to afford the students extra review time.

It is important to note that both the lesson plans and the Pacing Guide on p. ix are suggestions, and you can feel free to adjust them. We recommend striving to cover the core instruction in ¡Avancemos! from the Unit Opener (in Lesson 1) or Lesson Opener (in Lesson 2) through Todo junto. Once you complete the Todo junto section of a lesson, you can decide which remaining sections to teach and which to teach partially, assign as homework, or skip completely, as your schedule dictates. While the Todo junto section reviews the content from the entire lesson, we recommend assigning further review such as the Repaso de la lección pages prior to giving a Lesson or Unit Test.

The Unit Opener and Lesson Opener are important for establishing the cultural context and learning goals of the unit and lesson, in terms of location, culture, vocabulary, grammar, and communication. However, establishing the goals and the cultural context does not require a great deal of time. You might focus initially on pointing out the essential parts of these pages. Later in the program, if you find that you have extra time, you may choose to explore these pages more in-depth.

5. Keeping the pace: Adjusting for block scheduling

Block scheduling varies from school to school. Sometimes block schedule classes meet less frequently than traditional classes, or for only part of the school year. While they are always longer than traditional classes, their exact duration varies. For our purposes, we are assuming that block schedule classes are 90 minutes in duration. The lesson plans contained herein are easily adapted to this schedule. Since each lesson plan contains the material for a 45–50 minute class, two lesson plans can be taught in each 90-minute class. For 90-minute classes, each ¡Avancemos! lesson can be completed in about five days. Just as with the 50-minute classes, you can adapt the lesson plan and pacing guide as necessary.

You will note differences between the 50-Minute Pacing Guide and the 90-Minute Pacing Guide, especially in the sequence of instruction. For example, the Conexiones feature appears with the Lectura on day 7 of the 50-minute guide, followed by the Repaso de la lección on day 8. On the 90-minute guide, however, the Conexiones feature comes after the Lesson 1 Test on day 5. This change permits the teaching of the Repaso de la lección on day 4, giving students more time to review for the test. The only difference in Lesson 2 is the addition of the Proyectos culturales on day 9. Since this feature is optional, you may only want to teach it if you have ample time.

While the total amount of class time is the same for the 50- and 90-minute cycles of each unit (900 minutes), the time allotted to each lesson section is sometimes less in the 90-minute cycle. This difference never amounts to more than five minutes and is easily corrected by omitting the Warm Up for the second half of each day's lesson. However, you may find additional adjustments necessary in order to complete each lesson in the time allotted. In cases where time does not permit completion of the entire lesson, focus first on the core sections, then choose from the remaining sections based on your instructional needs.

Another difference between the 50- and 90-minute cycles is the assignment of homework. Since each class of the 90-minute guide essentially covers the same amount of material as two days of the 50-minute guide, then two days worth of homework is assigned on each day of the 90-minute guide. This amount of homework may or may not be realistic, depending on how frequently the 90-minute classes meet. You may need to be selective about the homework you assign, being careful to assign homework that will give students the chance to practice what they have learned without assigning excessive amounts.

6. Making choices for variety

The *¡Avancemos!* program affords many opportunities to vary instruction and assessment that enhance students' learning experience. For example, you can present the Telehistoria activities on video or on audio, or by reading the Telehistoria aloud while students follow along in the text. You can also have students read the script aloud or role play it with their classmates. You can choose from a great variety of in-class activities in the Pupil Edition, the Teacher's Edition, and ancillary materials, such as the Situational Transparencies from the Unit Transparency Books. Additional options for presenting new material include the Vocabulary and Grammar Presentation Transparencies.

As you know, students retain what they have learned more readily if it is reinforced with challenging and fun review and homework options. *¡Avancemos!* offers many different formats for homework and review. The Assess and Reteach portion of the Lesson Plans lists Para y piensa activities, *Cuaderno: práctica por niveles,* and *Cuaderno para hispanohablantes* for almost every section of the unit. The workbooks contain activities of different levels. Level A activities offer much more structure and guidance, level B activities are similar in difficulty to activities in the Pupil Edition, and level C activities require higher levels of critical thinking. These activity sections all focus on the same core grammar and vocabulary skills, and completion of these activities will move students toward mastery of these skills regardless of level.

Toward the end of each lesson, Repaso de la lección and En resumen pages are included under Assess and Reteach. These review pages, in addition to the Repaso inclusivo, can be used as homework or classwork during the unit, provided you assign material that the students have learned. The lesson plan for the Repaso de la lección day also lists the Review Games Online as a homework option. There are many other activities on Classzone.com that can be assigned throughout the unit as well. The Teacher s Edition contains many activities that can be used for classwork or homework expansion. You will also find specific references to the Reteaching and Practice Copymasters review pages from the Unit Resource Book in the Para y piensa Ongoing Assessment boxes in the Teacher s Edition. Many other ancillary materials also provide excellent reinforcement while piquing student interest, such as *Lecturas para todos, AvanzaCómics* comic books, *TPRS, Unit Resource Books,* and *Unit Transparency Books.*

¡Avancemos! also offers a four-tiered differentiated assessment program which includes Pre-AP Assessment, for more advanced students; On-level Assessment, for students working at the level of the Pupil Edition; Modified Assessment, for at-risk or slower-paced learners; and Heritage Learners Assessment, for native Spanish-speakers. These testing materials have leveling similar to the *Cuaderno.* Again, regardless of level, all testing materials assess comprehension of the same vocabulary and grammar.

The method of usage for leveled materials is at your discretion. Some teachers prefer to level classes as a whole, while other teaches find it useful to level individual students based on each student's learning needs and level of ability. For students who have specialized education plans that require modified testing and practice, you can use the level A *Cuaderno* activities and Modified Assessment book.

7. Making choices for pacing

If this is your first year using the *¡Avancemos!* program, you may want to plan to skip some of the Pupil Edition sections that are not considered core. Especially at the beginning of the school year, it is most important to give students ample time to practice the essential vocabulary and grammar before moving on to sections geared toward expansion. As the school year progresses and you become more comfortable with the program, you may find that you have the extra time to teach more sections from the Pupil Edition. If this is the case, try them out as the schedule allows. You will find that these sections provide a refreshing enhancement to language and culture practice in your classroom. You may wish to concentrate on teaching more of the expansion pages in your second year with the program, and adding more each subsequent year. This type of enrichment will give students a more complete (and fun!) language-learning experience.

Many teachers find themselves at the end of the school year but not the end of their textbook. The *¡Avancemos!* Pupil Edition has been designed with essential and non-essential units. Teachers are expected to complete Units 1-6, while Units 7 and 8 are optional. All material—vocabulary and grammar—from Units 7 and 8 are spiraled into the Pupil Edition of the next level. In other words, the vocabulary and grammar from Units 7 and 8 of Level 1b will all appear at some point during Units 1–6 of Level 2. In this way, students will learn no less if you do not teach Units 7 and 8. Furthermore, students who do go on to learn Units 7 and 8, or a portion thereof, will not see a traditional review of this material, but will be exposed to the material again as it is recycled throughout the Level 2 text.

50-Minute Sample Lesson Plan Pacing Guide
Unidad 1

Week 1	Day 1	Day 2	Day 3	Day 4	Day 5
	• Unit 1 Opener • Lesson 1 Opener • Presentación de vocabulario • Práctica de vocabulario	• Vocabulario en contexto	• Presentación de gramática • Práctica de gramática	• Gramática en contexto	• Presentación de gramática • Práctica de gramática
Week 2	**Day 6** • Todo junto • Juegos y diversiones	**Day 7** • Lectura • Conexiones	**Day 8** • Repaso de la lección	**Day 9** • Lesson 1 Test	**Day 10** • Lesson 2 Opener • Presentación de vocabulario • Práctica de vocabulario
Week 3	**Day 11** • Vocabulario en contexto	**Day 12** • Presentación de gramática • Práctica de gramática	**Day 13** • Gramática en contexto	**Day 14** • Presentación de gramática • Práctica de gramática	**Day 15** • Todo junto • Juegos y diversiones
Week 4	**Day 16** • Lectura cultural • Repaso de la lección	**Day 17** • Lesson 2 Test or Unit 1 Test	**Day 18** • Comparación cultural • Repaso inclusivo		

90-Minute Sample Lesson Plan Pacing Guide
Unidad 1

Week 1	Day 1	Day 2	Day 3	Day 4	Day 5
	• Unit 1 Opener • Lesson 1 Opener • Presentación de vocabulario • Práctica de vocabulario • Vocabulario en contexto	• Presentación de gramática • Práctica de gramática • Gramática en contexto	• Presentación de gramática • Práctica de gramática • Todo junto	• Lectura • Repaso de la lección	• Lesson 1 Test • Conexiones
Week 2	Day 6	Day 7	Day 8	Day 9	Day 10
	• Lesson 2 Opener • Presentación de vocabulario • Práctica de vocabulario • Vocabulario en contexto	• Presentación de gramática • Práctica de gramática • Gramática en contexto	• Presentación de gramática • Práctica de gramática • Todo junto • Juegos y diversiones	• Lectura cultural • Proyectos culturales • Repaso de la lección	• Lesson 2 Test or Unit 1 Test • Comparación cultural • Repaso inclusivo

Substitute Teacher Lesson Plans

Teacher name _____ Date _____ / _____ / _____

Class _____

Class period _____ Class location and meeting time _____

Culture

☐ Have students look at the *Celebraciones* Cultural Mini-lesson on pp. C____ – C____ of their text or have them preview it online at ClassZone.com. Before they read, have a pre-reading discussion about the topic based on the photos and students' prior knowledge. Have students read the text silently or do a round-robin reading by calling on different students to read aloud sentences from the text and photo captions. Have students answer the Comparación cultural questions on a separate sheet of paper. Follow up with a class discussion about the reading and students' answers to the Comparación cultural questions.

☐ Have students read the Comparación cultural spread for Unit ____ on pp. ____ – ____ of their text. If computer access is available, have students read the online version at ClassZone.com and click on the icons for expanded cultural information. After reading, have students complete the workbook pages in the *Cuaderno* that correspond to the spread (pp. ____ – ____).

☐ Copy and hand out the Fine Arts Activities for Unit ____, Lesson ____ found on pp. ____ – ____ in the Unit Resource Book for Unit ____. Post the corresponding Fine Art Transparencies (Transparencies ____ & ____ in the Unit Resource Book) on the overhead for students to view. Discuss the works and ask students to react to them. Have students complete the Fine Art Activities.

As a follow-up, have a class discussion where students share their responses to the questions.

☐ Have students review the information found in the Unit Opener for Unit ____ of their text on p. ____. If computer access is available, have students read the online version at ClassZone.com and click on the icons for expanded cultural information. Use the Map Transparency, found in the Unit Transparency Book for Unit ____. Show students the cultural segment of the video (DVD ____, Unit ____). As a follow-up, have students complete the Map/Culture Activities on pp. ____ – ____, of the Unit Resource Book for Unit ____. Use the Map/Culture Activities Answer Key on p. ____ of the Unit Resource Book to go over the answers as a class.

Additional information:

Teacher name _____ Date _____ / _____ / _____

Class _____

Class period _____ Class location and meeting time _____

Reading and Writing

☐ Have a Silent Reading Day. Have students preview and use the Strategy for the Lectura/Lectura cultural on pp. ____–____ of their text. Next, have students silently read the Lectura/Lectura cultural. After reading, have them complete the Para y piensa questions that follow. Refer to the Teacher's Edition for answers to the questions.

☐ Have students read and complete all activities for the selection on pp. ____–____ of the *Lecturas para todos* workbook. Guide students through the Reading Strategy and background information, as well as the activities that appear in the side columns of the pages. Use the Teacher's Edition of the *Lecturas para todos* text for answers to all activities. If time permits, have students listen to the recording of the reading as they follow along in their books (TXT CD ____, Track ____).

☐ Have students complete the following Escribir Activity from the Repaso inclusivo page for Unit ____ (p. ____):_____. Encourage students to plan out their writing and write a first draft before turning in their final draft. Allow students the opportunity for peer editing if time permits.

Video

☐ Copy and hand out the Video Activities Copymasters for Unit ____, Lesson ____, found on pp. ____–____ in the Unit Resource Book for Unit _____. Have students review the Presentación de vocabulario on pp. ____–____ of their text. Before viewing the video, have them complete the Pre-viewing Activity. Show the Vocabulary Video (DVD ____, Unit ____). Replay the video, and while students are watching the second time, have them complete the Viewing Activity. After they have viewed the video, have students complete the Post-viewing activity. Students can also view the video at ClassZone.com. Use the Video Activities Answer Key in the Unit Resource Book on pp. ____–____ to go over the activities as a class.

☐ Copy and hand out the Video Activities Copymasters for Unit ____, Lesson ____, found on pp. ____–____ in the Unit Resource Book for Unit _____. Have students review the Telehistoria Escena ____ on pp. ____–____ of their text. Before viewing the video, have them complete the Pre-viewing Activity. Show the Telehistoria Escena ____ Video (DVD ____, Unit ____). Replay the video, and while students are watching the second time, have them complete the Viewing Activity. After they have viewed the video, have students complete the Post-viewing Activity. Students can also view the video at ClassZone.com. Use the Video Activities Answer Key in the Unit Resource Book on pp. ____–____ to go over the activities as a class.

Additional information:

Teacher name _____ Date _____ / _____ / _____

Class _____

Class period _____ Class location and meeting time _____

ClassZone.com

☐ Have students complete the on-line Self-check Quiz(zes) for Unit ____, Lesson(s) ____ at ClassZone.com. Encourage them to use the Animated Grammar feature for further explanations of the lesson's grammar boxes and the Interactive Flashcards for help with the lesson's vocabulary.

☐ Have students click on the @HomeTutor feature at ClassZone.com and complete the self-guided leveled practice activities for Unit ____, Lesson(s) ____. Encourage them to use the Animated Grammar feature for further explanations of the lesson's grammar boxes and the Interactive Flashcards for help with the lesson's vocabulary.

☐ Have students complete the Review Games for Unit ____, Lesson(s) ____ at ClassZone.com. Encourage them to use the Animated Grammar feature for further explanations of the lesson's grammar boxes and the Interactive Flashcards for help with the lesson's vocabulary.

☐ Have students complete the practice activities for Unit _____, Lesson(s) _____ found in *The Conjugator* feature of ClassZone.com. Encourage them to use the Animated Grammar feature for further explanations of the lesson's grammar boxes and the Interactive Flashcards for help with the lesson's vocabulary.

☐ Have students complete the WebQuest for Unit _____ at ClassZone.com. Tell students to print out the charts and organizers included in the *Process* section and to follow all steps as they proceed with the activity.

Practice and Review

☐ Copy the Practice Games on pp. ____–____ of the Unit Resource Book for Unit ____ and have students complete the activities. Use the Answer Key provided on pp. ____–____ of the Unit Resource Book to go over the activities as a class.

☐ Copy the Did You Get It? Reteaching and Practice Copymasters on pp. ____–____ of the Unit Resource Book for Unit ____ and have students complete the activities. Encourage students to refer to their textbooks for help. Use the Answer Key provided on pp. ____–____ of the Unit Resource Book to go over the activities as a class.

☐ Copy the ¿Recuerdas? Reteaching and Practice Copymasters on pp. ____–____ of the Unit Resource Book for Unit ____ and have students complete the activities. Encourage students to reread those sections of their texts that introduce these topics. Use the Answer Key provided on pp. ____–____ of the Unit Resource Book to go over the activities as a class.

Additional information:

❑ Show students the Situational Transparency on p. ＿＿ of the Unit Transparency Book for Unit ＿＿ or copy and hand out the Situational Student Copymaster (without labels) on p. ＿＿ of the Unit Transparency Book. On a separate sheet of paper, have students write explanations or descriptions of what is happening in each of the illustrations. Encourage them to use as much of the unit's vocabulary as possible. Encourage students to refer to their textbooks for help. As a follow-up, have students read their descriptions aloud as others try to guess which drawing they are describing.

❑ Using the information included on the En resumen page (p. ＿＿) for Unit ＿＿, Lesson ＿＿ of their text, have students write sentences that include vocabulary words and grammar structures that were learned in the unit. Have student volunteers write their sentences on the board. Have other student volunteers come to the board and circle the vocabulary words and examples of the grammar structures used. While going over the sentences, ask students the meanings of the circled vocabulary words and have them explain the grammatical structures.

❑ Using their textbooks, have students answer all Para y piensa questions for Lesson(s) ＿＿ of Unit(s) ＿＿ on a separate sheet of paper. Encourage students to use their texts as a resource and encourage them to reread sections if they need to in order to answer the questions. Have students self-check their answers on pp. R＿＿–R＿＿ in their text when they finish.

❑ Have students complete pp. ＿＿–＿＿ in the *Cuaderno*. Encourage them to use their textbooks for help. Post answers for workbook activities (pp. ＿＿–＿＿ of the Unit Transparency Book for Unit ＿＿) on the overhead for students to see and go over them as a class.

❑ Have students complete the following Activities from Unit ＿＿, Lesson ＿＿ of their textbooks on a separate sheet of paper:

＿＿＿＿＿＿＿＿＿＿＿＿＿＿＿＿＿＿＿＿＿＿＿＿＿＿＿＿＿＿＿＿

＿＿＿＿＿＿＿＿＿＿＿＿＿＿＿＿＿＿＿＿＿＿＿＿＿＿＿＿＿＿＿＿

＿＿＿＿＿＿＿＿＿＿＿＿＿＿＿＿＿＿＿＿＿＿＿＿＿＿＿＿＿＿＿＿

Post answers for activities (pp. ＿＿–＿＿ of the Middle School Resource Book) on the overhead for students to see and go over them as a class.

❑ Provide each student with index cards and have them create their own set of flashcards for each of the words found on the En resumen page of Unit ＿＿, Lesson ＿＿ (p. ＿＿). Encourage students to draw pictures of words and terms when possible. Have students pair up and quiz each other on the vocabulary using their flashcards.

Additional information:

Feria de Málaga

OBJECTIVES
- Provide background for the topic: Feria de Málaga
- Familiarize students with the origin of the Feria de Málaga and its traditions

FOCUS AND MOTIVATE
❑ Direct students' attention to the pictures and elicit reactions.

TEACH
❑ Start by conducting the 50-minute lesson found on p. C2 of the Teacher's Edition.

❑ Direct students' attention to the pictures of the musicians on p. C2 and the *caseta* on p. C3. Tell them that, in addition to the street music, there are performances by top national stars in the *Príncipe de Asturias* Municipal Auditorium. Also tell them that the feria has a caseta— *la Caseta del Área de Juventud* —devoted entirely to younger people. Have students, in small groups, decide which three musical groups they would choose to perform at a fair in their community, and what activities and information they would present in a *caseta de juventud*. Ask them to share this information with the class.

❑ Have students do the Social Studies Connection on p. C2 of the Teacher's Edition. Have students work in small groups to research and list Málaga's imports and exports.

IEP Modification Ask students to describe *ferias* in their home countries, explaining what and how people celebrate.

PRACTICE AND APPLY
❑ Have students, in small groups, plan a fair in their community. Have them choose an occasion or theme for the fair, such as the first day of school, and decide what events they would like to include.

OPTIONAL RESOURCES

Plan
- Best Practices Toolkit

Present
- Atlas Map, UTB 1, Transparency 6

TECHNOLOGY TOOLS	
Teacher Tools	**Student Tools**
EasyPlanner CD-ROM	ClassZone.com
	Cultura interactiva
	eEdition Online or CD-ROM

Día de la Independencia

OBJECTIVES

- Provide background for the topic: Día de la Independencia.
- Familiarize students with Independence Day celebrations in Latin American countries.

STANDARDS
- 2.1 Practices and perspectives
- 3.1 Knowledge of other disciplines
- 4.2 Compare cultures

FOCUS AND MOTIVATE

- ❏ Direct students' attention to the pictures and elicit reactions. Discuss the meaning of the Fourth of July in the U.S. and how it is celebrated.

TEACH

- ❏ Start by conducting the 50-minute lesson found on p. C4 of the Teacher's Edition.
- ❏ When doing the *Cultura* section, ask students what other famous event features people carrying a torch (the Olympics). Discuss what students think that torch symbolizes.
- ❏ For the Timeline Enrichment Activity on p. C5 of the Teacher's Edition, have students work in groups of 3. Have them draw a separate time line for each of the 5 countries: Mexico, Chile, Guatemala, Costa Rica, and the U.S. Then have them create one master time line for all 5 countries.

IEP Modification Have students write a brief essay comparing the opening events of the Mexican War of Independence with those of the American Revolution.

PRACTICE AND APPLY

- ❏ Discuss how students could participate with their school in an Independence Day parade. Would they dance or sing? What would they wear?

Plan
- Best Practices Toolkit

Present
- Atlas Map, UTB 1, Transparencies 1–5

TECHNOLOGY TOOLS	
Teacher Tools	**Student Tools**
EasyPlanner CD-ROM	ClassZone.com
	Cultura interactiva
	eEdition Online or CD-ROM

El 12 de Octubre

OBJECTIVES

- Familiarize students with the meaning of El 12 de Octubre and the different ways people celebrate the holiday.
- Trace the route of Columbus's first voyage.

STANDARDS
- 2.1 Practices and perspectives
- 4.2 Compare cultures

FOCUS AND MOTIVATE

- ☐ Direct students' attention to the pictures and elicit reactions.

TEACH

- ☐ Start by conducting the 50-minute lesson found on p. C6 of the Teacher's Edition.
- ☐ Ask students to share what they know about Columbus's voyages to Latin American countries.
- ☐ Have students work in small groups to complete the Social Studies Connection on p. C6 of the Teacher's Edition. Have them draw or paste pictures of the food, plants, and animals on a map of the Americas. Display these maps in the classroom and discuss them.

IEP Modification   For the Language Arts activity on p. C7 of the Teacher's Edition, have students work with the simpler poem, *In 1492*. Review the rhyming words, read the poem to students, then have them underline the rhyming words. Have them take turns reading each verse.

PRACTICE AND APPLY

- ☐ Discuss what groups are indigenous to the U.S. What are some traditional clothes and dances students associate with them?

OPTIONAL RESOURCES

Plan
- Best Practices Toolkit

Present
- Atlas Map, UTB 1, Transparencies 1–6

TECHNOLOGY TOOLS	
Teacher Tools	**Student Tools**
EasyPlanner CD-ROM	ClassZone.com
	Cultura interactiva
	eEdition Online or CD-ROM

¡Día de los Muertos!

OBJECTIVES

- Familiarize students with Día de los Muertos celebrations in Mexico, the U.S., Central America, and South America.
- Locate Mexico, Guatemala, Ecuador, and the U.S. on a map.

> ### STANDARDS
> - 2.1 Practices and perspectives
> - 4.2 Compare cultures

FOCUS AND MOTIVATE

❑ Direct students' attention to the pictures and elicit reactions. Do these look like pictures of Halloween in the U.S.?

TEACH

❑ Start by conducting the 50-minute lesson found on p. C8 of the Teacher's Edition.

❑ Have students discuss their reactions to the dressed-up skeletons in the picture on p. C8. How are these similar to or different than Halloween costumes?

❑ For the Enrichment Family Project on p. C8, have students create a booklet, notebook, or poster commemorating the life of an ancestor or another historical figure and present it to the class.

IEP Modification   Some words in the text may be new to some English Learners, such as *cemeteries, gravesites, deceased, skulls, coincided, harvest, tissue paper.* Have students, in pairs, use a dictionary to look up new words, then share their results with the class.

PRACTICE AND APPLY

❑ Discuss what Halloween in the U.S. means to students and how they celebrate it. Does the holiday have anything to do with remembering their ancestors?

OPTIONAL RESOURCES

Plan
- Best Practices Toolkit

Present
- Atlas Map, UTB 1, Transparencies 1–5

TECHNOLOGY TOOLS	
Teacher Tools	**Student Tools**
EasyPlanner CD-ROM	ClassZone.com
	Cultura interactiva
	eEdition Online or CD-ROM

Las Navidades

OBJECTIVES

- Familiarize students with the differing ways people celebrate las navidades.
- Identify food enjoyed during the holiday.
- Locate the countries mentioned on a map.

STANDARDS
- 2.1 Practices and perspectives
- 2.2 Products and perspectives
- 4.2 Compare cultures

FOCUS AND MOTIVATE

❑ Direct students' attention to the pictures and elicit reactions. How do these pictures compare with the ways in which students and their families celebrate the winter holidays?

TEACH

❑ Start by conducting the 50-minute lesson found on p. C10 of the Teacher's Edition.

❑ Do the Language Arts Connection on p. C10. Ask students other idioms for *being old,* and write these on the board.

❑ When discussing *empanadas* in the *Cultura* section, tell students that most countries have various kinds of stuffed pastries. Ask students what kinds pastries they have eaten, what they were filled with, and what country they come from.

IEP Modification   Ask students to describe how *las navidades* are celebrated in their home countries or regions. Encourage them to bring in photos and share these with the class.

PRACTICE AND APPLY

❑ Discuss why December and January might be such big months for celebrations around the world. Discuss what it might be like to be in the southern hemisphere during December and January, when it is summer there.

OPTIONAL RESOURCES

Plan
- Best Practices Toolkit

PRESENT
- Atlas Map, UTB 1, Transparencies 3–6

TECHNOLOGY TOOLS	
Teacher Tools	**Student Tools**
EasyPlanner CD-ROM	ClassZone.com
	Cultura interactiva
	eEdition Online or CD-ROM

¡Año Nuevo!

OBJECTIVES

- Familiarize students with Año Nuevo celebratations.
- Locate the countries featured in the lesson on a map.

STANDARDS
- 2.1 Practices and perspectives
- 4.2 Compare cultures

FOCUS AND MOTIVATE

❑ Direct students' attention to the pictures and elicit reactions. What are ways in which people in the U.S. celebrate New Year's Eve?

TEACH

❑ Start by conducting the 50-minute lesson on p. C12 of the Teacher's Edition.

❑ For the Critical Thinking activity on p. C12, write the names of different types of calendars on the board: Gregorian, Julian, Mayan, Aztec, Islamic. Have students, in small groups, choose two to research and write about.

❑ For the Social Studies Enrichment Activity on p. C13, ask students to create comic strips illustrating an event in the past year.

IEP Modification   Go over the meaning of some of the idioms used in the text, such as *say good-bye to the old, make a toast, poke fun, final farewell*. Ask students if their native languages have idioms expressing the same ideas.

PRACTICE AND APPLY

❑ Why do students think New Year's is celebrated on Dec. 31/Jan. 1? If they were to choose another date to celebrate the new year, what would that be? How would they celebrate it?

OPTIONAL RESOURCES

Plan
- Best Practices Toolkit

Present
- Atlas Map, UTB 1, Transparencies 3–6

TECHNOLOGY TOOLS	
Teacher Tools	**Student Tools**
EasyPlanner CD-ROM	ClassZone.com
	Cultura interactiva
	eEdition Online or CD-ROM

¡Carnaval!

OBJECTIVES

- Familiarize students with Carnaval and its varied celebrations.
- Identify the traditional meaning of Carnaval and when it is held.

STANDARDS
- 2.1 Practices and perspectives
- 2.2 Products and perspectives
- 4.2 Compare cultures

FOCUS AND MOTIVATE

❑ Direct students' attention to the pictures and elicit reactions. Have any students ever seen a Carnaval parade?

TEACH

❑ Start by conducting the 50-minute lesson on p. C14 of the Teacher's Edition.

❑ Do the Social Studies Connection in p. C14. How many islands can students count? Are they closer to Spain or to Africa?

❑ For the Research Enrichment Activity on p. C15, have students, in pairs, create timelines of major milestones in UNESCO's history from its foundation on Nov. 16, 1945 to the present.

IEP Modification   Have students, in pairs, research Mardi Gras in New Orleans and the celebration of Carnaval in one Latin American country. Have them create a poster comparing and contrasting the two celebrations, and present these to the class.

PRACTICE AND APPLY

❑ Have students, in small groups, discuss how they could participate in a Carnaval parade: what costumes they would wear, what music they would have, what dances they would perform.

OPTIONAL RESOURCES

Plan
- Best Practices Toolkit

Present
- Atlas Map, UTB 1, Transparencies 1–6

TECHNOLOGY TOOLS	
Teacher Tools	**Student Tools**
EasyPlanner CD-ROM	ClassZone.com
	Cultura interactiva
	eEdition Online or CD-ROM

Las Fallas

OBJECTIVES

- Familiarize students with Las Fallas, the unusual holiday celebration in Valencia, Spain.

STANDARDS
- 2.1 Practices and perspectives
- 2.2 Products and perspectives
- 4.2 Compare cultures

FOCUS AND MOTIVATE

❑ Direct students' attention to the pictures and elicit reactions. Does this celebration remind them of any others? What is similar or different?

TEACH

❑ Start by conducting the 50-minute lesson on p. C16 of the Teacher's Edition.

❑ When discussing the photos, encourage students to recycle vocabulary they have learned, such as that for clothes, colors, and adjectives with **ser** and **estar**.

❑ Do the Critical Thinking activity on p. C16. Ask students if they have ever seen firemen or policemen at parades. What functions might they serve at public celebrations?

IEP Modification   Slower-paced Learners Have students, in pairs, create Venn diagrams comparing and contrasting Las Fallas with another celebration they have read about, such as Día de la Independencia or Año Nuevo. Have them choose three or four categories to compare, such as parades, costumes, food, fireworks, or dances.

PRACTICE AND APPLY

❑ Ask students what figures—in politics, sports, entertainment, recent events—people in their community would probably choose for *ninots*. Write these on the board. Then have students vote for the top ten.

OPTIONAL RESOURCES

Plan
- Best Practices Toolkit

Present
- Atlas Map, UTB 1, Transparency 6

TECHNOLOGY TOOLS	
Teacher Tools	**Student Tools**
EasyPlanner CD-ROM	ClassZone.com
	Cultura interactiva
	eEdition Online or CD-ROM

Semana Santa

OBJECTIVES

- Familiarize students with Semana Santa.
- Identify ways people in different countries celebrate Semana Santa.

STANDARDS
- 2.1 Practices and perspectives
- 2.2 Products and perspectives
- 4.2 Compare cultures

FOCUS AND MOTIVATE

- ❏ Direct students' attention to the pictures and elicit reactions. Have they ever seen rugs made of flowers or sand?

TEACH

- ❏ Start by conducting the 50-minute lesson on p. C18 of the Teacher's Edition.
- ❏ Ask students if the **bolitas de harina** remind them of any other food they have read about (**empanadas**). Have they ever eaten something similar?
- ❏ For the Critical Thinking activity on p. C18, pair weaker students with stronger students. Encourage them to use a dictionary or the glossary in their textbooks for support. Circulate around the room, giving assistance to the pairs.

IEP Modification   Review the meanings of those words in the text that might be unfamiliar to students, such as *relocated, hometown, countryside, twist, papier-mâché,* and *arch.*

PRACTICE AND APPLY

- ❏ Ask students what they do during spring break. Do they celebrate any holidays during the spring?

OPTIONAL RESOURCES

Plan
- Best Practices Toolkit

Present
- Atlas Map, UTB 1, Transparencies 3–5

TECHNOLOGY TOOLS	
Teacher Tools	**Student Tools**
EasyPlanner CD-ROM	ClassZone.com
	Cultura interactiva
	eEdition Online or CD-ROM

¡Cinco de Mayo!

OBJECTIVES

- Familiarize students with Cinco de Mayo.
- Differentiate Cinco de Mayo from Mexican independence celebrations.
- Identify Cinco de Mayo celebrations in the United States.

STANDARDS
- 2.1 Practices and perspectives
- 3.1 Knowledge of other disciplines
- 4.2 Compare cultures

FOCUS AND MOTIVATE

❑ Direct students' attention to the pictures and elicit reactions. What other names of holidays they have learned about refer to a specific day? (El 12 de Octubre, Año Nuevo, Día de la Independencia, Día de los Muertos)

TEACH

❑ Start by conducting the 50-minute lesson on p. C20 of the Teacher's Edition.

❑ For the Critical Thinking activity on p. C20, ask students to compare and contrast TV docudramas with news coverage of an event. Which do they prefer?

❑ For the Social Studies Enrichment Activity on p. C21, you might have students video their news reports and share them with the class.

IEP Modification   For the Social Studies Enrichment Activity found on p. C21 of the Teacher's Edition, have students, in pairs, complete a 5-Ws graphic organizer before they write their news reports.

PRACTICE AND APPLY

❑ Tell students that the word *holiday* comes from *holy day*. Have students brainstorm a list of holidays. Do most of these have a religious theme, or are they celebrations of a famous person or event in history?

OPTIONAL RESOURCES

Plan
- Best Practices Toolkit

Present
- Atlas Map, UTB 1, Transparencies 1–3

TECHNOLOGY TOOLS	
Teacher Tools	**Student Tools**
EasyPlanner CD-ROM	ClassZone.com
	Cultura interactiva
	eEdition Online or CD-ROM

Inti Raymi

OBJECTIVES

- Familiarize students with Inti Raymi.
- Differentiate between summer and winter solstices.

FOCUS AND MOTIVATE

❑ Direct students' attention to the pictures and elicit reactions. When does the winter solstice occur in the U.S.? Which is the longest day of the year (the summer solstice) in the U.S. and Peru?

TEACH

❑ Start by conducting the 50-minute lesson on p. C22 of the Teacher's Edition.

❑ Ask students to identify words within the reading and the captions that they think are not of Spanish origin. Then, share the information in the Teacher's Edition on Indigenous Languages on p. C22 with the class. Discuss the influence indigenous languages have had on regional variations in Spanish in the Americas.

IEP Modification   Have students, in groups of 3 or 4, research and write an explanation of the effect of the Earth's rotational axis factors on the number of hours of sunlight during the winter and summer solstices. Ask them to share their results with the class.

PRACTICE AND APPLY

❑ Have students, in small groups, write lists of what they tend to do during the winter and summer solstices. Do they tend to do more things indoors during either one?

OPTIONAL RESOURCES

Plan
- Best Practices Toolkit

Present
- Atlas Map, UTB 1, Transparency 5

TECHNOLOGY TOOLS	
Teacher Tools	**Student Tools**
EasyPlanner CD-ROM	ClassZone.com
	Cultura interactiva
	eEdition Online or CD-ROM

Día de Simón Bolivar

OBJECTIVES
- Provide biographical data on Simón Bolivar.
- Familiarize students with Día de Simón Bolivar.

STANDARDS
- 2.1 Practices and perspectives
- 2.2 Products and perspectives
- 3.1 Knowledge of other disciplines
- 4.2 Compare cultures

FOCUS AND MOTIVATE
- ❏ Direct students' attention to the pictures and elicit reactions. Do the painting and statue of Bolivar make them think of any other figures in history?

TEACH
- ❏ Start by conducting the 50-minute lesson on p. C24 of the Teacher's Edition.
- ❏ For the Critical Thinking activity on p. C24, have students work in small groups. Then ask them to design two new currency denominations, such as a $15 and a $40 bill, and decide whose image should be on each. Have them share their designs with the class.

IEP Modification   Heritage Language Learners Ask students to describe several famous leaders in the history of their country or region. Were any similar to Simón Bolivar? Are there public statues or paintings of them in their country or region?

PRACTICE AND APPLY
- ❏ Ask students to name famous people in the history of the United Sates who devoted their lives to freedom.

OPTIONAL RESOURCES
Plan
- Best Practices Toolkit

Present
- Atlas Map, UTB 1, Transparency 5

TECHNOLOGY TOOLS	
Teacher Tools	**Student Tools**
EasyPlanner CD-ROM	ClassZone.com
	Cultura interactiva
	eEdition Online or CD-ROM

Preliminary Lesson Opener, Hola, ¿qué tal?, pp. 1–5

OBJECTIVES

- Introduce lesson theme: ¡Hola!
- **Culture:** Learn about New York City's population and its cultural celebrations.
- Present and practice vocabulary: greetings and saying goodbye.
- Learn to say names in Spanish.
- Pronunciation: Learn about the letter **h** in Spanish.

STANDARDS

- 1.1 Engage in conversation, Acts. 2–3
- 1.2 Understand language
- 1.3 Present information, Acts. 2–3, PYP
- 2.1 Practices and perspectives
- 4.1 Compare languages, Pronunciación
- 4.2 Compare cultures

FOCUS AND MOTIVATE

☐ Preliminary Lesson Opener, p. 1: Have students look at the photos, and talk about Hispanic culture in the United States, and specifically in New York City and its surroundings, Connecticut (north) and New Jersey (south).

TEACH

☐ **Hola, ¿qué tal?,** pp. 2–3, paragraphs A–H.

☐ **Nombres de chicos** and **Nombres de chicas,** p. 4.

☐ Nota: **¿Cómo estás?** and **¿Cómo está usted?,** p. 5.

IEP Modification   Have students share any knowledge of Spanish greetings that they have, or any other Spanish expressions and proper names.

PRACTICE AND APPLY

☐ Preliminary Lesson Opener, page opposite to page 1. Read the brief presentation on **Nueva York.** Have students view the photographs and respond to the question *What cultural celebrations are there in your area?,* at the end of the brief presentation.

☐ Play TXT CD 1 track 2 to do ¡A responder! activity, p. 3.

☐ Práctica de vocabulario, Activities 1–2, p. 4. Have students work in pairs. Use reading, writing, and speaking skills listed next to the activity.

☐ Nota: **¿Cómo estás?** and **¿Cómo está usted?,** Activity 3, p. 5.

ASSESS AND RETEACH

☐ Para y piensa, p. 5. Have students practice formal and familiar greetings.

OPTIONAL RESOURCES

Plan
- Best Practices Toolkit
- PE Answers, MSRB, Transp. 24–27
- Workbook Answers, UTB 1, Transp. 34–45

Present
- Audio Script, URB 1, pp. 101–102

Practice
- Back to School Resources, URB 1, pp. 1–3

Assess
- Heritage Learner Diagnostic Test, Heritage Learners Assessment, pp. 1–6

TECHNOLOGY TOOLS	
Teacher Tools	**Student Tools**
Power Presentations	@Home Tutor
EasyPlanner CD-ROM	ClassZone.com
	Cultura interactiva
	eEdition Online or CD-ROM

¡AVANCEMOS!
Lección preliminar

¡Mucho gusto!, pp. 6–9

OBJECTIVES
- Present and practice greetings and making introductions.
- **Culture:** Discuss the murals of Manuel Vega.
- Practice asking someone's name.

STANDARDS
- 1.1 Engage in conversation, Acts. 6–7
- 1.2 Understand language
- 1.3 Present information, Acts. 4–7, Nota, PYP
- 2.1 Practices and perspectives, CC
- 4.2 Compare cultures, CC

FOCUS AND MOTIVATE
❑ ¡Mucho gusto! is vocabulary presentation of greetings and introductions, pp. 6–7.

TEACH
❑ **¡Mucho gusto!** vocabulary, pp. 6–7, paragraphs A–G.

❑ Audio Program TXT CD 1, track 4. Play audio for paragraphs A–G.

❑ Nota on familiar and formal introductions, p. 9.

PRACTICE AND APPLY
❑ Play TXT CD 1 track 5 to do ¡A responder! activity, p. 7.

❑ Práctica de vocabulario, Activities 4–6, p. 8. Have students work in pairs (activities 4–5) and in groups of four (activity 6). Use reading, writing, and speaking skills listed next to the activity.

❑ Nota: **¿Cómo te llamas?** and **¿Cómo se llama?,** Activity 7, p. 9.

IEP Modification   Have students share any other greetings that they use or know, and have them talk about when or with whom they use these.

ASSESS AND RETEACH
❑ Para y piensa, p. 9. Have students complete statements to introduce themselves and others.

OPTIONAL RESOURCES
Plan
- Best Practices Toolkit
- PE Answers, MSRB, Transp. 24–27
- Workbook Answers, UTB 1, Transp. 34–45

Practice
- Back to School Resources, URB 1, pp. 4–6

Present
- Warm-up Transp. 22, UTB 1
- Audio Script, URB 1, pp. 101–102

TECHNOLOGY TOOLS

Teacher Tools	Student Tools
Power Presentations	@Home Tutor
EasyPlanner CD-ROM	ClassZone.com
	eEdition Online or CD-ROM

El Abecedario, ¿De dónde eres?, pp. 10–15

OBJECTIVES

- To learn and say the Spanish alphabet.
- To practice spelling words in Spanish.
- To practice pronouncing the Spanish vowels **a, e, i, o, u.**
- Learn the names of countries in the Spanish-speaking world.
- Teach and practice saying where someone is from.
- Practice identifying countries in a map of Latin America.

STANDARDS

- 1.1 Engage in conversation, Acts. 9–10, 12–13
- 1.2 Understand language, Act. 8
- 1.3 Present information, Acts. 8–13, PYP
- 4.1 Compare languages, Pronunciación
- 4.2 Compare cultures, Acts. 11–13

FOCUS AND MOTIVATE

❑ Focus on the Spanish alphabet, on how to say the letters to spell words, and on the countries that make up the entire Spanish-speaking world, pp. 10 and 12–13.

TEACH

❑ Have students repeat the several letters of the Spanish alphabet, and the words on page 10.

❑ Use TXT CD 1 track 9 to practice the pronunciation of the Spanish vowels, p. 11.

❑ Introduce Los países hispanohablantes.

❑ Nota on p. 15.

PRACTICE AND APPLY

❑ Play TXT CD 1 track 8 to do activity 8, p. 11.

❑ In groups of three, do activity 9, p. 11.

❑ In pairs, do activity 10, p. 11.

❑ Play TXT CD 1 track 7 to do ¡A responder!, p. 10.

❑ Práctica, Activities 11–12, p. 14. Have students work in pairs on activity 12. Use reading, writing, and speaking skills listed next to the activity.

❑ Play TXT CD 1 track 11 to do ¡A responder!, p. 13.

❑ In pairs, do activity 13, p. 15.

IEP Modification   In activity 8, have students reinforce their writing of the names they hear by also spelling them out loud as they write down each name.

ASSESS AND RETEACH

❑ Para y piensa, p. 11. Have students recite the Spanish alphabet.

❑ Para y piensa, p. 15. Have students match each question with the correct response.

OPTIONAL RESOURCES

Plan
- Best Practices Toolkit
- PE Answers, MSRB, Transp. 24–27
- Workbook Answers, UTB 1, Transp. 34–45
- Easy Planner CD-ROM
- ClassZone.com

Present
- Warm-up Transp. 22, UTB 1
- Audio Script, URB 1, pp. 101–102

Practice
- Back to School Resources, URB 1, pp. 7–12

TECHNOLOGY TOOLS	
Teacher Tools	**Student Tools**
Power Presentations	@Home Tutor
EasyPlanner CD-ROM	ClassZone.com
	eEdition Online or CD-ROM

Mi número de teléfono, pp. 16–17

OBJECTIVES
- To say the numbers from zero to ten.
- To exchange phone numbers.

STANDARDS
- 1.1 Engage in conversation, Acts. 15–16

FOCUS AND MOTIVATE
❑ Have students repeat these first Spanish numbers after you.

TEACH
❑ Mi número de teléfono, p. 16.

IEP Modification · Pair up slower-paced learners with faster-paced learners to have each other ask what their home phone number or their own phone number is.

PRACTICE AND APPLY
❑ Play TXT CD 1 track 13 to do ¡A responder!, p. 16.

❑ Práctica, Activities 14–16, p. 17. Use reading, writing, and speaking skills listed next to the activity.

ASSESS AND RETEACH
❑ Para y piensa, p. 17. Have students practice the numbers.

OPTIONAL RESOURCES

Plan
- Best Practices Toolkit
- PE Answers, MSRB, Transp. 24–27
- Workbook Answers, UTB 1, Transp. 34–45

Present
- Warm-up Transp. 23, UTB 1
- Audio Script, URB 1, pp. 101–102

Practice
- Back to School Resources, URB 1, pp. 13–15

TECHNOLOGY TOOLS	
Teacher Tools	**Student Tools**
Power Presentations	@Home Tutor
EasyPlanner CD-ROM	ClassZone.com
	eEdition Online or CD-ROM

Los días de la semana, pp. 18–19

OBJECTIVES
- Learn and practice the days of the week.

FOCUS AND MOTIVATE
❏ Audio Program TXT CD 1, track 14.
  Play audio for paragraphs A–B.

STANDARDS
- 1.1 Engage in conversation, Act. 19
- 1.2 Understand language, Act. 18
- 1.3 Present information, Acts. 17–19, PYP

TEACH
❏ Los días de la semana, p. 18.

IEP Modification   Break down your class in pairs, making sure slower-paced learners are paired up with faster-paced learners. Have them ask the following hypothetical question to each other, back and forth:
Mañana es... ¿Qué día es hoy?

PRACTICE AND APPLY
❏ Play TXT CD 1 track 15 to do ¡A responder!, p. 18.
❏ Práctica, Activities 17–19, p. 19. Have students play TXT CD 1 track 16 to do activity 18. Have students work in pairs on activity 19. Use reading, writing, and speaking skills listed next to the activity.

ASSESS AND RETEACH
❏ Para y piensa, p. 19. Have students practice the days of the week.

OPTIONAL RESOURCES

Plan
- Best Practices Toolkit
- PE Answers, MSRB, Transp. 24–27
- Workbook Answers, UTB 1, Transp. 34–45

Present
- Warm-up Transp. 24, UTB 1
- Audio Script, URB 1, pp. 101–102

Practice
- Back to School Resources, URB 1, pp. 16–18

TECHNOLOGY TOOLS	
Teacher Tools	**Student Tools**
Power Presentations	@Home Tutor
EasyPlanner CD-ROM	ClassZone.com
	eEdition Online or CD-ROM

¿Qué tiempo hace?, pp. 20–21

OBJECTIVES
- Learn and practice weather expressions.
- Teach and practice saying where someone is from.
- Practice identifying countries in a map of Latin America.

STANDARDS
- 1.1 Engage in conversation, Acts. 21–22
- 1.2 Understand language, Act. 20
- 1.3 Present information, Acts. 20–22, PYP

FOCUS AND MOTIVATE
- ❑ Play Audio Program TXT CD 1, track 17 targeting expressions to describe the weather.

TEACH
- ❑ ¿Qué tiempo hace?, p. 20.

PRACTICE AND APPLY
- ❑ Activity 20, p. 21. Play TXT CD 1 track 19.
- ❑ Activities 21–22, p. 21. Have students work in pairs.
- ❑ Play TXT CD 1 track 18 to do ¡A responder!, p. 20.

IEP Modification In pairs have your class expand on activity 20 by going over the four items and saying out loud what the weather is like on each photo.

ASSESS AND RETEACH
- ❑ Para y piensa, p. 21. Have students match questions with the correct responses.

OPTIONAL RESOURCES
Plan
- Best Practices Toolkit
- PE Answers, MSRB, Transp. 24–27
- Workbook Answers, UTB 1, Transp. 34–45

Present
- Warm-up Transp. 24, UTB 1
- Audio Script, URB 1, pp. 101–102

Practice
- Back to School Resources, URB 1, pp. 19–21

TECHNOLOGY TOOLS	
Teacher Tools	**Student Tools**
Power Presentations	@Home Tutor
EasyPlanner CD-ROM	ClassZone.com
	eEdition Online or CD-ROM

En la clase, pp. 22–24

OBJECTIVES
- Learn and practice useful classroom phrases.

FOCUS AND MOTIVATE
- ❏ Have students repeat the useful phrases on page 22.

TEACH
- ❏ En la clase, p. 22.
- ❏ En el libro, p. 23.
- ❏ Play audio program TXT CD 1 track 20, useful phrases, pp. 22–23.

PRACTICE AND APPLY
- ❏ Play TXT CD 1 track 21 to do ¡A responder!, p. 23.
- ❏ Activities 23–25, p. 24. Practice using reading, writing, listening, speaking skills.

IEP Modification Have all students stand up and play Simon says . . . with you as facilitator, using some of the commands in **En la clase** list.

ASSESS AND RETEACH
- ❏ Para y piensa, p. 24. Have students practice useful classroom phrases.

> ### STANDARDS
> - 1.1 Engage in conversation, Acts. 24–25
> - 1.2 Understand language
> - 1.3 Present information, Acts. 24–25, PYP

OPTIONAL RESOURCES

Plan
- Best Practices Toolkit
- PE Answers, MSRB, Transp. 24–27
- Workbook Answers, UTB 1, Transp. 34–45

Present
- Warm-up Transp. 25, UTB 1
- Audio Script, URB 1, pp. 101–102

Practice
- Back to School Resources, URB 1, pp. 22–24

TECHNOLOGY TOOLS	
Teacher Tools	**Student Tools**
Power Presentations	@Home Tutor
EasyPlanner CD-ROM	ClassZone.com
Test Generator CD-ROM	eEdition Online or CD-ROM

Copyright © by McDougal Littell, a division of Houghton Mifflin Company.

¡AVANCEMOS!
Lección preliminar

¡Avancemos!
Level 1A Lección preliminar   **19**

En Resumen, Repaso de la Lección, pp. 25–27

OBJECTIVES
- Review lesson grammar and vocabulary.

STANDARDS
- 1.2 Understand language, Act. 1
- 1.3 Present information, Acts. 1–4

FOCUS AND MOTIVATE
❑ En resumen, p. 25. Review all vocabulary terms and grammar items.

TEACH
❑ En resumen. Assess which vocabulary terms need more practice and encourage students to form sentences with each.

❑ Repaso de la lección, pp. 26–27. Have students form two questions to ask classmates.

PRACTICE AND APPLY
❑ Repaso de la lección, Activity 1, p. 26. Play TXT CD 1 track 22 while they do Activity 1.

❑ Complete activities 2–4, pp. 26–27.

IEP Modification Have students do activity 2 in pairs, collaboratively.

ASSESS AND RETEACH
❑ Lesson Test, On-level Assessment, pp. 1–6.

OPTIONAL RESOURCES

Plan
- Best Practices Toolkit
- PE Answers, MSRB, Transp. 24–27
- Workbook Answers, UTB 1 Transp. 34–45

Present
- Warm-up Transp. 25, UTB 1
- Audio Script, URB 1, pp. 101–102

Assess
- Lesson Test, Modified Assessment, pp. 1–6
- Lesson Test, Pre-AP Assessment, pp. 1–6
- Lesson Test, Heritage Learners Assessment, pp. 7–12

TECHNOLOGY TOOLS	
Teacher Tools	**Student Tools**
Power Presentations	@Home Tutor
EasyPlanner CD-ROM	ClassZone.com
	eEdition Online or CD-ROM

Unit and Lesson Opener,
Presentación y práctica de vocabulario, pp. 28–35

OBJECTIVES

- **Culture:** compare everyday activities.
- Present and practice vocabulary about everyday activities, snack foods, and likes and dislikes.
- State preferences about favorite activities.

STANDARDS

- 1.1 Engage in conversation
- 1.2 Understand language, Act. 1
- 1.3 Present information, Acts. 1–2, PYP
- 2.1 Practices and perspectives
- 4.2 Compare cultures

FOCUS AND MOTIVATE

❑ Unit 1 Opener, pp. 28–29: Have students study the map of the U.S., look at the photos, and talk about Hispanic culture in the United States.

TEACH

❑ Presentación de vocabulario, pp. 32–34, paragraphs A–F.

❑ Video Program DVD 1, Unit 1. View Vocabulary Presentation video.

IEP Modification Ask students what activities they like by giving them a choice: e.g., "¿Te gusta hablar por télefono o escuchar música?" Model the answer: "Me gusta _____." Then ask about foods.

PRACTICE AND APPLY

❑ Lesson 1 Opener, pp. 30–31. Read Comparación cultural. Have students view the photographs and respond to the ¿Qué ves? questions.

❑ Play TXT CD 1 track 16 to do ¡A responder! activity, p. 34,

❑ Práctica de vocabulario, Activities 1–2, p. 35. Have students work in pairs. Use reading, writing, and speaking skills listed next to the activity. Review **Me gusta** and **No me gusta.**

ASSESS AND RETEACH

❑ Para y piensa, p. 35. Pair students and do the exercise. Expand to other activities, such as renting a DVD, eating ice cream, drinking water.

❑ Vocabulary Recognition Quiz, On-level Assessment, p. 11.

❑ Homework: *Cuaderno:* pp. 1–3; *Cuaderno para hispanohablantes,* pp. 1–4.

OPTIONAL RESOURCES

Plan
- Family Letter, URB 1, p. 123
- Family letters in Haitian Creole and Spanish on ClassZone.com
- Best Practices Toolkit
- Absent Student Copymasters, URB 1, p. 125
- PE Answers, MSRB, Transparencies 28–31
- Workbook Answers, UTB 1, Transparencies 54–61

- Música del mundo hispano
- Vocabulary Transp. 12–13, UTB 1
- TPRS, pp. 1–7
- Video Script, URB 1, pp. 97–98
- Audio Script, URB 1, pp. 103–107
- Vocabulary Video, DVD 1
- Fine Art Activities, URB 1, pp. 118–120
- Fine Art Transp. 9–11, UTB 1

Present
- Warm-up Transp. 26, UTB 1
- Atlas Map, UTB 1, Transp. 4
- Map Transp. 7, UTB 1
- Map-Culture Activities, URB 1, pp. 113–114

Practice
- Practice Games, URB 1, p. 57
- Video Activities URB 1, pp. 79–80

Assess
- Reteaching Copymasters, URB 1, pp. 29–30

TECHNOLOGY TOOLS	
Teacher Tools	**Student Tools**
Power Presentations	@Home Tutor
EasyPlanner CD-ROM	ClassZone.com
	Cultura interactiva
	eEdition Online or CD-ROM

Vocabulario en contexto, pp. 36–37

OBJECTIVES

- Understand what others say about activities.
- Practice talking about activities they and others like to do.
- **Recycle:** weather expressions, p. 20.

STANDARDS

- 1.1 Engage in conversation, Acts. 4–5
- 1.2 Understand language, Act. 3
- 1.3 Present information, Acts. 3–5, PYP

FOCUS AND MOTIVATE

☐ Telehistoria escena 1, Strategies. Read Cuando lees strategy, p. 36.

TEACH

☐ Telehistoria escena 1, p. 36. Have students repeat the dialogue after you for correct pronunciation and intonation.

☐ Video Program DVD 1, Unit 1. Show the video for scene 1. Listen for the activity expressions and raise hands each time they hear a new activity. Write the expression on the board.

☐ Audio Program TXT CD 1, track 25. Play audio for scene 1.

☐ Ask what activities students like or don't like to do. Give them a choice and model the answer: "Me gusta _____. No me gusta _____."

PRACTICE AND APPLY

☐ Comprensión del episodio, Activity 3, p. 37. Play TXT CD 1 track 25. Call on students to give the answers.

☐ Review weather expression on p. 20 before doing Activity 4, p. 37. work in pairs.

☐ Have students work in groups to do Activity 5, p. 37.

IEP Modification Ask students to assume the role of Sandra in the dialog and respond to Alicia according to what they like and do not like.

ASSESS AND RETEACH

☐ Para y piensa, p. 37. Do a quick review of activity expressions beforehand.

☐ Vocabulary Production Quiz, On-level Assessment, p. 12.

OPTIONAL RESOURCES

Plan

- Best Practices Toolkit
- PE Answers, MSRB, Transparencies 28–31
- Workbook Answers, UTB 1, Transparencies 54–61
- Absent Student Copymasters, URB 1, p. 126

Present

- Warm-up Transp. 26, UTB 1
- Audio Script, URB 1, pp. 103–107
- Video Script, URB 1, pp. 97–98

Practice

- Video Activities, URB 1, pp. 81–82
- Practice Games, URB 1, p. 58

Assess

- Reteaching Copymasters, URB 1, pp. 29, 31, 38

TECHNOLOGY TOOLS	
Teacher Tools	**Student Tools**
Power Presentations	@Home Tutor
EasyPlanner CD-ROM	ClassZone.com
Test generator CD-ROM	eEdition Online or CD-ROM

Presentación y práctica de gramática 1, pp. 38–41

OBJECTIVES

- Present and practice subject pronouns and the verb **ser.**
- Practice using **ser de** + location to tell where someone is from.

STANDARDS

- 1.1 Engage in conversation, Act. 10
- 1.2 Understand language
- 1.3 Present information, Acts. 6–11, PYP
- 3.1 Knowledge of other disciplines
- 4.1 Compare languages

FOCUS AND MOTIVATE

❑ Presentación de gramática, p. 38: Using gestures, establish the difference between the subject pronouns **yo** and **tú.** Say, "Yo soy de ____". Ask individual students; "¿Y tú?" to elicit "Yo soy de ____" responses.

TEACH

❑ Explain that **nosotras, vosotras,** and **ellas** are used when all the people in a group are female. The masculine forms (**nosotros, vosotros, ellos**) are used with a mixed group.

❑ Explain the difference between **tú** and **usted** and give the plural form of each. Explain that **vosotros** is used only in Spain and **ustedes** will be used in class.

❑ Nota grammatical, p. 39. Have students use different forms of **ser** plus **de** to tell where someone is from.

IEP Modification   Presentación de gramática, p. 38: Ask: "¿Tú eres de ____?" Elicit response: "Sí, yo soy de ____."

PRACTICE AND APPLY

❑ Práctica de gramática, Activities 6–9, 11, pp. 39–41. Write the answers.

❑ Práctica de gramática, Activity 10, p. 41. Practice orally in pairs. Call on students to ask and answer questions for the whole class to hear. Ask for volunteer pairs to ask and answer original questions in front of the class.

ASSESS AND RETEACH

❑ Para y piensa, p. 41. Write other subjects and endings on the board and have students draw lines between the two to match.

❑ Homework: *Cuaderno:* pp. 4–6; *Cuaderno para hispanohablantes,* pp. 5–7.

OPTIONAL RESOURCES

Plan

- Best Practices Toolkit
- PE Answers, MSRB, Transparencies 28–31
- Workbook Answers, UTB 1, Transparencies 54–61
- Absent Student Copymasters, URB 1, p. 127
- Easy Planner CD-ROM
- ClassZone.com

Present

- Warm-up Transp. 27, UTB 1
- Grammar Presentation Transp. 16, UTB 1
- Audio Script, URB 1, pp. 103–107

Practice

- Practice Games, URB 1, p. 59

Assess

- Reteaching Copymasters, URB 1, pp. 32–33

TECHNOLOGY TOOLS	
Teacher Tools	**Student Tools**
Power Presentations	@Home Tutor
EasyPlanner CD-ROM	ClassZone.com
Test generator CD-ROM	eEdition Online or CD-ROM

Gramática en contexto, pp. 42–43

OBJECTIVES

- Practice the verb **ser** in context.
- **Culture:** discussion of a well-known Latino award show in Miami.
- Practice names of Latin American countries.

STANDARDS

- 1.1 Engage in conversation, Acts. 13–14
- 1.2 Understand language, Act. 10
- 2.2 Products and perspectives, Act. 13
- 4.2 Compare cultures, Act. 13

FOCUS AND MOTIVATE

- ❑ Telehistoria escena 2, Strategies, p. 42. Read the Cuando escuchas strategy.

TEACH

- ❑ Telehistoria escena 2, p. 42. Direct students' attention to the photo and have them guess what is happening in the scene.
- ❑ Video Program DVD 1, Unit 1. Show video for scene 2. Listen for the use of subject pronouns and forms of **ser** with **de.** Have students raise their hands each them they hear one of these expressions.
- ❑ Audio Program TXT CD 1, track 26. Play audio for scene 2.
- ❑ Telehistoria escena 2, p. 42: Read the dialog and have students repeat after you.

IEP Modification   Explain that the placement of prepositions in questions often varies between English and Spanish: "Where are you _from_?" "¿_De_ dónde eres?"

PRACTICE AND APPLY

- ❑ **Comprensión del episodio,** Activity 12, p. 43. Play TXT CD 1 track 26. Call on students to give the answers.
- ❑ **Los famosos en Miami,** Activity 13, p. 43. Read **Los Premios Juventud** as a class. Have students talk about where the nominees are from and share the names of their favorite stars and where they are from.

ASSESS AND RETEACH

- ❑ Para y piensa, p. 43. Complete the sentences based on the Telehistoria. Ask the following questions: "¿De dónde eres? ¿De dónde son tus amigos?"
- ❑ Grammar Quiz 1, On-level Assessment, p. 13.

OPTIONAL RESOURCES

Plan
- Best Practices Toolkit
- PE Answers, MSRB, Transparencies 28–31
- Workbook Answers, UTB 1, Transparencies 54–61
- Absent Student Copymasters, URB 1, p. 128

Present
- Warm-up Transp. 27, UTB 1
- Audio Script, URB 1, pp. 103–107
- Video Script, URB 1, pp. 97–98

Practice
- Practice Games, URB 1, p. 60
- Video Activities, URB 1, pp. 83–84

Assess
- Reteaching Copymasters, URB, pp. 32, 34

TECHNOLOGY TOOLS	
Teacher Tools	**Student Tools**
Power Presentations	@Home Tutor
EasyPlanner CD-ROM	ClassZone.com
Test generator CD-ROM	eEdition Online or CD-ROM

Presentación y práctica de gramática 2, pp. 44–47

OBJECTIVES
- Present and practice **gustar** + infinitives.
- Present personal **a** + noun/pronoun.
- Compare pronunciation of the letters **p** and **t** in Spanish and English.

STANDARDS
- 1.1 Engage in conversation, Acts. 16, 19
- 1.2 Understand language, Act. 18, Pronunciación
- 1.3 Present information, Acts. 15–19, PYP
- 3.1 Knowledge of other disciplines
- 4.1 Compare languages, Pronunciación
- 4.2 Compare cultures, CC

FOCUS AND MOTIVATE
❏ Presentación de gramática, p. 44. Present all the pronouns with the same infinitive, using gestures to illustrate about whom you are talking.

TEACH
❏ Presentación de gramática, p. 44. Make a chart on the board, illustrating the relationship between the subject pronouns and the indirect object pronouns.

❏ Explain the infinitive form of the verb. Use **me gusta** and te **gusta** to introduce the other indirect object pronouns: **le, nos, les.**

❏ Comparación cultural, **El arte de Miami,** p. 45. Have students study the painting and answer the questions.

IEP Modification: Explain that to clarify who likes something, use a before the noun or pronoun that identifies that person. Make another chart on the board, this time illustrating the relationship between the indirect object pronouns and pronouns used after prepositions.

PRACTICE AND APPLY
❏ **Pronunciación,** p. 47. Play TXT CD 1, track 27. Direct students to compare the Spanish and English pronunciation of these letters orally.

❏ Activity 15, p. 45. Have students write their answers.

❏ Activity 16, 17, 19, pp. 46–47. Have students work in pairs.

❏ Activity 18, p. 44. Play TXT CD 1 track 28.

ASSESS AND RETEACH
❏ Para y piensa, p. 47. Expand by using more pronouns (**a mí, a él, a usted, a ustedes, a ellos(as)**).

❏ Homework: *Cuaderno:* pp. 7–9; *Cuaderno para hispanohablantes,* pp. 8–11.

OPTIONAL RESOURCES
Plan
- Best Practices Toolkit
- PE Answers, MSRB, Transparencies 28–31
- Workbook Answers, UTB 1, Transparencies 54–61
- Absent Student Copymasters, URB 1, p. 129

Present
- Warm-up Transp. 18, UTB 1
- Grammar Presentation Transp. 17, UTB 1
- Fine Art Activities, URB 1, p. 117
- Fine Art Transp. 8, UTB 1

Practice
- Practice Games, URB 1, p. 61
- Audio Script, URB 1, pp. 103–107

Assess
- Reteaching Copymasters, URB 1, pp. 35–36

TECHNOLOGY TOOLS

Teacher Tools	Student Tools
Power Presentations	@Home Tutor
EasyPlanner CD-ROM	ClassZone.com
Test generator CD-ROM	eEdition Online or CD-ROM

Todo junto, Juegos y Diversiones, pp. 48–51

OBJECTIVES

- Integrate lesson content.
- Practice using and integrating lesson vocabulary and grammar.

> ### STANDARDS
>
> - 1.1 Engage in conversation, Act. 22
> - 1.2 Understand language, Acts. 20, 23
> - 1.3 Present information, Acts. 21–24, PYP
> - 5.2 Life-long learners, Juegos y diversiones

FOCUS AND MOTIVATE

- ❏ Todo junto, p. 48. Instruct students to form small groups and say: "¿De dónde eres? Soy de _____. El (Ella) es de _____. ¿Ellos(as) son de _____?"

TEACH

- ❏ Telehistoria completa, p. 48. Read Cuando escuchas. Write on the board a list of the cognates they hear.
- ❏ Video Program DVD 1, Unit 1. Show Telehistoria scenes 1 and 2 as a review before showing scene 3.
- ❏ Audio Program TXT CD 1 tracks 25 and 26. Play Telehistoria scenes 1 and 2 as a review before listening to scene 3 (TXT CD 1 track 29).
- ❏ Telehistoria escena 3. In groups of three, play the roles of Alicia, Miguel, and Teresa.
- ❏ Activity 24, p. 50. Use the rubric to assess students' writings.

PRACTICE AND APPLY

- ❏ **Comprensión de los episodios,** p. 49. Play TXT CD 1 tracks 25, 26, and 29 to do Activities 20–21.
- ❏ Activities 22–24, pp. 49–50. Practice using reading, writing, listening, speaking skills.

IEP Modification   Encourage students to write their self-introductions before speaking them in Activity 22.

- ❏ Juegos y diversiones, p. 51

ASSESS AND RETEACH

- ❏ Para y piensa, p. 50. Create an original description using the characters.
- ❏ Grammar Quiz 2, On-level Assessment, p. 14.
- ❏ Homework: *Cuaderno:* pp. 10–11; *Cuaderno para hispanohablantes,* pp. 12–13.

OPTIONAL RESOURCES

Plan

- Best Practices Toolkit
- PE Answers, MSRB, Transparencies 28–31
- Workbook Answers, UTB 1, Transparencies 54–61
- Absent Student Copymasters, URB 1, p. 130

Present

- Warm-up Transp. 28, UTB 1
- Audio Script, URB 1, pp. 103–107
- Video Script, URB 1, pp. 97–98

Practice

- Learning Scenarios on Easy Planner
- Conversation cards on Easy Planner and ClassZone
- Video activities, URB 1, pp. 85–86
- Practice Games, URB 1, p. 62

Assess

- Reteaching Copymasters, URB 1, pp. 35, 37

| TECHNOLOGY TOOLS ||
Teacher Tools	Student Tools
Power Presentations	@Home Tutor
EasyPlanner CD-ROM	ClassZone.com
Test generator CD-ROM	eEdition Online or CD-ROM

Lectura/Conexiones, pp. 52–54

OBJECTIVES

- Use surveys to talk about favorite activities.
- Read and compare what students in another schools like to do.
- Read about Hernando de Soto's exploration of the US.

STANDARDS

- 1.2 Understand language
- 2.1 Practices and perspectives
- 2.2 Products and perspectives
- 3.1 Knowledge of other disciplines
- 4.2 Compare cultures

FOCUS AND MOTIVATE

❏ Lectura, pp. 52–53. Complete the survey as a class.

TEACH

❏ **¿Qué te gusta hacer?** pp. 52–53. Play TXT CD 1, track 32. Ask what other activities students like to do. Write them on the board.

❏ Conexiones, **La geografía,** p. 54. In small groups, hold a contest to see which one can name the cities first.

PRACTICE AND APPLY

❏ **¿Qué te gusta hacer?** In pairs, ask and answer: "¿Qué te gusta hacer?" Circulate around the class and check for proper intonation, pronunciation.

❏ **La geografía,** In Proyecto 2, share results with the class. In Proyecto 3, bring samples of Tex-Mex music to share.

IEP Modification   Based on Proyecto 2 of **La geografía,** ask students to list the English meanings of some place names from their countries of origin.

ASSESS AND RETEACH

❏ Para y piensa, p. 53. Tally the results of the class survey taken earlier. Compare the class with the survey in the book.

❏ Culture Quiz, On-level Assessment, p. 15.

OPTIONAL RESOURCES

Plan

- Best Practices Toolkit
- PE Answers, MSRB, Transparencies 28–31
- Workbook Answers, UTB 1, Transparencies 54–61
- Absent Student Copymasters, URB 1, p. 131

Present

- Warm-up Transp. 29, UTB 1

Practice

- Lecturas para todos pp. 2–6
- Lecturas para hispanohablantes
- Practice Games, URB 1, p. 63

TECHNOLOGY TOOLS	
Teacher Tools	**Student Tools**
Power Presentations	@Home Tutor
EasyPlanner CD-ROM	ClassZone.com
Test generator CD-ROM	eEdition Online or CD-ROM

En resumen, Repaso de la lección, pp. 55–57

OBJECTIVES

- Review using **gustar** with the infinitive.
- Review conjugating **ser** in the present tense.
- Review using **ser de** to tell where they and others are from.

STANDARDS

- 1.2 Understand language, Acts. 1, 3
- 1.3 Present information, Acts. 2, 4
- 4.2 Compare cultures, Act. 5

FOCUS AND MOTIVATE

❑ En resumen, p. 55. Review all vocabulary terms and grammar items.

TEACH

❑ En resumen. Assess which vocabulary terms need more practice and encourage students to form sentences with each.

❑ Repaso de la lección, pp. 56–57. Have students form two questions to ask classmates.

PRACTICE AND APPLY

❑ Repaso de la lección, Activity 1, p. 56. Play TXT CD 1 track 33 while they do Activity 1.

❑ Complete activities 2–5, pp. 56–57.

IEP Modification   Instruct students to answer the items in Activity 5 in Spanish.

ASSESS AND RETEACH

❑ Homework: Study En resumen, p. 55; *Cuaderno:* pp. 12–23;, *Cuaderno para hispanohablantes,* pp. 14–23.

❑ Lesson Test, On-level Assessment, pp. 16–22.

OPTIONAL RESOURCES

Plan

- Best Practices Toolkit
- PE Answers, MSRB, Transparencies 28–31
- Workbook Answers, UTB 1, Transparencies 54–61
- Absent Student Copymasters, URB 1, p. 132

Present

- Warm-up Transp. 29, UTB 1
- Audio Script, URB 1, pp. 103–107

Practice

- Practice Games, URB 1, p. 64
- Sing-along Audio CD

Assess

- Review Games Online
- Lesson Test, Modified Assessment, pp. 11–17
- Lesson Test, Pre-AP Assessment, pp. 11–17
- Lesson Test, Heritage Learners Assessment, 17–23

TECHNOLOGY TOOLS	
Teacher Tools	**Student Tools**
Power Presentations	@Home Tutor
EasyPlanner CD-ROM	ClassZone.com
Test generator CD-ROM	eEdition Online or CD-ROM
McDougal Littell Assessment System	

Lesson Opener,
Presentación y práctica de vocabulario, pp. 58–63

OBJECTIVES

- Teach about Hispanic culture in the U.S.
- Present and practice vocabulary: adjectives, likes and dislikes.
- **Recycle:** **ser** to describe people, p. 38.

STANDARDS

- 1.2 Understand language, Act. 1
- 1.3 Present information, Act. 2
- 2.1 Practices and perspectives
- 4.2 Compare cultures

FOCUS AND MOTIVATE

- ❑ Presentación de vocabulario, pp. 60–62. Guess the descriptions of the people in the photos.

TEACH

- ❑ Presentación de vocabulario, pp. 60–62, paragraphs A–F. Read the paragraphs.
- ❑ Video Program DVD 1, Unit 1. View Vocabulary Presentation video.
- ❑ Play TXT CD 1 track 34 and do ¡A responder! activity, p. 57, TXT CD 1 track 35.

IEP Modification   Nota gramatical, p. 63. Review the present-tense conjugations of the verb **ser** on p. 38.

PRACTICE AND APPLY

- ❑ Lesson Opener, pp. 58–59. Read the Comparación cultural, discuss the questions. Have students view the photographs and respond to the ¿Qué ves? questions.
- ❑ Play TXT CD 1 track 35 to do ¡A responder! activity, p. 62.
- ❑ Práctica de vocabulario, p. 63, Activities 1–2. Review **gustar** with infinitive.

ASSESS AND RETEACH

- ❑ Para y piensa, p. 63. Complete activity.
- ❑ Vocabulary Recognition Quiz, On-level Assessment, p. 28.
- ❑ Homework: *Cuaderno:* pp. 24–26; *Cuaderno para hispanohablantes,* pp. 24–27.

OPTIONAL RESOURCES

Plan
- Best Practices Toolkit
- Absent Student Copymasters, URB 1, p. 133
- PE Answers, MSRB, Transparencies 32–35
- Workbook Answers, UTB 1, Transparencies 62–69

Present
- Warm-up Transp. 30, UTB 1
- Vocabulary Transp. 14–15, UTB 1

- TPRS, pp. 8–14
- Video Script, URB 1, pp. 99–100
- Audio Script, URB 1, pp. 108–112
- Vocabulary Video, DVD 1

Practice
- Practice Games, URB 1, p. 65
- Video Activites URB 1, pp. 87–88

Assess
- Reteaching Copymasters, URB 1, pp. 39–40

TECHNOLOGY TOOLS	
Teacher Tools	**Student Tools**
Power Presentations	@Home Tutor
EasyPlanner CD-ROM	ClassZone.com
	Cultura interactiva
	eEdition Online or CD-ROM

Vocabulario en contexto, pp. 64–65

OBJECTIVES

- Understand and practice vocabulary in context: descriptive words.
- **Culture:** Compare Mexican and Tex-Mex food.

STANDARDS

- 1.1 Engage in conversation, Act. 4
- 1.2 Understand language, Acts. 3–4
- 1.3 Present information, Acts. 3–4
- 2.2 Products and perspectives, CC

FOCUS AND MOTIVATE

❑ Telehistoria escena 1, Strategies. Read Cuando lees, p. 64.

TEACH

❑ Telehistoria escena 1, p. 64. Have students read the dialog out loud for correct pronunciation and intonation.

❑ Video Program, DVD 1, Unit 1. Show the DVD. Have students listen for the adjectives, and raise their hands each time they hear one. Write the adjectives on the board.

❑ Audio Program TXT CD 1, track 36. Play audio for scene 1.

❑ To teach hair color vocabulary, point to your own hair and say: "Tengo pelo rubio (castaño) or Soy pelirrojo(a). Then ask a blond student "¿Tienes pelo rubio?" and model the answer.

❑ Comparacíon cultural, Comida mexicana y Tex-Mex, p. 65. Do Compara con tu mundo activity.

PRACTICE AND APPLY

❑ Comprensión del episodio, Activity 3, p. 65. Play TXT CD 1 track 36 to compare Ricardo and Alberto. Have students draw and fill in their Venn diagrams on the board.

❑ Activity 4, p. 65. In pairs, read the interview and prepare a list of adjectives.

ASSESS AND RETEACH

❑ Para y piensa, p. 65. Expand the activity to use other adjectives.

❑ Vocabulary Production Quiz, On-level Assessment, p. 29.

OPTIONAL RESOURCES

Plan

- Best Practices Toolkit
- PE Answers, MSRB, Transparencies 32–35
- Workbook Answers, UTB 1, Transparencies 62–69
- Absent Student Copymasters, URB 1, p. 134

Present

- Warm-up Transp. 30, UTB 1
- Audio Script, URB 1, pp. 108–112
- Video Script, URB 1, pp. 99–100

Practice

- Video Activities, URB 1, pp. 89–90
- Practice Games, URB 1, p. 66

Assess

- Reteaching Copymasters, URB 1, pp. 39, 41

TECHNOLOGY TOOLS	
Teacher Tools	**Student Tools**
Power Presentations	@Home Tutor
EasyPlanner CD-ROM	ClassZone.com
Test generator CD-ROM	eEdition Online or CD-ROM

Presentación y práctica de gramática 1, pp. 66–69

OBJECTIVES

- Present and practice definite and indefinite articles.
- **Recycle:** snack foods, p. 33; **gustar** + infinitive, 44.

FOCUS AND MOTIVATE

❑ Presentación de gramática, p. 66. Orally introduce the definite, indefinite articles.

TEACH

❑ Presentación de gramática, p. 66. Relate the Spanish definite and indefinite articles to the English articles *the, a, an, some*.

❑ Introduce the concepts of gender and number. Explain that all nouns in Spanish are either masculine or feminine.

❑ Write the Spanish definite and indefinite articles on the board, then fill in the correct forms of **amigo**.

IEP Modification Hold up pictures of the snacks they learned and elicit the indefinite article first, then the definite article.

PRACTICE AND APPLY

❑ Práctica de gramática, pp. 67–69. Complete Activities 5–11.

❑ Play TXT CD 1 track 37 to do Activity 6.

❑ Review **gustar** with infinitive. Then have students to work in pairs for Activity 10.

ASSESS AND RETEACH

❑ Para y piensa: page 69. Expand the activity by writing other nouns on the board and asking students to give the correct definite and indefinite articles.

❑ Homework: *Cuaderno:* pp. 27–29; *Cuaderno para hispanohablantes*, pp. 28–30.

STANDARDS

- 1.1 Engage in conversation, Acts. 9–11
- 1.2 Understand language
- 1.3 Present information, Acts. 5–11, PYP
- 4.1 Compare languages

OPTIONAL RESOURCES

Plan

- Best Practices Toolkit
- PE Answers, MSRB, Transparencies 32–35
- Workbook Answers, UTB 1, Transparencies 62–69
- Absent Student Copymasters, URB 1, p. 135
- Easy Planner CD-ROM
- ClassZone.com

Present

- Warm-up Transp. 31, UTB 1
- Grammar Presentation Transp. 18, UTB 1
- Audio Script, URB 1, pp. 73–77

Practice

- Practice Games, URB 1, p. 67

Assess

- Reteaching Copymasters, URB 1, pp. 42, 43, 48, 49

TECHNOLOGY TOOLS	
Teacher Tools	**Student Tools**
Power Presentations	@Home Tutor
EasyPlanner CD-ROM	ClassZone.com
Test generator CD-ROM	eEdition Online or CD-ROM

Gramática en contexto, pp. 70–71

OBJECTIVES

- Practice using definite and indefinite articles to talk about people.
- Teach the pronunciation of the letter ñ.
- **Recycle:** after-school activities, pp. 32–33.

STANDARDS

- 1.1 Engage in conversation, Act. 13
- 1.2 Understand language, Act. 12, Pronunciación
- 1.3 Present information, Act. 13
- 4.1 Compare languages, Pronunciación

FOCUS AND MOTIVATE

❑ Telehistoria escena 2, Strategies. Read Cuando escuchas, p. 70.

TEACH

❑ Video Program DVD 1, Unit 1. Show the video for scene 2. Ask students to raise their hands when they hear an article and write it with the accompanying noun on the board.

❑ Audio Program TXT CD 1, track 38. Play audio for scene 2.

❑ Telehistoria escena 2, p. 70. Have students read the dialog out loud for correct pronunciation and intonation. Emphasize the definite and indefinite articles.

❑ Pronunciación, p. 71. Play TXT CD 1 track 39. Have students practice the sound of ñ out loud.

PRACTICE AND APPLY

❑ Comprensión del episodio, Activity 12, p. 71. Play TXT CD 1 track 38.

❑ Activity 13, p. 71. Review after-school activities on pp. 32–33, before doing this activity.

IEP Modification   Ask students to write on the board other words they know that use the letter ñ. Practice pronouncing those words as a class.

ASSESS AND RETEACH

❑ Para y piensa, p. 71. To expand the activity, write more sentences on the board.

❑ Grammar Quiz 1, On-level Assessment, p. 30.

OPTIONAL RESOURCES

Plan

- Best Practices Toolkit
- PE Answers, MSRB, Transparencies 32–35
- Workbook Answers, UTB 1, Transparencies 62–69
- Absent Student Copymasters, URB 1, p. 136

Present

- Warm-up Transp. 31, UTB 1
- Audio Script, URB 1, pp. 108–112
- Video Script, URB 1, pp. 99–100

Practice

- Practice Games, URB 1, p. 68
- Video Activities, URB 1, pp. 91–92

Assess

- Reteaching Copymasters, URB 1, pp. 42, 44, 50

| TECHNOLOGY TOOLS ||
Teacher Tools	Student Tools
Power Presentations	@Home Tutor
EasyPlanner CD-ROM	ClassZone.com
Test generator CD-ROM	eEdition Online or CD-ROM

Presentación y práctica de gramática 2, pp. 72–75

OBJECTIVES
- Present and practice noun-adjective agreement.
- Practice using adjectives to describe people.
- **Culture:** Recognize or discuss the influence of cultural traditions on an artist's work.

FOCUS AND MOTIVATE
❏ Go around the room pointing to different students, using different nouns and adjectives.

STANDARDS
- 1.1 Engage in conversation, Acts. 18–19
- 1.2 Understand language, Act. 18
- 1.3 Present information, Acts. 14–19
- 2.1 Practices and perspectives, Act. 19
- 3.1 Knowledge of other disciplines
- 4.1 Compare languages, Act. 19
- 4.2 Compare cultures, Act. 19

TEACH
❏ Presentación de gramática, p. 72. Copy the noun-adjective chart on the board, and underline the endings. After you have presented the principles of gender and number agreement, erase **alto** and substitute another adjective.

❏ Presentación de gramática, p. 72. Present adjectives that end in **-e** or a consonant and have students pair them with masculine, feminine, singular, and plural nouns.

PRACTICE AND APPLY
❏ Práctica de gramática, Activity 14, p. 73. Have students work in pairs.

❏ Activity 15, p. 73. Stress that students should show noun-adjective agreement in their descriptions.

❏ Activities 16, 17, p. 74. Have students write their answers.

❏ Activity 18, p. 75. Ask for volunteers to present their descriptions.

❏ Activity 19, Comparacíon cultural, El arte tejano, p. 75. Discuss the Compara con tu mundo question and do the exercise based on the painting.

ASSESS AND RETEACH
❏ Para y piensa, p. 75. Complete activity.

❏ Homework: *Cuaderno:* pp. 30–32; *Cuaderno para hispanohablantes*, pp. 31–34.

IEP Modification Expand Para y piensa by writing more examples on the board.

OPTIONAL RESOURCES
Plan
- Best Practices Toolkit
- PE Answers, MSRB, Transparencies 32–35
- Workbook Answers, UTB 1, Transparencies 62–69
- Absent Student Copymasters, URB 1, p. 137

Present
- Warm-up Transp. 32, UTB 1
- Grammar Presentation Transp. 19, UTB 1

Practice
- Practice Games, URB 1, p. 69
- Audio Script, URB 1, pp. 108–112

Assess
- Reteaching Copymasters, URB 1, pp. 45, 46

TECHNOLOGY TOOLS

Teacher Tools	Student Tools
Power Presentations	@Home Tutor
EasyPlanner CD-ROM	ClassZone.com
Test generator CD-ROM	eEdition Online or CD-ROM

Todo junto, Juegos y Diversiones, pp. 76–79

OBJECTIVES

- Use definite, indefinite articles, adjectives to tell what someone is like.
- Juegos y diversiones, p. 79.

STANDARDS

- 1.1 Engage in conversation, Act. 22
- 1.2 Understand language, Acts. 20, 22–23
- 1.3 Present information, Acts. 21–24, PYP
- 5.2 Life-long learners, Juegos y diversiones

FOCUS AND MOTIVATE

❑ Pair students and have them describe each other using articles and descriptive adjectives.

TEACH

❑ Video Program DVD 1, Unit 1. After viewing escena 3, have students form groups of three and play the roles of Alberto, Ricardo, and Sandra.

❑ Audio Program TXT CD 1 tracks 36 and 38. Play Telehistoria scenes 1 and 2 as a review before listening to scene 3 (TXT CD 1 track 40).

❑ Telehistoria completa, p. 76. Read the Resumen sections for scenes 1 and 2 before reading scene 3.

❑ Activity 24, p. 78. Use the rubric to assess students' writings.

IEP Modification   View scenes 1 and 2 in preparation for the Activities 20–21, p. 77.

PRACTICE AND APPLY

❑ Comprensión de los episodios, p. 77. Play TXT CD 1 tracks 36, 38, and 40 to do Activities 20–21. Have students do Activity 20 in teams. A representative from each group will come to the board and write the answer. Opposing groups will approve or correct the answer.

❑ Activity 22, p. 77. Have students work in pairs.

❑ Activity 23, p. 78. Play TXT CD 1, track 41–42.

❑ Activity 24, p. 78. Students may want to draw a picture of their ideal friend.

❑ Juegos y diversiones, p. 79. Have students play 20 *preguntas* to review descriptive adjectives, noun-adjective agreement, and indefinite articles.

ASSESS AND RETEACH

❑ Para y piensa, p. 78. Alter completing this exercise, have students create an original sentence on the characters and following the model.

❑ Grammar Quiz 2, On-level Assessment, p. 31.

❑ Homework: *Cuaderno:* pp. 33–34, *Cuaderno para hispanohablantes,* pp. 35–36.

OPTIONAL RESOURCES

Plan
- Best Practices Toolkit
- PE Answers, MSRB, Transparencies 32–35
- Workbook Answers, UTB 1, Transparencies 62–69
- Absent Student Copymasters, URB 1, p. 138

Practice
- Learning Scenarios on Easy Planner
- Conversation cards on Easy Planner and ClassZone
- Video activities, URB 1, pp. 93–94
- Practice Games, URB 1, p. 70

Present
- Warm-up Transp. 32, UTB 1
- Audio Script, URB 1, pp. 108–112
- Video Script, URB 1, pp. 99–100

Assess
- Reteaching Copymasters, URB 1, pp. 45, 47

TECHNOLOGY TOOLS	
Teacher Tools	**Student Tools**
Power Presentations	@Home Tutor
EasyPlanner CD-ROM	ClassZone.com
Test generator CD-ROM	eEdition Online or CD-ROM

Lectura/Proyectos culturales, pp. 80–82

OBJECTIVES

- Read and discuss things to do in San Antonio and Miami.
- Compare what teenagers like to do.
- Learn why traditional Hispanic dishes change when prepared in the U.S.

FOCUS AND MOTIVATE

- ❑ Lectura cultural pp. 80–81. Have students scan the reading and make a comparison chart of San Antonio and Miami.

STANDARDS

- 1.2 Understand language
- 2.1 Practices and perspectives
- 3.1 Knowledge of other disciplines
- 4.2 Compare cultures
- 5.1 Spanish in the community

TEACH

- ❑ Lectura cultural, pp. 80–81. Request volunteers to read out loud. Ask them why they think the Mexican influence is strong in San Antonio and why the Cuban influence is strong in Miami.
- ❑ Proyectos culturales, p. 82. Have students investigate En tu comunidad.

PRACTICE AND APPLY

- ❑ Lectura cultural, p. 80. Ask questions about San Antonio and Miami, based on the comparison chart, such as: "¿Cuáles actividades les gustan hacer a los estudiantes en San Antonio / en Miami? ¿Cuáles son los sitios de interés en San Antonio / en Miami? ¿Es mexicana o cubana la comida en San Antonio / en Miami?"
- ❑ Proyectos culturales, p. 82. Bring all the ingredients for **salsa fresca** (or ask for volunteers) and have a small group of students prepare the salsa fresca for the whole class. Instruct them to say the ingredients in Spanish as they use them. Then invite the entire class to partake, saying ¡Buen provecho!

IEP Modification   Ask students what similarities and differences they see between these two cities and how they compare to where they live.

ASSESS AND RETEACH

- ❑ Para y piensa, p. 81. Answer the ¿Comprendiste? and ¿Y tú? questions.
- ❑ Culture Quiz, On-level Assessment, p. 32.

OPTIONAL RESOURCES

Plan

- Best Practices Toolkit
- PE Answers, MSRB, Transparencies 32–35
- Workbook Answers, UTB 1, Transparencies 62–69
- Absent Student Copymasters, URB 1, p. 139

Present

- Warm-up Transp. 33, UTB 1

Practice

- Lecturas para todos pp. 7–11
- Lecturas para hispanohablantes
- Practice Games, URB 1, p. 71

TECHNOLOGY TOOLS	
Teacher Tools	**Student Tools**
Power Presentations	@Home Tutor
EasyPlanner CD-ROM	ClassZone.com
Test generator CD-ROM	eEdition Online or CD-ROM

En resumen, Repaso de la lección, pp. 83–85

OBJECTIVES

- Review describing what someone is like using **ser.**
- Review using articles, and descriptive adjectives to talk about people.
- Review article-noun agreement and noun-adjective agreement.

STANDARDS

- 1.2 Understand language, Acts. 1, 3
- 1.3 Present information, Acts. 2, 4
- 4.2 Compare cultures, Act. 5

FOCUS AND MOTIVATE

❑ En resumen, p. 83. Review all vocabulary terms and grammar items.

TEACH

❑ En resumen, p. 83. Assess which vocabulary terms need more practice and encourage students to form sentences with each.

❑ Repaso de la lección, pp. 84–85. Review **ser** to tell what someone is like, p. 63.

❑ Review definite and indefinite articles, p. 66. Write **amigo, amiga, amigos, amigas** on the board and ask students to give the definite and indefinite articles.

❑ Ask students to describe someone in the class.

❑ Review Comparación cultural, pp. 65, 75, and 80–81.

PRACTICE AND APPLY

❑ Repaso de la lección, Activity 1, p. 84. Play TXT CD 1 track 46 while they do Activity 1.

❑ Activities 2–5, pp. 84–85. Have students work in pairs or small groups.

IEP Modification: Instruct students to answer the items in Activity 5 in Spanish.

ASSESS AND RETEACH

❑ Homework: Study En resumen, p. 83; *Cuaderno:* pp. 35–46, *Cuaderno para hispanohablantes,* pp. 37–46.

❑ Lesson Test, On-level Assessment, pp. 33–39.

OPTIONAL RESOURCES

Plan
- Best Practices Toolkit
- PE Answers, MSRB, Transparencies 32–35
- Workbook Answers, UTB 1, Transparencies 62–69
- Absent Student Copymasters, URB 1, p. 141

Present
- Warm-up Transp. 33, UTB 1
- Audio Script, URB 1, pp. 108–112

Practice
- Practice Games, URB 1, p. 72
- Sing-along Audio CD

Assess
- Review Games Online
- Lesson Test, Modified Assessment, pp. 23–29
- Lesson Test, Pre-AP Assessment, pp. 23–29
- Lesson Test, Heritage Learners Assessment, 29–35

TECHNOLOGY TOOLS	
Teacher Tools	**Student Tools**
Power Presentations	@Home Tutor
EasyPlanner CD-ROM	ClassZone.com
Test generator CD-ROM	eEdition Online or CD-ROM
McDougal Littell Assessment System	

Comparación cultural, Repaso inclusivo, pp. 86–89

OBJECTIVES
- Read three personal accounts about personal descriptions and favorite activities.
- Compare favorite activities of teens with your favorite activities.
- Cumulative review.

Copyright © by McDougal Littell, a division of Houghton Mifflin Company.

STANDARDS
- 1.2 Understand language, Acts. 1, 3
- 1.3 Present information, Acts. 2–6
- 2.1 Practices and perspectives, Act. 1
- 4.2 Compare cultures, Act. 1

FOCUS AND MOTIVATE
- ❏ Using the chart on p. 86, ask a question for each language category.

TEACH
- ❏ Comparación cultural, p. 87. Call on students to read the descriptions of José Manuel, Martina, and Mónica. Encourage them to note similarities between the three in language and theme.
- ❏ Comparación cultural, p. 86. Use the writing strategy to guide students in their own descriptions.
- ❏ Repaso inclusivo, pp. 88–89. Review the En resumen pages in Unit 1 to prepare students for Activities 1–6.

PRACTICE AND APPLY
- ❏ Comparación cultural, p. 86. Help students increase their cultural awareness by doing the **Compara con tu mundo** activity.
- ❏ Repaso inclusivo, p. 88. Play TXT CD 1 track 46 to complete Activity 1.
- ❏ Repaso inclusivo, pp. 88–89. Complete Activities 2–6.

ASSESS AND RETEACH
- ❏ Homework: *Cuaderno*, pp. 47–49; *Cuaderno para hispanohablantes*, pp. 47–49.
- ❏ Unit Test, On-level Assessment, pp. 45–51.

OPTIONAL RESOURCES

Plan
- Absent Student Copymasters, URB 1, pp. 142, 143

Present
- Audio Script, URB 1, pp. 108–112

Practice
- Situational Transp. and Copymasters, UTB 1, Transp. 20–21, pp. 1–2
- Family Involvement Activity, URB 1, p. 124

Assess
- Unit Test, Modified Assessment, pp. 35–41
- Unit Test, Pre-AP Assessment, pp. 35–41
- Unit Test, Heritage Learners Assessment, pp. 41–47

TECHNOLOGY TOOLS	
Teacher Tools	**Student Tools**
EasyPlanner CD-ROM	ClassZone.com
Test generator CD-ROM	Cultura interactiva
McDougal Littell Assessment System	eEdition Online or CD-ROM

Unit and Lesson Opener,
Presentación y práctica de vocabulario, pp. 90–97

OBJECTIVES
- Introduce lesson theme: **Somos estudiantes.**
- Learn about Mexican culture.
- Present and practice vocabulary: time, school and class schedules, numbers, school subjects, classroom activities.

STANDARDS
- 1.1 Engage in conversation, Act. 2
- 1.2 Understand language
- 1.3 Present information, Act. 1
- 2.1 Practices and perspectives
- 4.1 Compare languages, Nota gramatical
- 4.2 Compare cultures

FOCUS AND MOTIVATE
- ❑ Unit 2 Opener, p. 90. Ask simple questions about the facts and photos presented on page 90. Let students find the information.

TEACH
- ❑ Presentación de vocabulario, pp. 92–93, paragraphs. Have students read the paragraphs.
- ❑ Video Program DVD 1, Unit 2. Show Vocabulary Presentation video. Review Pablo and Claudia's schedule
- ❑ Practice **tener** and **tener que** with infinitives.
- ❑ Audio Program TXT CD 2, track 3. Listen to Vocabulary Presentation audio.

IEP Modification   Provide a list of class subjects using cognates such as: Matemáticas, Literatura, Física, etc.

PRACTICE AND APPLY
- ❑ Lesson Opener, pp. 92–93: Have students read Comparación cultural. Have students view photos and respond to "¿Qué ves? ¿Qué hay?" questions.
- ❑ Review vocabulary for after school activities and numbers, p. 94.
- ❑ Listen to TXT CD 2 track 2 to do ¡A responder! activity, p. 96.
- ❑ Práctica de vocabulario. Do Activity 1, and Activity 2 (in pairs), p. 97.

IEP Modification   Have students talk about their after-school classes. Ask them to provide details.

ASSESS AND RETEACH
- ❑ Para y piensa, p. 97. Have students to work in pairs.
- ❑ Vocabulary Recognition Quiz, On-level Assessment, p. 57.
- ❑ Homework: *Cuaderno*, pp. 51–53; *Cuaderno para hispanohablantes*, pp. 51–54.

OPTIONAL RESOURCES
Plan
- Family Letter, URB 2, p. 91
- Family letters in Haitian Creole and Spanish on ClassZone.com
- Best Practices Toolkit
- Absent Student Copymasters, URB 2, p. 93
- PE Answers, MSRB, Transparencies 36–39
- Workbook Answers, UTB 2, Transparencies 32–39

Present
- Warm-up Transp. 16, UTB 2
- Atlas Map, UTB 1, Transp. 3
- Map Transp. 7, UTB 2
- Map-Culture Activities, URB 2, pp. 81–82

- Música del mundo hispano
- Vocabulary Transp. 6–7, UTB 2
- TPRS, pp. 15–21
- Video Script, URB 2, pp. 67–68
- Audio Script, URB 2, pp. 71–75
- Vocabulary Video, DVD 1
- Fine Art Activities, URB 2, pp. 86, 88
- Fine Art Transp. 3, 5, UTB 2

Practice
- Practice Games, URB 2, p. 27

Assess
- Reteaching Copymasters, URB 2, pp. 1–2

TECHNOLOGY TOOLS

Teacher Tools	Student Tools
Power Presentations	@Home Tutor
EasyPlanner CD-ROM	ClassZone.com
	Cultura interactiva
	eEdition Online or CD-ROM

Vocabulario en contexto, pp. 98–99

OBJECTIVES
- Talk about daily routines.
- Practice words for telling the time.

STANDARDS
- 1.2 Understand language, Act. 3, PYP
- 1.3 Present information, Act. 4
- 4.1 Compare languages, Nota gramatical

FOCUS AND MOTIVATE
- ❏ Telehistoria escena 1, p. 98. Read the Cuando escuchas strategy.

TEACH
- ❏ Telehistoria escena 1, p. 98. Direct students' attention to the photo and have them guess what is happening in the scene.
- ❏ Video Program DVD 1, Unit 2. Show the video for scene 1. Have students listen for the time expressions.
- ❏ Audio Program TXT CD 2 track 3. Listen to audio for scene 1.
- ❏ Telehistoria escena 1, p. 98. Have students read the dialog out loud for correct pronunciation and intonation.

PRACTICE AND APPLY
- ❏ Comprensión del episodio, Activity 3, p. 99. Listen to TXT CD 2 track 3. Call on students to give the answers.
- ❏ Nota gramatical, p. 99. Practice time expressions by having students say what time it is now and what time they will say it is in five minutes, twenty minutes, etc.

IEP Modification   Have students talk about after school activities. Encourage them to give details by asking questions: "A qué hora es? ¿Qué tienes que hacer?"

ASSESS AND RETEACH
- ❏ Para y piensa, p. 99. Have students complete the sentences with the appropriate time. Also personalize questions by asking, "¿A qué hora tienes la clase de español?"
- ❏ Vocabulary Production Quiz, On-level Assessment, p. 58.

OPTIONAL RESOURCES

Plan
- Best Practices Toolkit
- PE Answers, MSRB, Transp. 36–39
- Workbook Answers, UTB 2, Transp. 32–39
- Absent Student Copymasters, URB 2, p. 94

Present
- Warm-up Transp. 16, UTB 2
- Audio Script, URB 2, pp. 71–75
- Video Script, URB 2, pp. 67–68

Practice
- Video Activities, URB 2, pp. 51–52
- Practice Games, URB 2, p. 28

Assess
- Reteaching Copymasters, URB 2, pp. 1, 3

TECHNOLOGY TOOLS	
Teacher Tools	**Student Tools**
Power Presentations	@Home Tutor
EasyPlanner CD-ROM	ClassZone.com
Test Generator CD-ROM	eEdition Online or CD-ROM

¡AVANCEMOS!
Unidad 2 Lección 1

Presentación y práctica de gramática 1, pp. 100–103

OBJECTIVES

- Present and practice the verb **tener.**
- Practice lesson vocabulary and expressions of frequency.
- **Recycle:** after school activities, p. 32.
- Practice pronouncing the **ch** combination.

STANDARDS
- 1.1 Engage in conversation, Acts. 7, 9
- 1.2 Understand language, Act. 8, Pronunciación
- 1.3 Present information, Acts. 5–9
- 2.1 Practices and perspectives, CC
- 4.1 Compare languages, Pronunciación
- 4.2 Compare cultures, CC

FOCUS AND MOTIVATE

❑ Presentación de gramática, p. 100. Read the English Grammar Connection to the class as an introduction to the verb **tener.**

TEACH

❑ Presentación de gramática, p. 100. Ask students to write sentences using at least three forms of the verb **tener** that describe what they or others in the class have.

❑ Pronunciación, p. 98. Listen to TXT CD 2, track 6. Call on students to say the words and the sentence out loud.

❑ Práctica de gramática, Comparación cultural, p. 102. Have students read about school uniforms, then lead a discussion about whether or not schools should use them.

❑ Práctica de gramática, Nota gramatical, p. 103. Write expressions of frequency on the board. Emphasize their placement in sentences and compare to English.

IEP Modification If the **ch** sound is unfamiliar to students, allow them extra time to listen to the audio and practice pronunciation.

PRACTICE AND APPLY

❑ Práctica de gramática, p. 103. Activity 5. Have students write their answers.

❑ For Activity 6, ask six different students to form the required sentences.

❑ Play TXT CD 2 track 4 to do Activity 8.

❑ Activity 7, 9. Have students work in pairs.

IEP Modification Pair students with good role models in pair work so that they can learn by peer example.

ASSESS AND RETEACH

❑ Para y piensa: p. 103. Have students answer the questions with the given expressions of frequency.

❑ Homework: *Cuaderno,* pp. 54–56; *Cuaderno para hispanohablantes,* pp. 55–57.

OPTIONAL RESOURCES

Plan
- Best Practices Toolkit
- PE Answers, MSRB, Transparencies 36–39
- Workbook Answers, UTB 2, Transparencies 32–39
- Absent Student Copymasters, URB 2, p. 95
- Easy Planner CD-ROM
- ClassZone.com

Present
- Warm-up Transp. 17, UTB 2
- Grammar Presentation Transp. 10, UTB 2
- Audio Script, URB 2, pp. 71–75

Practice
- Practice Games, URB 2, p. 29

Assess
- Reteaching Copymasters, URB, pp. 4, 5, 10

TECHNOLOGY TOOLS	
Teacher Tools	**Student Tools**
Power Presentations	@Home Tutor
EasyPlanner CD-ROM	ClassZone.com
Test Generator CD-ROM	eEdition Online or CD-ROM

Gramática en contexto, pp. 104–105

OBJECTIVES
- Practice using **tener** and **tener que** to talk daily activities on different days of the week.
- **Recycle:** Days of the week, p. 18.

> **STANDARDS**
> - 1.2 Understand language, Act. 10
> - 1.3 Present information, Acts. 11–12, PYP

FOCUS AND MOTIVATE
- ❑ Telehistoria escena 2, p. 104. Read the Cuando lees strategy.

TEACH
- ❑ Telehistoria escena 2, p. 104. Direct students' attention to the photo and have them guess what is happening in the scene.
- ❑ Telehistoria escena 2. Have students read the dialog out loud for correct pronunciation and intonation.
- ❑ Video Program DVD 1, Unit 2. Show the video for scene 2.
- ❑ Audio Program TXT CD 2, track 5. Listen to audio for scene 2. Have students to listen for the tag questions. Ask them how many they hear.

PRACTICE AND APPLY
- ❑ Comprensión del episodio, Activity 10, p. 105. Listen to TXT CD 2, track 5. Call on students to answer the questions.
- ❑ Activity 11, p. 105. Have students to do the activity in pairs so they can e-mail each other.
- ❑ Activity 12, p. 105. After students do the activity, have them work in groups to take a survey of responses to three of the items. Then ask them to make a chart of the responses.

ASSESS AND RETEACH
- ❑ Para y piensa, p. 105. Have students complete sentences based on the Telehistoria.
- ❑ Grammar Quiz 1, On-level Assessment, p. 59.

IEP Modification   Confirm students' understanding of the task by having them repeat directions orally.

OPTIONAL RESOURCES

Plan
- Best Practices Toolkit
- PE Answers, MSRB, Transparencies 36–39
- Workbook Answers, UTB 2, Transparencies 32–39
- Absent Student Copymasters, URB 2, p. 96

Present
- Warm-up Transp. 17, UTB 2
- Audio Script, URB 2, pp. 71–75
- Video Script, URB 2, pp. 67–68

Practice
- Practice Games, URB 2, p. 30
- Video Activities, URB 2, pp. 53–54

Assess
- Reteaching Copymasters, URB 2, pp. 4, 6

TECHNOLOGY TOOLS	
Teacher Tools	**Student Tools**
Power Presentations	@Home Tutor
EasyPlanner CD-ROM	ClassZone.com
Test Generator CD-ROM	eEdition Online or CD-ROM

Presentación y práctica de gramática 2, pp. 106–109

OBJECTIVES
- Present and practice the present tense of regular **-ar** verbs.
- Compare English equivalencies.

FOCUS AND MOTIVATE
- ❏ Presentación de gramática, p. 106. Read the English Grammar Connection to the class as an introduction to the Spanish present tense.

TEACH
- ❏ Presentación de gramática, p. 106. Write the present-tense **-ar** verb endings on the board in one color. Give students other regular **-ar** verbs and invite them to come up and complete the conjugation in another color to demonstrate that the verb stems are the same in all forms.
- ❏ Práctica de gramática, Act. 18, Comparación cultural, p. 109. Have students read the passage. Encourage them to investigate other themes depicted in murals and then to brainstorm answers to Compara con tu mundo.

PRACTICE AND APPLY
- ❏ Práctica de gramática, Activity 13, p. 107. Have students write their answers.
- ❏ Activity 14, p. 107. Ask different students to form the required sentences.
- ❏ Activity 15. Ask other students to complete the paragraph with the correct form of the appropriate verb.
- ❏ Práctica de gramática, p. 108–109. Pair and group students to do Activities 16–19.

ASSESS AND RETEACH
- ❏ Para y piensa, p. 109. Change the subjects of each sentence and have students redo the activity.
- ❏ Homework: *Cuaderno*, pp. 57–59; *Cuaderno para hispanohablantes*, pp. 58–61.

OPTIONAL RESOURCES

Plan
- Best Practices Toolkit
- PE Answers, MSRB, Transparencies 36–39
- Workbook Answers, UTB 2, Transparencies 32–39
- Absent Student Copymasters, URB 2, p. 97

Present
- Warm-up Transp. 18, UTB 2
- Fine Art Activities, URB 2, p. 85
- Fine Art Transp. 2, UTB 2
- Grammar Presentation Transp. 11, UTB 2

Practice
- Practice Games, URB 2, p. 31
- Audio Script, URB 2, pp. 71–75

Assess
- Reteaching Copymasters, URB 2, pp. 7, 8

TECHNOLOGY TOOLS	
Teacher Tools	**Student Tools**
Power Presentations	@Home Tutor
EasyPlanner CD-ROM	ClassZone.com
Test Generator CD-ROM	eEdition Online or CD-ROM

¡AVANCEMOS!
Unidad 2 Lección 1

Todo junto, Juegos y diversiones, pp. 110–113

OBJECTIVES

- Practice **tener** and **–ar** verbs.
- Review school activities vocabulary.
- Review numbers by playing a game.

STANDARDS

- 1.1 Engage in conversation, Act. 22
- 1.2 Understand language, Acts. 20, 23
- 1.3 Present information, Acts. 20–24, PYP
- 5.2 Life-long learners, Juegos y diversiones

FOCUS AND MOTIVATE

- ❏ Telehistoria completa, p. 110. Direct students to read the two Resúmenes as a review the previous Telehistoria scenes.

TEACH

- ❏ Video Program DVD 1, Unit 2. Show Telehistoria scenes 1 and 2 as a review before showing scene 3.
- ❏ Audio Program TXT CD 2 tracks 3 and 5. Listen to Telehistoria scenes 1 and 2 as a review before listening to scene 3 (TXT CD 2 track 7).
- ❏ Telehistoria escena 3, p. 110. Have students read the dialog out loud for correct pronunciation and intonation. Ask them to identify cognates.

IEP Modification   Ask for three volunteers to role-play the dialog and encourage the person playing Pablo to use proper intonation and the corresponding facial expressions to show surprise.

PRACTICE AND APPLY

- ❏ Comprensión de los episodios, p. 111. Listen to TXT CD 2 tracks 3, 5, and 7 to do Activities 20–21 in pairs. Ask two or three pairs to share their dialogs.
- ❏ Activity 22, p. 111. Have students work in pairs.
- ❏ Activity 23, p. 112. Read Manuel's schedule and listen to the principal's message. Audio Program TXT CD 2 tracks 8, 9.
- ❏ Activity 24, p. 112. After students have written about their schedules, ask for three volunteers to share what they wrote.
- ❏ Juegos y diversiones, p. 113. Have students play silencio to review numbers.

ASSESS AND RETEACH

- ❏ Para y piensa, p. 112. Ask students to complete the exercise writing the correct form of the indicated verbs.
- ❏ Grammar Quiz 2, On-level Assessment, p. 60.
- ❏ Homework: *Cuaderno,* pp. 60–61; *Cuaderno para hispanohablantes,* pp. 62–63.

OPTIONAL RESOURCES

Plan
- Best Practices Toolkit
- PE Answers, MSRB, Transparencies 36–39
- Workbook Answers, UTB 2, Transparencies 32–39
- Absent Student Copymasters, URB 2, p. 98

Present
- Warm-up Transp. 18, UTB 2
- Audio Script, URB 2, pp. 71–75
- Video Script, URB 2, pp. 67–68

Practice
- Learning Scenarios on Easy Planner
- Conversation cards on Easy Planner and ClassZone
- Video activities, URB 2, pp. 55–56
- Practice Games, URB 2, p. 32

Assess
- Reteaching Copymasters, URB 2, pp. 7, 9

TECHNOLOGY TOOLS	
Teacher Tools	**Student Tools**
Power Presentations	@Home Tutor
EasyPlanner CD-ROM	ClassZone.com
Test Generator CD-ROM	eEdition Online or CD-ROM

¡Avancemos!
44   Level 1A Unidad 2
   Lección 1

Lectura/Conexiones, pp. 114–116

OBJECTIVES
- Read about and discuss a bilingual school in Mexico.
- Make cultural comparisons.
- Analyze an antique map to learn about an ancient Mexican city.

STANDARDS
- 1.2 Understand language
- 1.3 Present information
- 2.1 Practices and perspectives
- 3.1 Knowledge of other disciplines
- 3.2 Acquire information
- 4.2 Compare cultures

FOCUS AND MOTIVATE
- ❑ Lectura, p. 115. Have students scan the list of classes at Colegio Americano and compare them to the classes they are taking.

TEACH
- ❑ Lectura, pp. 114–115. Review the reading strategies before reading the handbook. Have students read the class requirements out loud.
- ❑ Audio Program: TXT CD 2 track 10. Listen to the audio for the Colegio Americano handbook.
- ❑ Conexiones, p. 116. Have students read the passage El pueblo de Zempoala.

PRACTICE AND APPLY
- ❑ Lectura, pp. 114–115. After students read or listen to the audio, ask them to work in pairs to write a similar handbook for your school. They should include a student testimonial and a list of the course requirements for their grade.
- ❑ Conexiones, p. 116. Divide students into three subgroups, with each group assigned to one of the Proyectos. Then have them share their projects as a class.

IEP Modification When organizing groups, have stronger students partner with slower-paced learners.

ASSESS AND RETEACH
- ❑ Para y piensa, p. 115. Help students to identify similarities and differences between the bilingual program and their school.
- ❑ Culture Quiz, On-level Assessment, p. 61.

OPTIONAL RESOURCES

Plan
- Best Practices Toolkit
- PE Answers, MSRB, Transp. 36–39
- Workbook Answers, UTB 2, Transp. 32–39
- Absent Student Copymasters, URB 2, p. 99

Present
- Warm-up Transp. 19, UTB 2

Practice
- Lecturas para todos pp. 12–16
- Lecturas para hispanohablantes
- Practice Games, URB 2, p. 23

TECHNOLOGY TOOLS	
Teacher Tools	**Student Tools**
Power Presentations	@Home Tutor
EasyPlanner CD-ROM	ClassZone.com
Test Generator CD-ROM	eEdition Online or CD-ROM

En resumen, Repaso de la lección, pp. 117–119

OBJECTIVES

- Review lesson grammar and vocabulary.

STANDARDS
- 1.2 Understand language, Act. 1
- 1.3 Present information, Acts. 2–5
- 4.2 Compare cultures, Act. 5

FOCUS AND MOTIVATE

❑ En resumen, p. 117. Review all vocabulary terms and grammar items.

TEACH

❑ En resumen. Assess which vocabulary terms need more practice and encourage students to form sentences with each.

❑ Repaso de la lección, pp. 118–119. Do a quick review of how to conjugate **tener** and present tense of **-ar** verbs.

❑ Repaso de la lección, pp. 118–119. Ask personal questions using adverbs of frequency and **-ar** verbs. Ask students to come up with 3–5 questions of their own.

PRACTICE AND APPLY

❑ Repaso de la lección, Activity 1, p. 118. Listen to TXT CD 2 track 11 while they do Activity 1.

❑ Complete activities 2–5, pp. 118–119. You can pair students to complete Activity 5.

IEP Modification   Instruct students to answer the items in Activity 5 in Spanish.

ASSESS AND RETEACH

❑ Homework: Study En resumen, p. 118; *Cuaderno*, pp. 62–73, *Cuaderno para hispanohablantes*, pp. 64–73.

❑ Lesson Test, On-level Assessment, pp. 62–68.

OPTIONAL RESOURCES

Plan
- Best Practices Toolkit
- PE Answers, MSRB, Transp. 36–39
- Workbook Answers, UTB 2, Transp. 32–39
- Absent Student Copymasters, URB 2, p. 100

Present
- Warm-up Transp. 19, UTB 2
- Audio Script, URB 2, pp. 71–75

Practice
- Practice Games, URB 2, p. 34
- Sing-along Audio CD

Assess
- Review Games Online
- Lesson Test, Modified Assessment, pp. 47–53
- Lesson Test, Pre-AP Assessment, pp. 47–53
- Lesson Test, Heritage Learners Assessment, pp. 53–59

TECHNOLOGY TOOLS	
Teacher Tools	**Student Tools**
Power Presentations	@Home Tutor
EasyPlanner CD-ROM	ClassZone.com
Test Generator CD-ROM	eEdition Online or CD-ROM
McDougal Littell Assessment System	

Left margin: ¡AVANCEMOS! Unidad 2 Lección 1

Lesson Opener,
Presentación y práctica de vocabulario, pp. 120–125

OBJECTIVES
- Teach classroom vocabulary.
- Teach expressions with the verbs **estar** and **ir**.

STANDARDS
- 1.1 Engage in conversation, Act. 3
- 1.2 Understand language
- 1.3 Present information, Acts. 1–3, PYP
- 4.2 Compare cultures

FOCUS AND MOTIVATE
- ❏ Lesson Opener, p. 120. Read Compara con tu mundo and discuss the question.

TEACH
- ❏ Presentación de vocabulario, pp. 122–124, paragraphs A–D. Read the paragraphs.
- ❏ Video Program DVD 1, Unit 2. Show Vocabulary Presentation video. Ask students which items mentioned can be found in your classroom.
- ❏ Audio Program TXT CD 2, track 12. Listen to Vocabulary Presentation audio. Have students note any cognates they hear.

PRACTICE AND APPLY
- ❏ Lesson 1 Opener, pp. 120–121. Read Comparación cultural. Have students view the photographs and respond to the ¿Qué ves? questions.
- ❏ Listen to TXT CD 2 track 13 to do ¡A responder! activity, p. 124.
- ❏ Práctica de vocabulario, p. 125. Allow students to check each other's work on Activities 1 and 2. Pair students to complete Activity 3.

ASSESS AND RETEACH
- ❏ Para y piensa, p. 125. Ask students to name their three favorite rooms in school.
- ❏ Vocabulary Recognition Quiz, On-level Assessment, p. 74.
- ❏ Homework: *Cuaderno*, pp. 74–76; *Cuaderno para hispanohablantes*, pp. 74–77.

IEP Modification Ask students about their favorite place(s) in school. How do they feel there? Model: "En la cafetería, estoy contento(a)".

OPTIONAL RESOURCES
Plan
- Best Practices Toolkit
- Absent Student Copymasters, URB 2, p. 101
- PE Answers, MSRB, Transp. 40–43
- Workbook Answers, UTB 2, Transp. 40–47

Present
- Warm-up Transp. 20, UTB 2
- Vocabulary Transp. 6–7, UTB 3
- TPRS, pp. 22–28

- Video Script, URB 3, pp. 69–70
- Audio Script, URB 2, pp. 76–80
- Vocabulary Video, DVD 1

Practice
- Practice Games, URB 2, p. 35
- Video Activities URB 2, pp. 57–58

Assess
- Reteaching Copymasters, URB 2, pp. 11–12

TECHNOLOGY TOOLS	
Teacher Tools	**Student Tools**
Power Presentations	@Home Tutor
EasyPlanner CD-ROM	ClassZone.com
	Cultura interactiva
	eEdition Online or CD-ROM

Vocabulario en contexto, pp. 126–127

OBJECTIVES

- Identify words for after school activities.
- Describe classes and classroom objects.
- **Recycle:** class subjects, p. 95.

STANDARDS
- 1.1 Engage in conversation, Act. 5
- 1.2 Understand language, Act. 4
- 1.3 Present information, Act. 5, PYP

FOCUS AND MOTIVATE

❑ Telehistoria escena 1, p. 126. Read the Cuando lees strategy.

TEACH

❑ Telehistoria escena 1, p. 126. Direct students' attention to the photos and have them guess what is happening in the scene. What class is Pablo in?

❑ Telehistoria escena 1, p. 126. Have students read the dialog out loud for correct pronunciation and intonation. Encourage them to pay attention to exclamations.

❑ Video Program DVD 1, Unit 2. Show the video for scene 1. Ask students what emotions are evident among the characters.

❑ Audio Program TXT CD 2, track 14. Listen to audio for scene 1.

IEP Modification   Ask students if they know other words from their country of origin that mean the same thing as **pizarrón.**

PRACTICE AND APPLY

❑ Comprensión del episodio, Activity 4, p. 127. Listen to TXT CD 2 track 14 to describe what happens in the scene.

❑ Activity 5, p. 127. Have students work in pairs.

ASSESS AND RETEACH

❑ Para y piensa, p. 127. Ask students to write complete sentences. Model: **Pablo y Claudia tienen que estudiar en la biblioteca.**

❑ Vocabulary Production Quiz, On-level Assessment, p. 75.

OPTIONAL RESOURCES

Plan
- Best Practices Toolkit
- PE Answers, MSRB, Transp. 40–43
- Workbook Answers, UTB 2, Transp. 40–47
- Absent Student Copymasters, URB 2, p. 102

Present
- Warm-up Transp. 20, UTB 2
- Audio Script, URB 2, pp. 76–80
- Video Script, URB 2, pp. 69–70

Practice
- Video Activities, URB 2, pp. 59–60
- Practice Games, URB 2, p. 36

Assess
- Reteaching Copymasters, URB 2, pp. 11, 13, 20

TECHNOLOGY TOOLS	
Teacher Tools	**Student Tools**
Power Presentations	@Home Tutor
EasyPlanner CD-ROM	ClassZone.com
Test Generator CD-ROM	eEdition Online or CD-ROM

Presentación y práctica de gramática 1, pp. 128–131

OBJECTIVES
- Present and practice the uses of the verb **estar.**
- Practice vocabulary to express feelings.
- Practice prepositions of place.

STANDARDS
- 1.1 Engage in conversation, Acts. 8, 9, 12
- 1.3 Present information, Acts. 6–12, PYP
- 3.1 Knowledge of other disciplines, Act. 9
- 4.1 Compare languages
- 4.2 Compare cultures, Act. 9

FOCUS AND MOTIVATE
- ❏ Presentación de gramática, p. 128. Refer students to page 38 for a review of the verb **ser** and contrast with **estar.**

TEACH
- ❏ Presentación de gramática, p. 128. Elicit conjugation of the verb **estar** by stating a subject and allowing students to respond with the correct form.
- ❏ Presentación de gramática. Illustrate words of location by placing students at various places in the classroom and describing their relative locations.
- ❏ Comparación cultural, Activity 9, p. 130. Lead students in a discussion of the Compara con tu mundo question.
- ❏ Nota gramatical, p. 130. Make simple statements and have students turn them into questions.

IEP Modification   Place different objects, such as a pen, in different places in the classroom. Pair students with a stronger partner to tell where the object is now located. Model: La pluma está en el libro.

PRACTICE AND APPLY
- ❏ Práctica de gramática, p. 129. Allow students to check each other's work on Activity 6.
- ❏ Activities 7, 10, 11. Have students write their answers.
- ❏ Activities 8, 12. Pair students to complete the activities.
- ❏ Activity 9. Expand the activity by using a map of your community. Have students say where certain businesses or buildings are located relative to each other.

ASSESS AND RETEACH
- ❏ Para y piensa: p. 131. Pair students to talk about where they are and how they are feeling. Model: **Estoy al lado de Jim. Estoy bien.**
- ❏ Homework: *Cuaderno*, pp. 77–79; *Cuaderno para hispanohablantes*, pp. 78–80.

OPTIONAL RESOURCES
Plan
- Best Practices Toolkit
- PE Answers, MSRB, Transp. 40–43
- Workbook Answers, UTB 2, Transp. 40–47
- Absent Student Copymasters, URB 2, p. 103
- Easy Planner CD-ROM
- ClassZone.com

Present
- Warm-up Transp. 21, UTB 2
- Grammar Presentation Transp. 12, UTB 2
- Audio Script, URB 2, pp. 76–80

Practice
- Practice Games, URB 2, p. 37

Assess
- Reteaching Copymasters, URB 2, pp. 14–15

TECHNOLOGY TOOLS	
Teacher Tools	**Student Tools**
Power Presentations	@Home Tutor
EasyPlanner CD-ROM	ClassZone.com
Test Generator CD-ROM	eEdition Online or CD-ROM

Gramática en contexto, pp. 132–133

OBJECTIVES
- Practice **estar** in context.

STANDARDS
- 1.1 Engage in conversation, Acts. 14–15
- 1.2 Understand language, Act. 13
- 1.3 Present information, Acts. 14–15, PYP

FOCUS AND MOTIVATE
- ❑ Telehistoria escena 2, p. 132. Read the Cuando escuchas strategy.

TEACH
- ❑ Telehistoria escena 2, p. 132. Direct students' attention to the photos and have them guess what is happening in the scene.
- ❑ Video Program DVD 1, Unit 2. Show the video for scene 2. Encourage students to note feelings through the characters' words and facial expressions.
- ❑ Audio Program TXT CD 2, track 15. Listen to audio for scene 2.
- ❑ Telehistoria escena 2, p. 132. Read dialogue two lines at a time with students, emphasizing expression and intonation.

IEP Modification   Pair students to act out two lines of dialogue, changing one word in each exchange.

PRACTICE AND APPLY
- ❑ Comprensión del episodio, Activity 13, p. 133. Listen to TXT CD 2, track 15 to determine which statements are false.
- ❑ Activities 14, 15, p. 133. Pair or group students to do the activities. Ask some of them to share their answers with the group.

ASSESS AND RETEACH
- ❑ Para y piensa, p. 133. Have students write three sentences about Pablo and Claudia.
- ❑ Grammar Quiz 1, On-level Assessment, p. 76.

OPTIONAL RESOURCES

Plan
- Best Practices Toolkit
- PE Answers, MSRB, Transp. 40–43
- Workbook Answers, UTB 2, Transp. 40–47
- Absent Student Copymasters, URB 2, p. 104

Present
- Warm-up Transp. 21, UTB 2
- Audio Script, URB 2, pp. 76–80
- Video Script, URB 2, pp. 69–70

Practice
- Practice Games, URB 2, p. 38
- Video Activities, URB 2, pp. 61–62

Assess
- Reteaching Copymasters, URB 2, pp. 14, 16

TECHNOLOGY TOOLS	
Teacher Tools	**Student Tools**
Power Presentations	@Home Tutor
EasyPlanner CD-ROM	ClassZone.com
Test Generator CD-ROM	eEdition Online or CD-ROM

Presentación y práctica de gramática 2, pp. 134–137

OBJECTIVES

- Present and practice the verb **ir**.
- Practice naming places in school.
- Practice pronouncing the difference sounds of the letter **d**.

STANDARDS

- 1.1 Engage in conversation, Act. 20
- 1.2 Understand language, Act. 18
- 1.3 Present information, Acts. 16–17, 19–21, PYP
- 2.2 Products and perspectives, CC
- 4.1 Compare languages, Pronunciación
- 4.2 Compare cultures, CC

FOCUS AND MOTIVATE

- ❏ Presentación de gramática, p. 134. Refer students back to page 100 to review conjugating verbs.

TEACH

- ❏ Presentación de gramática, p. 134. Elicit conjugation of the verb **ir** by stating a subject and allowing students to respond with the correct form.
- ❏ Presentación de gramática. Present the interrogative **¿Adónde (vas)?** Then ask different students where they go after Spanish class or after school.
- ❏ Comparación cultural, p. 137. Read El autorretrato and have students work in pairs to answer the Compara con tu mundo question.

PRACTICE AND APPLY

- ❏ Práctica de gramática, p. 135. Allow students to check each other's work on Activity 16.
- ❏ Activities 17, 19. Have students write their answers.
- ❏ Pronunciación, p. 135. Listen to TXT CD 2 track 17. Have students practice the two pronunciations of the letter **d** out loud.
- ❏ Activity 18. Listen to TXT CD 2 track 16 to complete the activity.
- ❏ Activity 20, p. 137. Pair students to complete the activity. Activity 21 can be set up as an interview between two students.

IEP Modification Before doing speaking activities, allow students time to write down their answers first.

ASSESS AND RETEACH

- ❏ Para y piensa, p. 137. Ask students to form sentences.
- ❏ Homework: *Cuaderno*, pp. 80–82; *Cuaderno para hispanohablantes*, pp. 81–84.

OPTIONAL RESOURCES

Plan

- Best Practices Toolkit
- PE Answers, MSRB, Transp. 40–43
- Workbook Answers, UTB 2, Transp. 40–47
- Absent Student Copymasters, URB 2, p. 105

Present

- Warm-up Transp. 22, UTB 2
- Fine Art Activities, URB 2, p. 87

- Fine Art Transp. 4, UTB 2
- Grammar Presentation Transp. 13, UTB 2

Practice

- Practice Games, URB 2, p. 39
- Audio Script, URB 2, pp. 76–80

Assess

- Reteaching Copymasters, URB 2, pp. 17, 18

TECHNOLOGY TOOLS	
Teacher Tools	**Student Tools**
Power Presentations	@Home Tutor
EasyPlanner CD-ROM	ClassZone.com
Test Generator CD-ROM	eEdition Online or CD-ROM

Todo junto, Juegos y diversiones, pp. 138–141

OBJECTIVES

- Practice the verbs **ir** and **estar.**
- **Recycle:** telling time, p. 99.
- Review **estar,** classroom objects, and location words by playing a game.

STANDARDS
- 1.1 Engage in conversation, Act. 24
- 1.2 Understand language, Acts. 22–23, 25
- 1.3 Present information, Act. 24–26, PYP
- 5.2 Life-long learners, Juegos y diversiones

FOCUS AND MOTIVATE

❏ Telehistoria completa, p. 138. Have students talk about the scene 3 photo. Ask: "¿Dónde están? ¿Cómo están?"

TEACH

❏ Video Program DVD 1, Unit 2. Show Telehistoria scenes 1 and 2 as a review before showing scene 3.

❏ Audio Program TXT CD 2 tracks 14 and 15. Listen to Telehistoria scenes 1 and 2 as a review before listening to scene 3 (TXT CD 2 track 18).

❏ Telehistoria escena 3, p. 138. Have students read the dialog and note the problems that Pablo is experiencing.

IEP Modification   Ask students to write a short paragraph that summarizes the Telehistoria storyline in Lesson 2.

PRACTICE AND APPLY

❏ Comprensión de los episodios, p. 139. Listen to TXT CD 2 tracks 14, 15, and 18 to do Activities 22–23. Allow students to work in pairs.

❏ Activity 24. Ask students to describe their daily routine with as many details as they can: "¿Qué clases tomas? ¿A qué hora es tu clase favorita? ¿A qué hora vas a la cafetería? ¿Adónde vas después?"

❏ Activity 25, p. 140. Listen to TXT CD 2 tracks 19 and 20 to determine when Raquel and Mario can study.

❏ Juegos y diversiones, p. 141. Have students play ¿Cierto o falso? for review.

ASSESS AND RETEACH

❏ Para y piensa, p. 140.

❏ Grammar Quiz 2, On-level Assessment, p. 77.

❏ Homework: *Cuaderno,* pp. 83–84; *Cuaderno para hispanohablantes,* pp. 85–86.

OPTIONAL RESOURCES

Plan
- Best Practices Toolkit
- PE Answers, MSRB, Transp. 40–43
- Workbook Answers, UTB 2, Transp. 40–47
- Absent Student Copymasters, URB 2, p. 106

Present
- Warm-up Transp. 22, UTB 2
- Audio Script, URB 2, pp. 76–80
- Video Script, URB 2, pp. 69–70

Practice
- Learning Scenarios on Easy Planner
- Conversation cards on Easy Planner and ClassZone
- Video activities, URB 2, pp. 63–64
- Practice Games, URB 2, p. 40

Assess
- Reteaching Copymasters, URB 2, pp. 17, 19

TECHNOLOGY TOOLS	
Teacher Tools	**Student Tools**
Power Presentations	@Home Tutor
EasyPlanner CD-ROM	ClassZone.com
Test Generator CD-ROM	eEdition Online or CD-ROM

Lectura/Proyectos culturales, pp. 142–144

OBJECTIVES
- Read and discuss descriptions of favorite classes.
- Read about yarn painting in Mexico and rock drawing in the Dominican Republic.

STANDARDS
- 1.2 Understand language
- 1.3 Present information
- 2.2 Products and perspectives
- 4.2 Compare cultures
- 5.1 Spanish in the community

FOCUS AND MOTIVATE
- ❏ Lectura cultural, pp. 142–143. Ask students: "¿Cuál es tu clase favorita? ¿Por qué?"

TEACH
- ❏ Lectura cultural, pp. 142–143. Read Mi clase favorita as a class. Afterward, encourage students to find at least one similarity between the two essays.
- ❏ Proyectos culturales, p. 144. Prepare materials to do one of the two cultural projects in class.

PRACTICE AND APPLY
- ❏ Lectura cultural, Mi clase favorita, pp. 142–143. Ask students to write an essay about their favorite class. Call on some students to share their essays.
- ❏ Proyectos culturales, p. 144. Encourage students to research more about the Huichol and the Taino, especially what other contributions they may have made to modern culture.

IEP Modification   Ask students about traditional art forms from other Spanish-speaking countries and have them organize a project to create that art.

ASSESS AND RETEACH
- ❏ Para y piensa, p. 143.
- ❏ Culture Quiz, On-level Assessment, p. 78.

OPTIONAL RESOURCES

Plan
- Best Practices Toolkit
- PE Answers, MSRB, Transp. 40–43
- Workbook Answers, UTB 2, Transp. 40–47
- Absent Student Copymasters, URB 2, p. 107

Present
- Warm-up Transp. 23, UTB 2

Practice
- Lecturas para todos pp. 17–21
- Lecturas para hispanohablantes
- Practice Games, URB 2, p. 41

TECHNOLOGY TOOLS

Teacher Tools	Student Tools
Power Presentations	@Home Tutor
EasyPlanner CD-ROM	ClassZone.com
Test Generator CD-ROM	eEdition Online or CD-ROM

¡AVANCEMOS!
Unidad 2 Lección 2

En resumen, Repaso de la lección, pp. 145–147

OBJECTIVES
- Review lesson grammar and vocabulary.

STANDARDS
- 1.2 Understand language, Act. 1
- 1.3 Present information, Acts. 1–5
- 4.2 Compare cultures, Act. 5

FOCUS AND MOTIVATE
- ❏ En resumen, p. 145. Review all vocabulary terms and grammar items.

TEACH
- ❏ En resumen. Assess which vocabulary terms need more practice and encourage students to form sentences with each.
- ❏ Repaso de la lección, p. 146. Model sentences with **estar**: "Estoy contento(a)." Then ask: "¿Y tú, cómo estás? ¿Y ella?" etc.
- ❏ Repaso de la lección. Model sentences with **ir**: "Esta tarde voy al cine." Then ask various students: "¿Y tú? ¿adónde vas esta tarde? ¿Y ella?"

PRACTICE AND APPLY
- ❏ Repaso de la lección, Activity 1, p. 146. Listen to TXT CD 2 track 22 while they do Activity 1.
- ❏ Complete activities 2–5, pp. 146–147.

IEP Modification   Instruct students to answer the items in Activity 5 in Spanish.

ASSESS AND RETEACH
- ❏ Homework: En resumen, p. 145. *Cuaderno*, pp. 85–96. *Cuaderno para hispanohablantes*, pp. 87–96.
- ❏ Lesson Test, On-level Assessment, pp. 79–85.

OPTIONAL RESOURCES

Plan
- Best Practices Toolkit
- PE Answers, MSRB, Transp. 40–43
- Workbook Answers, UTB 2, Transp. 40–47
- Absent Student Copymasters, URB 2, p. 109

Present
- Warm-up Transp. 23, UTB 2
- Audio Script, URB 2, pp. 76–80

Practice
- Practice Games, URB 2, p. 42
- Sing-along Audio CD

Assess
- Review Games Online
- Lesson Test, Modified Assessment, pp. 60–65
- Lesson Test, Pre-AP Assessment, pp. 60–65
- Lesson Test, Heritage Learners Assessment, pp. 65–71

TECHNOLOGY TOOLS	
Teacher Tools	**Student Tools**
Power Presentations	@Home Tutor
EasyPlanner CD-ROM	ClassZone.com
Test Generator CD-ROM	eEdition Online or CD-ROM
McDougal Littell Assessment System	

¡AVANCEMOS!
Unidad 2 Lección 2

Comparación cultural, Repaso inclusivo, pp. 148–151

OBJECTIVES

- Read personal narratives about school and classes in three different countries.
- Have students compare the favorite classes of the authors with their own favorite classes.
- Ask students to write about their school schedule.

STANDARDS

- 1.2 Understand language
- 1.3 Present information
- 2.1 Practices and perspectives
- 4.2 Compare cultures

FOCUS AND MOTIVATE

- ❑ Comparación cultural, pp. 148–149. Ask students to get out their school schedules to prepare for the writing activity.

TEACH

- ❑ Comparación cultural, p. 149. Call on students to read the descriptions of Rafael, Andrea, and Juan Carlos. Encourage them to note similarities between the three in language and theme.
- ❑ Audio Program TXT CD 2 track 23. Listen to Rafael, Andrea, and Juan Carlos.
- ❑ Comparación cultural, p. 132. Use the writing strategy to guide students in the descriptions of their schedules.
- ❑ Repaso inclusivo, pp. 150–151. Review the En resumen pages in Units 1 and 2 to prepare students for Activities 1–6.

PRACTICE AND APPLY

- ❑ Comparación cultural, p. 148. Help students increase their cultural awareness by doing the Compara con tu mundo activity.
- ❑ Repaso inclusivo, p. 150. Listen to TXT CD 2 track 24 to complete Activity 1.
- ❑ Repaso inclusivo, pp. 150–151. Complete Activities 2–6.

IEP Modification Allow students to time organize their ideas and write the first draft of their paragraph in English.

ASSESS AND RETEACH

- ❑ Homework: *Cuaderno*, pp. 97–99; *Cuaderno para hispanohablantes*, pp. 97–99.
- ❑ Unit Test, On-level Assessment, pp. 91–97.

OPTIONAL RESOURCES

Plan
- Absent Student Copymasters, URB 2, pp. 110, 111

Present
- Audio Script, URB 2, pp. 76–80

Practice
- Situational Transp. and Copymasters, UTB 2, Transp. 14–15, pp. 1–2
- Family Involvement Activity, URB 2, p. 92

Assess
- Unit Test, Modified Assessment, pp. 71–77
- Unit Test, Pre-AP Assessment, pp. 71–77
- Unit Test, Heritage Learners Assessment, pp. 77–83

TECHNOLOGY TOOLS	
Teacher Tools	**Student Tools**
EasyPlanner CD-ROM	ClassZone.com
Test Generator CD-ROM	Cultura interactiva
McDougal Littell Assessment System	eEdition Online or CD-ROM

Unit and Lesson Opener,
Presentación y práctica de vocabulario, pp. 152–159

OBJECTIVES
- Teach about Puerto Rican culture.
- Teach students to express what they like to eat for breakfast, lunch, and dinner.
- **Recycle:** the verb **gustar** with an infinitive, p. 44.

STANDARDS
- 1.1 Engage in conversation, Act. 2
- 1.2 Understand language
- 1.3 Present information, Acts. 1–2, PYP
- 2.2 Products and perspectives
- 4.2 Compare cultures

FOCUS AND MOTIVATE
- ❏ Unit 3 Opener, p. 152. Review interrogatives by forming questions based on information about Puerto Rico.

TEACH
- ❏ Presentación de vocabulario, pp. 156–158, paragraphs A–D. Have students repeat the labeled foods after you.
- ❏ Video Program DVD 1, Unit 3. Show Vocabulary Presentation video. Review Pablo and Claudia's schedule.
- ❏ Practice **gustar** with infinitives and **tener** expressions by asking questions such as: "Cuando tienes hambre, ¿te gusta comer huevos o cereal? Cuando tienes sed, ¿te gusta beber jugo de naranja o leche?"
- ❏ Audio Program TXT CD 3 track 1. Listen to Vocabulary Presentation audio.

IEP Modification Bring in pictures of the foods mentioned in the lesson. Hold up pictures and have the class repeat the words after you. Next hold up the pictures and have students generate the words themselves.

PRACTICE AND APPLY
- ❏ Lesson Opener, pp. 154–155: Have students read Comparación cultural. Have students view photos and respond to "¿Qué ves?" questions.
- ❏ Listen to TXT CD 3 track 2 to do ¡A responder! activity, p. 158.
- ❏ Práctica de vocabulario, Activity 1. Allow students to check each other's work.
- ❏ Activity 2. Review **gustar** with infinitive on page 44.

ASSESS AND RETEACH
- ❏ Para y piensa, p. 159. Have students ask each other, "¿Cuál es tu comida favorita? ¿Por qué?"
- ❏ Vocabulary Recognition Quiz, On-level Assessment, p. 103.
- ❏ Homework: *Cuaderno*, pp. 101–103; *Cuaderno para hispanohablantes*, pp. 101–104.

OPTIONAL RESOURCES
Plan
- Family Letter, URB 3, p. 91
- Family letters in Haitian Creole and Spanish on ClassZone.com
- Best Practices Toolkit
- Absent Student Copymasters, URB 3, p. 93
- PE Answers, MSRB, Transp. 44–47
- Workbook Answers, UTB 3, Transp. 32–39

Present
- Warm-up Transp. 16, UTB 3
- Atlas Map, UTB 1, Transp. 4
- Map Transp. 1, UTB 3
- Map-Culture Activities, URB 3, pp. 83–84
- Música del mundo hispano

- Vocabulary Transp. 6–7, UTB 3
- TPRS, pp. 29–35
- Video Script, URB 3, pp. 69–70
- Audio Script, URB 3, pp. 73–77
- Vocabulary Video, DVD 1
- Fine Art Activities, URB 3, pp. 87, 89
- Fine Art Transp. 3, 5, UTB 3

Practice
- Practice Games, URB 3, p. 31
- Video Activities URB 3, pp. 51–52

Assess
- Reteaching Copymasters, URB 3, pp. 1–2, 10

TECHNOLOGY TOOLS	
Teacher Tools	**Student Tools**
Power Presentations	@Home Tutor
EasyPlanner CD-ROM	ClassZone.com
	Cultura interactiva
	eEdition Online or CD-ROM

Vocabulario en contexto, pp. 160–161

OBJECTIVES

- Present and practice interrogative words.
- **Recycle:** snack foods, p. 33.

STANDARDS

- 1.1 Engage in conversation, Act. 4
- 1.2 Understand language, Act. 3
- 1.3 Present information, Act. 4, PYP

FOCUS AND MOTIVATE

❑ Telehistoria escena 1, p. 160. Read the Cuando lees strategy.

TEACH

❑ Telehistoria escena 1, p. 160. Direct students' attention to the photo and have them guess what is happening in the scene. "¿Quién es la chica? ¿Quién es el chico? ¿Dónde están? ¿Adónde van? ¿De qué hablan?"

❑ Telehistoria escena 1, p. 160. Have students read the dialog out loud, making clear differences in tone between questions and statements.

❑ Video Program DVD 1, Unit 3. Show the video for scene 1. Suggest that they count or write down all the question words they hear.

❑ Audio Program TXT CD 3 track 3. Listen to audio for scene 1.

❑ Nota gramatical, p. 161. Remind students that questions in English are formed in the same way, with a conjugated verb after the interrogative word.

PRACTICE AND APPLY

❑ Comprensión del episodio, Activity 3, p. 161. Listen to TXT CD 3 track 3. Call on students to say the correct interrogative word, then ask them the complete question for them to respond.

❑ Activity 4. Encourage students to ask each other questions about the food served in their cafeteria.

IEP Modification For Activity 4, allow students to write down the names of the food before speaking, and then pair them with stronger students to facilitate the activity.

ASSESS AND RETEACH

❑ Para y piensa, p. 161. Have students choose the correct interrogative word.

❑ Vocabulary Production Quiz, On-level Assessment, p. 104.

OPTIONAL RESOURCES

Plan

- Best Practices Toolkit
- PE Answers, MSRB, Transp. 44–47
- Workbook Answers, UTB 3, Transp. 32–39
- Absent Student Copymasters, URB 3, p. 94

Present

- Warm-up Transp. 16, UTB 3
- Audio Script, URB 3, pp. 73–77
- Video Script, URB 3, pp. 69–70

Practice

- Video Activities, URB 3, pp. 53–54
- Practice Games, URB 3, p. 32

Assess

- Reteaching Copymasters, URB 3, pp. 1, 3, 11

TECHNOLOGY TOOLS	
Teacher Tools	**Student Tools**
Power Presentations	@Home Tutor
EasyPlanner CD-ROM	ClassZone.com
Test Generator CD-ROM	eEdition Online or CD-ROM

¡AVANCEMOS!
Unidad 3 Lección 1

Presentación y práctica de gramática 1, pp. 162–165

OBJECTIVES

- Present and practice using **gustar** with nouns.
- Pronunciation: the letters **r** and **rr**.
- **Recycle: gustar** with infinitives.

STANDARDS

- 1.1 Engage in conversation, Acts. 7–9
- 1.2 Understand language, Pronunciación
- 1.3 Present information, Acts. 5–11, PYP
- 2.2 Products and perspectives, Act. 7
- 4.1 Compare languages
- 4.2 Compare cultures, Act. 7

FOCUS AND MOTIVATE

- ❏ Presentación de gramática, p. 162. Review **gustar** with infinitives by asking students the following questions: "¿Te gusta estudiar? ¿Te gusta mirar la televisión? ¿Te gusta comer?"

TEACH

- ❏ Presentación de gramática, p. 162. Write on the board: "Me gusta la pizza. Me gusta la leche." Underline the final "a" of **gusta.** Now write: "Me gustan los sándwiches. Me gustan las manzanas." Underline the final "n" of **gustan.** Ask students to explain when gusta is used and when **gustan** is used.
- ❏ Presentación de gramática. Explain how the translation of **me gusta** as "I like" is not literal.
- ❏ Pronunciación, p. 163. Listen to TXT CD 3 track 4. Call on students to practice the both pronunciations of the Spanish **r.**

PRACTICE AND APPLY

- ❏ Práctica de gramática, p. 163. Activity 5. Have students write or say their answers.
- ❏ Activity 6. Ask students to say that they do or do not like each of the foods mentioned.
- ❏ Comparación cultural, p. 164. Activity 7. Have students work in pairs to talk about which traditional foods they like.
- ❏ Have students do Activities 8, 9 in pairs or groups.
- ❏ Have students use the questions in Activity 10 to interview other students.
- ❏ Activity 11. Have students write their answers and share them with the class.

ASSESS AND RETEACH

- ❏ Para y piensa: p. 165. Have students express likes and dislikes.
- ❏ Homework: *Cuaderno: práctica por niveles,* pp. 104–106; *Cuaderno para hispanohablantes,* pp. 105–107.

IEP Modification Extend the deadline on homework assignments for students that need more time.

OPTIONAL RESOURCES

Plan
- Best Practices Toolkit
- PE Answers, MSRB, Transp. 44–47
- Workbook Answers, UTB 3, Transp. 32–39
- Absent Student Copymasters, URB 3, p. 95
- Easy Planner CD-ROM
- ClassZone.com

Present
- Warm-up Transp. 17, UTB 3
- Grammar Presentation Transp. 10, UTB 3
- Audio Script, URB 3, pp. 73–77

Practice
- Practice Games, URB 3, p. 33

Assess
- Reteaching Copymasters, URB 3, pp. 4–5

TECHNOLOGY TOOLS	
Teacher Tools	**Student Tools**
Power Presentations	@Home Tutor
EasyPlanner CD-ROM	ClassZone.com
Test Generator CD-ROM	eEdition Online or CD-ROM

¡AVANCEMOS!
Unidad 3 Lección 1

Gramática en contexto, pp. 166–167

OBJECTIVES

- Teach students learn to use **gustar** to express likes and dilikes.
- Practice using this structure with foods.

STANDARDS
- 1.1 Engage in conversation, Act. 14
- 1.3 Present information, Acts. 12–14, PYP

FOCUS AND MOTIVATE

- ❑ Telehistoria escena 2, p. 166. Read the Cuando escuchas strategy.

TEACH

- ❑ Telehistoria escena 2, p. 166. Direct students' attention to the photo and have them guess what is happening in the scene.
- ❑ Video Program DVD 1, Unit 3. Show the video for scene 2. As students watch, have them write down all the foods they hear. Then ask them to write a sentence stating whether they like or do not like each item.
- ❑ Audio Program TXT CD 3, track 5. Listen to audio for scene 2.
- ❑ Telehistoria escena 2. Have students read the dialog out loud for correct pronunciation and intonation.

PRACTICE AND APPLY

- ❑ Comprensión del episodio, Activity 12, p. 167. Listen to TXT CD 3, track 5. Call on students to answer the questions.
- ❑ Activity 13, p. 167. Expand the activity by having students relate what they do and do not like for dinner.
- ❑ Activity 14, p. 167. Have students keep a tally of who likes what. Then call on them to say who likes the same things.

IEP Modification On Activity 13, have students work in pairs, with one writing down what the other says. Then switch roles. Together, they check the written work for accuracy.

ASSESS AND RETEACH

- ❑ Para y piensa, p. 167. Ask students follow-up questions: "¿Piensan ustedes que a Marisol le gusta el qchocolate? ¿Le gustan los caramelos? ¿Por qué piensan así?"
- ❑ Grammar Quiz 1, On-level Assessment, p. 105.

OPTIONAL RESOURCES

Plan
- Best Practices Toolkit
- PE Answers, MSRB, Transp. 44–47
- Workbook Answers, UTB 3, Transp. 32–39
- Absent Student Copymasters, URB 3, p. 96

Present
- Warm-up Transp. 17, UTB 3
- Audio Script, URB 3, pp. 73–77
- Video Script, URB 3, pp. 69–70

Practice
- Practice Games, URB 3, p. 34
- Video Activities, URB 3, pp. 55–56

Assess
- Reteaching Copymasters, URB 3, pp. 4, 6

TECHNOLOGY TOOLS	
Teacher Tools	**Student Tools**
Power Presentations	@Home Tutor
EasyPlanner CD-ROM	ClassZone.com
Test Generator CD-ROM	eEdition Online or CD-ROM

Presentación y práctica de gramática 2, pp. 168–171

OBJECTIVES
- Present and practice present tense **-er, -ir** verbs.
- Introduce the verb **hacer** and connect it to **-er** verbs.
- **Recycle:** the verb **estar**, p. 128.

STANDARDS
- 1.1 Engage in conversation, Acts. 18, 20
- 1.2 Understand language, Act. 17
- 1.3 Present information, Acts. 15–20, PYP
- 2.2 Products and perspectives, CC
- 4.1 Compare languages
- 4.2 Compare cultures, CC

FOCUS AND MOTIVATE
- ❑ Presentación de gramática, p. 168. Review the forms of regular **-ar** verbs on page 106.

TEACH
- ❑ Presentación de gramática, p. 168. Introduce the present tense of **-er** and **-ir** verbs. First, give the verb forms and tell students to call out the subject. Then do the opposite, stating the subject pronoun and asking for the verb form.
- ❑ Presentación de gramática, p. 168. Ask students which endings of **-er** and **-ir** verbs are the same. Which are different?
- ❑ Nota gramatical, p. 170. Review and practice the irregular conjugation of the verb **hacer.**

IEP Modification   Reinforce the similarities and differences between **-er** and **-ir** verb forms on the board. Illustrate their common endings, and the variations for **nosotros** and **vosotros.**

PRACTICE AND APPLY
- ❑ Práctica de gramática, p. 169, Activities 15, 16. Allow students to form pairs and check each other's work.
- ❑ Activity 17, p. 169. Listen to TXT CD 3 track 6 to complete the activity.
- ❑ Activities 18, 19, 20, pp. 170–171. Have students work in pairs.
- ❑ Comparación cultural, p. 170. Begin a discussion with the Compara con tu mundo question.

ASSESS AND RETEACH
- ❑ Para y piensa, p. 171. Have students practice **-er** verb conjugations by completing the exercise.
- ❑ Homework: *Cuaderno: práctica por niveles*, pp. 107–109; *Cuaderno para hispanohablantes*, pp. 108–111.

OPTIONAL RESOURCES
Plan
- Best Practices Toolkit
- PE Answers, MSRB, Transp. 44–47
- Workbook Answers, UTB 3, Transp. 32–39
- Absent Student Copymasters, URB 3, p. 97

Present
- Warm-up Transp. 18, UTB 3
- Fine Art Activities, URB 3, p. 86

- Fine Art Transp. 2, UTB 3
- Grammar Presentation Transp. 11, UTB 3

Practice
- Practice Games, URB 3, p. 35
- Audio Script, URB 3, pp. 73–77

Assess
- Reteaching Copymasters, URB 3, pp. 7, 8, 12

TECHNOLOGY TOOLS	
Teacher Tools	**Student Tools**
Power Presentations	@Home Tutor
EasyPlanner CD-ROM	ClassZone.com
Test Generator CD-ROM	eEdition Online or CD-ROM

¡AVANCEMOS!
Unidad 3 Lección 1

Todo junto, Juegos y Diversiones, pp. 172–175

OBJECTIVES

- Practice using -er and -ir verbs and **gustar** to talk about lunchtime in the cafeteria.
- **Recycle:** telling time, p. 99.
- Review food vocabulary by playing a game of Fly Swatter.

FOCUS AND MOTIVATE

- ❑ Telehistoria completa, p. 172. Direct students to read the two Resúmenes as a review the previous Telehistoria scenes.

TEACH

- ❑ Video Program DVD 1, Unit 2. Show Telehistoria scenes 1 and 2 as a review before showing scene 3.
- ❑ Audio Program TXT CD 2 tracks 3 and 5. Listen to Telehistoria scenes 1 and 2 as a review before listening to scene 3 (TXT CD 2 track 7).
- ❑ Telehistoria escena 3, p. 172. Have students read the dialog and note the shift in Rodrigo's attitude.

IEP Modification   Have students write a four-line dialog between Rodrigo and Marisol based only on what they see in the picture. Compare it later to what actually happens in the scene.

PRACTICE AND APPLY

- ❑ Comprensión de los episodios, p. 173. Listen to TXT CD 3 tracks 3, 5, and 7 to do Activities 21–22 in pairs. For Activity 21, ask for pairs to read their articles out loud.
- ❑ Activity 23, p. 173. Have students work in groups of three.
- ❑ Activity 24, p. 174. Read the supermarket print ad and listen to the supermarket radio ad. Audio Program TXT CD 3 tracks 8, 9.
- ❑ Activity 25, p. 174. After students have written their letters, have them exchange and edit each other's work.
- ❑ Juegos y diversiones, p. 175. Have students play Matamoscas to review food vocabulary.

ASSESS AND RETEACH

- ❑ Para y piensa, p. 174. After completing this exercise, have students create one original sentence based on the characters and following the model.
- ❑ Grammar Quiz 2, On-level Assessment, p. 106.
- ❑ Homework: *Cuaderno: práctica por niveles*, pp. 110–111; *Cuaderno para hispanohablantes*, pp. 112–113.

OPTIONAL RESOURCES

Plan
- Best Practices Toolkit
- PE Answers, MSRB, Transp. 44–47
- Workbook Answers, UTB 3, Transp. 32–39
- Absent Student Copymasters, URB 3, p. 98

Present
- Warm-up Transp. 18, UTB 3
- Audio Script, URB 3, pp. 73–77
- Video Script, URB 3, pp. 69–70

Practice
- Learning Scenarios on Easy Planner
- Conversation cards on Easy Planner and ClassZone
- Video activities, URB 3, pp. 57–58
- Practice Games, URB 3, p. 36

Assess
- Reteaching Copymasters, URB 3, pp. 7, 9, 12

TECHNOLOGY TOOLS	
Teacher Tools	**Student Tools**
Power Presentations	@Home Tutor
EasyPlanner CD-ROM	ClassZone.com
Test Generator CD-ROM	eEdition Online or CD-ROM

¡AVANCEMOS!
Unidad 3 Lección 1

Lectura/Conexiones, pp. 176–178

OBJECTIVES

- Have students read and discuss the items on a supermarket circular and make cultural comparisons.
- Read about the conditions that contribute to the formation of hurricanes.
- Learn about Hurricane Georges and its effect on Puerto Rico.

STANDARDS

- 1.1 Engage in conversation
- 1.2 Understand language
- 1.3 Present information
- 2.1 Practices and perspectives
- 3.1 Knowledge of other disciplines
- 3.2 Acquire information
- 4.2 Compare cultures

FOCUS AND MOTIVATE

- ❏ Lectura, p. 177. Have students scan the supermarket circular for items that they may not find in a supermarket in their community.

TEACH

- ❏ Lectura, pp. 176–177. Prepare students to read or listen to the circular by teaching them words they may not know, such as **onza, libra,** and **centavos.**
- ❏ Audio Program: TXT CD 3 track 10. Listen to the audio for the Supermercados La Famsoa circular. Ask them to note of any unfamiliar words they hear.
- ❏ Conexiones, p. 178. Do a brainstorming activity with students in which they generate words that they freely associate with hurricanes.

PRACTICE AND APPLY

- ❏ Lectura, pp. 176–177. Have students bring in circulars of local supermarkets for comparison. Assign them to write a summary of the comparison between products and prices.
- ❏ Conexiones, p. 178. Divide students into three subgroups, with each group assigned to one of the Proyectos. Then have them share their projects as a class.

IEP Modification   Give students who are reluctant to speak in Spanish the opportunity to contribute more to this class discussion as the material is presented in English.

ASSESS AND RETEACH

- ❏ Para y piensa, p. 177. Help students to identify similarities and differences between the bilingual program and their school.
- ❏ Culture Quiz, On-level Assessment, p. 107.

OPTIONAL RESOURCES

Plan
- Best Practices Toolkit
- PE Answers, MSRB, Transp. 44–47
- Workbook Answers, UTB 3, Transp. 32–39
- Absent Student Copymasters, URB 3, p. 99

Present
- Warm-up Transp. 19, UTB 3

Practice
- Lecturas para todos pp. 22–26
- Lecturas para hispanohablantes
- Practice Games, URB 3, p. 37

TECHNOLOGY TOOLS	
Teacher Tools	**Student Tools**
Power Presentations	@Home Tutor
EasyPlanner CD-ROM	ClassZone.com
Test Generator CD-ROM	eEdition Online or CD-ROM

¡AVANCEMOS!
Unidad 3 Lección 1

En resumen, Repaso de la lección, pp. 179–181

OBJECTIVES

- Talk about foods and beverages, likes and dislikes.
- Use **gustar** with nouns.
- Use the present tense of **-er** and **-ir** verbs and **hacer.**

STANDARDS

- 1.2 Understand language, Act. 1
- 1.3 Present information, Acts. 2–5
- 4.2 Compare cultures, Act. 5

FOCUS AND MOTIVATE

❑ En resumen, p. 179. Review all vocabulary terms and grammar items.

TEACH

❑ En resumen. Assess which vocabulary terms need more practice and encourage students to form sentences with each.

❑ Repaso de la lección, pp. 180–181. Do a quick review of how to say who likes what.

❑ Repaso de la lección, pp. 180–181. Review the present-tense endings of **-er** and **-ir** verbs.

PRACTICE AND APPLY

❑ Repaso de la lección, Activity 1, p. 180. Listen to TXT CD 3 track 11 while they do Activity 1.

❑ Complete activities 2–5, pp. 180–181. To expand Activity 3, have students form questions with **¿qué?, ¿dónde?, ¿cómo?, ¿quién?, ¿cuándo?, ¿cuánto (a, os, as)?** and **¿adónde?**

ASSESS AND RETEACH

❑ Homework: Study En resumen, p. 179; *Cuaderno,* pp. 112–123; *Cuaderno para hispanohablantes,* pp. 114–123.

❑ Lesson Test, On-level Assessment, pp. 108–114.

IEP Modification   Hold a common review session before or after class or during a free period for students who want extra help.

OPTIONAL RESOURCES

Plan

- Best Practices Toolkit
- PE Answers, MSRB, Transp. 44–47
- Workbook Answers, UTB 3, Transp. 32–39
- Absent Student Copymasters, URB 3, p. 100

Present

- Warm-up Transp. 19, UTB 3
- Audio Script, URB 3, pp. 73–77

Practice

- Practice Games, URB 3, p. 38
- Sing-along Audio CD

Assess

- Review Games Online
- Lesson Test, Modified Assessment, pp. 83–89
- Lesson Test, Pre-AP Assessment, pp. 83–89
- Lesson Test, Heritage Learners Assessment, pp. 89–95

TECHNOLOGY TOOLS

Teacher Tools	Student Tools
Power Presentations	@Home Tutor
EasyPlanner CD-ROM	ClassZone.com
Test Generator CD-ROM	eEdition Online or CD-ROM
McDougal Littell Assessment System	

Lesson Opener,
Presentación y práctica de vocabulario, pp. 182–187

OBJECTIVES

- Teach more about Puerto Rican culture.
- Teach dates and numbers from 200–1,000,000.
- Express possession using **de.**

STANDARDS
- 1.2 Understand language, Act. 2
- 1.3 Present information, Acts. 1–2, PYP
- 2.1 Practices and perspectives
- 4.1 Compare languages, Nota gramatical
- 4.2 Compare cultures

FOCUS AND MOTIVATE

❏ Lesson Opener, p. 182. Read Compara con tu mundo and discuss the questions.

TEACH

❏ Presentación de vocabulario, pp. 184–186, paragraphs A–C. Read the paragraphs. Have students repeat the words for family members and numbers after you.

❏ Video Program DVD 1, Unit 3. Show Vocabulary Presentation video. Have students recite their birthdays: day + month + year.

❏ Audio Program TXT CD 3, track 12. Listen to Vocabulary Presentation audio. Dictate random numbers between 200 and 1,000,000 and have students write them numerically.

❏ Nota gramatical, p. 187. Ask students to look on each other's desktops and point out possession of items using **de.**

PRACTICE AND APPLY

❏ Lesson 1 Opener, pp. 182–183. Read Comparación cultural. Have students view the photograph and respond to the ¿Qué ves? questions.

❏ Listen to TXT CD 3 track 13 to do ¡A responder! activity, p. 186.

❏ Práctica de vocabulario, p. 187. Allow students to check each other's work on Activities 1 and 2.

IEP Modification   Use mnemonic devices for the family vocabulary to help students memorize the words. For example, **abuelo(a)** starts with "a" is at the top of the family; **primo(a)** is like "primary" or "first", as in "first *cousin*", etc.

ASSESS AND RETEACH

❏ Para y piensa, p. 187. For further assessment, rewrite the items on the board, filling in the second word and leaving the last word blank.

❏ Vocabulary Recognition Quiz, On-level Assessment, p. 120.

❏ Homework: *Cuaderno,* pp. 124–126; *Cuaderno para hispanohablantes,* pp. 124–127.

OPTIONAL RESOURCES

Plan
- Best Practices Toolkit
- Absent Student Copymasters, URB 3, p. 101
- PE Answers, MSRB, Transp. 48–51
- Workbook Answers, UTB 3, Transp. 40–47

Present
- Warm-up Transp. 20, UTB 3
- Vocabulary Transp. 8–9, UTB 3
- TPRS, pp. 36–42

- Video Script, URB 3, pp. 71–72
- Audio Script, URB 3, pp. 78–82
- Vocabulary Video, DVD 1

Practice
- Practice Games, URB 3, p. 39

Assess
- Reteaching Copymasters, URB 3, pp. 13–14

TECHNOLOGY TOOLS	
Teacher Tools	**Student Tools**
Power Presentations	@Home Tutor
EasyPlanner CD-ROM	ClassZone.com
	Cultura interactiva
	eEdition Online or CD-ROM

¡AVANCEMOS!
Unidad 3 Lección 2

Vocabulario en contexto, pp. 188–189

OBJECTIVES

- Present and practice family and birthday vocabulary.
- Review talking about age.
- **Recycle:** the verb **tener,** p. 100; numbers from 11–100, p. 94.

STANDARDS
- 1.1 Engage in conversation, Act. 4
- 1.2 Understand language, Act. 3, PYP
- 1.3 Present information, Act. 4

FOCUS AND MOTIVATE

- ❏ Telehistoria escena 1, p. 188. Read the Cuando escuchas strategy.

TEACH

- ❏ Telehistoria escena 1, p. 188. Direct students' attention to the photo and have them guess what is happening in the scene. Who in the photo is related and how?
- ❏ Video Program DVD 1, Unit 3. Show the video for scene 1. As students watch, have them write down all the dates and ages they hear.
- ❏ Audio Program TXT CD 3, track 14. Listen to audio for scene 1. Have students listen for the verb **tener** and guess why it is used so frequently in the scene.
- ❏ Telehistoria escena 1, p. 188. Have students read the dialog out loud for correct pronunciation and intonation. Ask them what the problem is at the end.
- ❏ Nota gramatical, p. 189. After presenting the Nota, direct students back to the Telehistoria to see how many times the characters talk about age.

PRACTICE AND APPLY

- ❏ Comprensión del episodio, Activity 3, p. 189. Listen to TXT CD 3 track 14 to determine which statements are false.
- ❏ Activity 4, p. 189. Personalize the activity by asking students how old they are, how old a friend or relative is, and how old a classmate is.

IEP Modification Pair reluctant speakers with those who have stronger verbal skills and allow them a few minutes to organize before speaking out loud.

ASSESS AND RETEACH

- ❏ Para y piensa, p. 189. Ask students to write three more sentences in the same manner about friends, relatives, or pets.
- ❏ Vocabulary Production Quiz, On-level Assessment, p. 121.

OPTIONAL RESOURCES

Plan
- Best Practices Toolkit
- PE Answers, MSRB, Transp. 48–51
- Workbook Answers, UTB 3, Transp. 40–47
- Absent Student Copymasters, URB 3, p. 102

Present
- Warm-up Transp. 20, UTB 3
- Audio Script, URB 3, pp. 78–82
- Video Script, URB 3, pp. 71–72

Practice
- Video Activities, URB 3, pp. 61–62
- Practice Games, URB 3, p. 40

Assess
- Reteaching Copymasters, URB 3, pp. 13, 15, 22, 23

TECHNOLOGY TOOLS	
Teacher Tools	**Student Tools**
Power Presentations	@Home Tutor
EasyPlanner CD-ROM	ClassZone.com
Test Generator CD-ROM	eEdition Online or CD-ROM

¡AVANCEMOS!
Unidad 3 Lección 2

Presentación y práctica de gramática 1, pp. 190–193

OBJECTIVES
- Present and practice possessive adjectives.
- Use possessive adjectives to discuss family.
- **Recycle:** after-school activities, pp. 32–33; describing others, p. 63.
- Practice pronunciation of the letter j in Spanish.

STANDARDS
- 1.3 Present information, Acts. 5–6
- 4.1 Compare languages, Pronunciación

FOCUS AND MOTIVATE
- ❏ Presentación de gramática, p. 190. Model possessive adjectives by pointing to objects and using the correct form. Model: "Es mi libro. Son mis libros."

TEACH
- ❏ Presentación de gramática, p. 190. Draw a simple family tree on the board and describe your family members with possessive adjectives. Then have students repeat what you say, changing the possessives appropriately.
- ❏ Pronunciación, p. 191. Listen to TXT CD 3 track 16. Remind students that the English "j" sound is not used in Spanish, while the Spanish **h** is silent.
- ❏ Comparación cultural, p. 193. Ask for a volunteer to read about elections in Puerto Rico. Then discuss the Compara con tu mundo question.
- ❏ Nota gramatical, p. 192. Have students practice saying today's date, the date a week from now, and their birthdays, including the year.

PRACTICE AND APPLY
- ❏ Práctica de gramática, p. 191. Allow students to check each other's work on Activities 5, 6. Refer them to pp. 32–33 to review after-school activities.
- ❏ Pronunciación, p. 191. Have students practice the Spanish **j** by giving them turns to read the words and the sentence out loud.
- ❏ Activity 7. Remind students to avoid saying years as is done in English: "mil novecientos setenta y siete", not "diez y nueve setenta y siete."
- ❏ Activity 8, p. 192. Refer students to page 63 to review how to describe others.

ASSESS AND RETEACH
- ❏ Para y piensa: p. 193. Expand the activity by changing **cumpleaños** to **fecha de nacimiento,** and adding random years to the dates.
- ❏ Homework: *Cuaderno,* pp. 127–129; *Cuaderno para hispanohablantes,* pp. 128–130.

OPTIONAL RESOURCES
Plan
- Best Practices Toolkit
- PE Answers, MSRB, Transp. 48–51
- Workbook Answers, UTB 3, Transp. 40–47
- Absent Student Copymasters, URB 3, p. 103
- Easy Planner CD-ROM
- ClassZone.com

Present
- Warm-up Transp. 21, UTB 3
- Grammar Presentations Transp. 12, UTB 3
- Audio Script, URB 3, pp. 78–82

Practice
- Practice Games, URB 3, p. 41

Assess
- Reteaching Copymasters, URB 3, pp. 16, 17, 24

TECHNOLOGY TOOLS	
Teacher Tools	**Student Tools**
Power Presentations	@Home Tutor
EasyPlanner CD-ROM	ClassZone.com
Test Generator CD-ROM	eEdition Online or CD-ROM

¡AVANCEMOS!
Unidad 3 Lección 2

Gramática en contexto, pp. 194–195

OBJECTIVES

- Practice possessive adjectives.
- Use possessive adjectives to discuss friends' birthdays.

STANDARDS

- 1.1 Engage in conversation, Act. 11
- 1.2 Understand language, Act. 10
- 1.3 Present information, Acts. 11–12, PYP

FOCUS AND MOTIVATE

- ❑ Telehistoria escena 2, p. 194. Read the Cuando lees strategy.

TEACH

- ❑ Telehistoria escena 2, p. 194. Direct students' attention to the photo and have them guess why Sra. Vélez is on the phone.
- ❑ Telehistoria escena 2, p. 194. Read dialog with students, pausing every time a name is mentioned. Ask, "Quién es _____?". Students shoud respond with possessive adjectives.
- ❑ Video Program DVD 1, Unit 3. Show the video for scene 2. Ask them to write down every family member they hear and then to draw a small family tree of Rodrigo and his relatives.
- ❑ Audio Program TXT CD 3, track 15. Listen to audio for scene 2.

PRACTICE AND APPLY

- ❑ Comprensión del episodio, Activity 10, p. 195. Listen to TXT CD 3, track 15 to complete the sentences.
- ❑ Activity 11 p. 195. Have groups present their findings out loud, with each person reading at least one birthdate.
- ❑ Activity 12. Allow students to exchange their paragraphs with a classmate to peer assess their work.

IEP Modification In group and pair work, evenly distribute students according to skill level to help slower-paced learners retain vocabulary and grammar.

ASSESS AND RETEACH

- ❑ Para y piensa, p. 195. Remind students that in Spanish, the day comes before the month.
- ❑ Grammar Quiz 1, On-level Assessment, p. 122.

OPTIONAL RESOURCES

Plan
- Best Practices Toolkit
- PE Answers, MSRB, Transp. 48–51
- Workbook Answers, UTB 3, Transp. 40–47
- Absent Student Copymasters, URB 3, p. 104

Present
- Warm-up Transp. 21, UTB 3
- Audio Script, URB 3, pp. 78–82
- Video Script, URB 3, pp. 71–72

Practice
- Practice Games, URB 3, p. 42
- Video Activities, URB 3, pp. 63–64

Assess
- Reteaching Copymasters, URB 3, pp. 16, 18

TECHNOLOGY TOOLS	
Teacher Tools	**Student Tools**
Power Presentations	@Home Tutor
EasyPlanner CD-ROM	ClassZone.com
Test Generator CD-ROM	eEdition Online or CD-ROM

¡AVANCEMOS!
Unidad 3 Lección 2

Presentación y práctica de gramática 2, pp. 196–199

OBJECTIVES
- Teach students to make comparisons.
- Practice comparing traits of friends and family.

STANDARDS
- 1.2 Understand language, Act. 17
- 1.3 Present information, Acts. 13–18
- 2.2 Products and perspectives, Act. 18
- 3.1 Knowledge of other disciplines, Act. 18
- 4.1 Compare languages

FOCUS AND MOTIVATE
- ❏ Presentación de gramática, p. 196. Introduce comparisons by calling two students with diverse characteristics to the front of the class. Make statements of comparison about them.

TEACH
- ❏ Presentación de gramática, p. 196. Explain the difference between unequal and equal comparisons. Remind students who know the word **que** as "that" that in comparisons it means "than".

IEP Modification Provide visual redundancy by bringing in pictures or objects that you can use to model comparisons and to have students generate original comparisons.

PRACTICE AND APPLY
- ❏ Práctica de gramática, p. 197. Allow students to check each other's work on Activities 13 and 14.
- ❏ Activities 15, 16, p. 198. Have students write their answers and share them with the class.
- ❏ Activity 17, p. 199. Listen to TXT CD 3 track 17 to complete the activity.
- ❏ Comparación cultural, p. 199. Expand Activity 18 by asking students to say how old each person is and to state their birthdates.

ASSESS AND RETEACH
- ❏ Para y piensa, p. 199. Ask students to consider if the statements are true for them and to correct them if they are false.
- ❏ Homework: *Cuaderno*, pp. 130–132; *Cuaderno para hispanohablantes*, pp. 131–134.

OPTIONAL RESOURCES
Plan
- Best Practices Toolkit
- PE Answers, MSRB, Transp. 48–51
- Workbook Answers, UTB 3, Transp. 40–47
- Absent Student Copymasters, URB 3, p. 105

Present
- Warm-up Transp. 22, UTB 3
- Fine Art Activities, URB 3, p. 88

- Fine Art Transp. 4, UTB 3
- Grammar Presentation Transp. 13, UTB 3

Practice
- Practice Games, URB 3, p. 43
- Audio Script, URB 3, pp. 78–82

Assess
- Reteaching Copymasters, URB 3, pp. 19, 20

TECHNOLOGY TOOLS

Teacher Tools	Student Tools
Power Presentations	@Home Tutor
EasyPlanner CD-ROM	ClassZone.com
Test Generator CD-ROM	eEdition Online or CD-ROM

Todo junto, Juegos y diversiones, pp. 200–203

OBJECTIVES
- Practice comparisons and possessive adjectives.
- Review family-based vocabulary.
- Review possessive adjectives and possession using **de** by playing a game.

STANDARDS
- 1.1 Engage in conversation, Act. 21
- 1.2 Understand language, Acts. 19–20, 22
- 1.3 Present information, Acts. 19–20, 22–23, PYP
- 5.2 Life-long learners, Juegos y diversiones

FOCUS AND MOTIVATE
- ❑ Telehistoria completa, p. 200. Based on the summaries for scenes 1 and 2, ask students to look at the photos and guess what has happened.

TEACH
- ❑ Video Program DVD 1, Unit 3. Show Telehistoria scenes 1 and 2 as a review before showing scene 3. Based on the video, have students compare Tito to his cousin Rodrigo.
- ❑ Audio Program TXT CD 3 tracks 14 and 15. Listen to Telehistoria scenes 1 and 2 as a review before listening to scene 3 (TXT CD 3 track 18).
- ❑ Telehistoria escena 3, p. 200. Have students read the dialog. Ask them to make predictions as to what happens to the T-shirt after the scene.

PRACTICE AND APPLY
- ❑ Comprensión de los episodios, p. 201. Listen to TXT CD 3 tracks 14, 15, and 18 to do Activities 19–20. Allow students to work in pairs.
- ❑ Activity 21. Once students have reached a conclusion, ask them to say if they know any families that meet their description.
- ❑ Activity 22, p. 202. Read the flyer and listen to TXT CD 3 tracks 19 and 20 to determine what homes would be best for the pets mentioned.
- ❑ Activity 23. Have students write their letters and exchange them with partners for peer editing.
- ❑ Juegos y diversiones, p. 203. Have students play ¿De quién es? to review talking about possession.

IEP Modification   For Activity 21, reluctant speakers may find trouble participating. Assign two of the Para organizarte questions specifically to them to answer, and encourage them to share their opinions with their group.

ASSESS AND RETEACH
- ❑ Para y piensa, p. 202. Ask students to compare two other characters from the Telehistoria.
- ❑ Grammar Quiz 2, On-level Assessment, p. 123.
- ❑ Homework: *Cuaderno*, pp. 133–134; *Cuaderno para hispanohablantes*, pp. 135–136.

OPTIONAL RESOURCES
Plan
- Best Practices Toolkit
- PE Answers, MSRB, Transp. 48–51
- Workbook Answers, UTB 3, Transp. 40–47
- Absent Student Copymasters, URB 3, p. 106

Present
- Warm-up Transp. 22, UTB 3
- Audio Script, URB 3, pp. 78–82
- Video Script, URB 3, pp. 71–72

Practice
- Learning Scenarios on Easy Planner
- Conversation cards on Easy Planner and ClassZone
- Video activities, URB 3, pp. 65–66
- Practice Games, URB 3, p. 44

Assess
- Reteaching Copymasters, URB 3, pp. 19, 21

TECHNOLOGY TOOLS	
Teacher Tools	**Student Tools**
Power Presentations	@Home Tutor
EasyPlanner CD-ROM	ClassZone.com
Test Generator CD-ROM	eEdition Online or CD-ROM

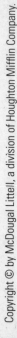

¡AVANCEMOS!
Unidad 3 Lección 2

Lectura/Proyectos culturales, pp. 204–206

OBJECTIVES

- Learn about the **quinceañera** celebration.
- Compare birthday traditions.
- Read about musical instruments of Puerto Rico and Peru.

FOCUS AND MOTIVATE

- ❑ Lectura cultural, pp. 204–205. Ask students what a typical birthday celebration is like in their families.

TEACH

- ❑ Lectura cultural, pp. 204–205. Before reading, start a discussion based on the photos, asking if they bring to mind any kinds of celebrations that students know. Then ask for four volunteers to read a paragraph each out loud.
- ❑ Lectura cultural. Play TXT CD 3 track 21 to hear audio for correct pronunciation.
- ❑ Proyectos culturales, p. 206. Prepare materials to do one of the two cultural projects in class. Bring in music samples that use these instruments.

PRACTICE AND APPLY

- ❑ Lectura, La quinceañera, pp. 204–205. Have students note at least three differences in how the **quince** is celebrated in Peru and Puerto Rico.
- ❑ Proyectos culturales, p. 206. Encourage students to investigate other musical instruments used in the traditional music of these countries.

IEP Modification Ask students about musical styles from other Spanish-speaking countries and have them organize a project to create an instrument commonly used in them.

ASSESS AND RETEACH

- ❑ Para y piensa, p. 205. Allow a discussion in which students compare birthday celebrations they know to the celebrations they just read about.
- ❑ Culture Quiz, On-level Assessment, p. 124.

OPTIONAL RESOURCES

Plan

- Best Practices Toolkit
- PE Answers, MSRB, Transp. 48–51
- Workbook Answers, UTB 3, Transp. 40–47
- Absent Student Copymasters, URB 3, p. 107

Present

- Warm-up Transp. 23, UTB 3

Practice

- Lecturas para todos pp. 27–31
- Lecturas para hispanohablantes
- Practice Games, URB 3, p. 45

TECHNOLOGY TOOLS	
Teacher Tools	**Student Tools**
Power Presentations	@Home Tutor
EasyPlanner CD-ROM	ClassZone.com
Test Generator CD-ROM	eEdition Online or CD-ROM

¡AVANCEMOS!
Unidad 3 Lección 2

En resumen, Repaso de la lección, pp. 207–209

OBJECTIVES

- Review lesson vocabulary and grammar.

FOCUS AND MOTIVATE

❑ En resumen, p. 207. Review all vocabulary terms and grammar items.

TEACH

❑ En resumen. Assess which vocabulary terms need more practice and encourage students to form sentences with each.

❑ Repaso de la lección, p. 208. Reinforce understanding of comparisons using items in the classroom. If item belongs to someone, have students express possession.

PRACTICE AND APPLY

❑ Repaso de la lección, Activity 1, p. 208. Listen to TXT CD 3 track 22 while they do Activity 1.

❑ Complete activities 2–5, pp. 208–209. As an alternative, divide class into groups and assign ach group one activity to prepare and present to the class.

ASSESS AND RETEACH

❑ Homework: Study En resumen, p. 207. *Cuaderno,* pp. 135–146. *Cuaderno para hispanohablantes,* pp. 137–146.

❑ Lesson Test, On-level Assessment, pp. 125–131.

IEP Modification   Determine which review activities best fit each student's skill level and assign them as homework accordingly.

OPTIONAL RESOURCES

Plan
- Best Practices Toolkit
- PE Answers, MSRB, Transp. 48–51
- Workbook Answers, UTB 3, Transp. 40–47
- Absent Student Copymasters, URB 3, p. 109

Present
- Warm-up Transp. 23, UTB 3
- Audio Script, URB 3, pp. 78–82

Practice
- Practice Games, URB 3, p. 46
- Sing-along Audio CD

Assess
- Review Games Online
- Lesson Test, Modified Assessment, pp. 95–101
- Lesson Test, Pr e-AP Assessment, pp. 95–101
- Lesson Test, Heritage Learners Assessment, pp. 101–107

TECHNOLOGY TOOLS	
Teacher Tools	**Student Tools**
Power Presentations	@Home Tutor
EasyPlanner CD-ROM	ClassZone.com
Test Generator CD-ROM	eEdition Online or CD-ROM
McDougal Littell Assessment System	

Comparación cultural, Repaso inclusivo, pp. 210–213

OBJECTIVES

- Read three personal accounts about Sunday gatherings written by teens from Puerto Rico, El Salvador, and Peru.
- Compare Sunday meals with one of the three students in the text.
- Cumulative review.

STANDARDS

- 1.1 Engage in conversation, Acts. 2, 3, 5
- 1.2 Understand language, Act. 1
- 1.3 Present information, Acts. 2–6
- 2.1 Practices and perspectives
- 4.2 Compare cultures

FOCUS AND MOTIVATE

- ❏ Comparación cultural, pp. 210–211. If students don't typically have a large Sunday meal, ask them to think about Thanksgiving.

TEACH

- ❏ Comparación cultural, p. 211. Call on students to read the descriptions of María Luisa, Silvia, and José. Encourage them to note similarities between the three in language and theme.
- ❏ Audio Program TXT CD 3 track 23. Listen to María Luisa, Silvia, and José.
- ❏ Comparación cultural, p. 210. Use the writing strategy to guide students in the descriptions of their Sunday meals.
- ❏ Repaso inclusivo, pp. 212–213. Review the En resumen pages in Units 1, 2, and 3 to prepare students for Activities 1–6.

PRACTICE AND APPLY

- ❏ Comparación cultural, p. 210. Help students increase their cultural awareness by doing the Compara con tu mundo activity.
- ❏ Repaso inclusivo, p. 212. Listen to TXT CD 3 track 24 to complete Activity 1.
- ❏ Repaso inclusivo, pp. 212–213. Complete Activities 2–6.

ASSESS AND RETEACH

- ❏ Homework: *Cuaderno*, pp. 147–149, *Cuaderno para hispanohablantes*, pp. 147–149.
- ❏ Unit Test, On-level Assessment, pp. 137–143.

IEP Modification   Prepare a brief True/False oral comprehension check based on descriptions of the three people on p. 211.

OPTIONAL RESOURCES

Plan
- Absent Student Copymasters, URB 3, pp. 110, 111

Present
- Audio Script, URB 3, pp. 78–82

Practice
- Situational Transp. and Copymasters, UTB 3, Transp. 14–15, pp. 1–2
- Family Involvement Activity, URB 3, p. 92

Assess
- Unit Test, Modified Assessment, pp. 107–113
- Unit Test, Pre-AP Assessment, pp. 107–113
- Unit Test, Heritage Learners Assessment, pp. 113–119

TECHNOLOGY TOOLS	
Teacher Tools	**Student Tools**
EasyPlanner CD-ROM	@Home Tutor
Test Generator CD-ROM	ClassZone.com
McDougal Littell Assessment System	eEdition Online or CD-ROM

Unit and Lesson Opener,
Presentación y práctica de vocabulario, pp. 214–221

OBJECTIVES
- Teach about Spain.
- Have students talk about clothing.
- **Recycle:** numbers 11–100, p. 94.

STANDARDS
- 1.1 Engage in conversation, Act. 2
- 1.2 Understand language
- 1.3 Present information, Act. 1
- 2.1 Practices and perspectives
- 4.2 Compare cultures

FOCUS AND MOTIVATE
- ❑ Unit 4 Opener, pp. 214–215: Review numbers, interrogatives and present tense verbs by having students scan facts and ask and answer questions about Spain.

TEACH
- ❑ Presentación de vocabulario: pp. 218–220, paragraphs A–E. Read the paragraphs. Have students repeat the labeled words after you. Afterward, ask students to describe the clothing they see in the photo on pp. 219–220.
- ❑ Video Program, DVD 1, Unit 4. Show Vocabulary Presentation video.
- ❑ Audio Program TXT CD 4, track 1. Listen to Vocabulary Presentation audio.
- ❑ Based on the readings on pp. 218–220, ask students questions such as: "¿Adónde va Enrique?, ¿Con quién va?, ¿Qué quieren comprar?, ¿Cuánto cuesta el vestido de Maribel?"

IEP Modification   Point to articles of clothing in the room and have students identify and describe them.

PRACTICE AND APPLY
- ❑ Lesson 1 opener, pp. 216–217. Read Comparación cultural. Have students view the photographs and respond to the ¿Qué ves? questions.
- ❑ Listen to TXT CD 4, track 2 to do ¡A responder! Activity, p. 220.
- ❑ Review numbers from 11–100, p. 94. Do Activities 1–2 p. 221. Have students work in pairs to complete Activity 2.

ASSESS AND RETEACH
- ❑ Para y piensa, p. 221.
- ❑ Vocabulary Recognition Quiz, On-level Assessment, p. 149.
- ❑ Homework: *Cuaderno*, pp. 151–153. *Cuaderno para hispanohablantes*, pp. 151–154.

OPTIONAL RESOURCES
Plan
- Family Letter, URB 4, p. 91
- Family letters in Haitian Creole and Spanish on ClassZone.com
- Best Practices Toolkit
- Absent Student Copymasters, URB 4, p. 93
- PE Answers, MSRB, Transp. 52–55
- Workbook Answers, UTB 4, Transp. 32–39

Present
- Warm-up Transp. 16, UTB 4
- Atlas Map, UTB 1, Transp. 6
- Map Transp. 1, UTB 1
- Map-Culture Activities, URB 4, pp. 83–84
- Música del mundo hispano

- Vocabulary Transp. 6–7, UTB 4
- TPRS, pp. 43–49
- Video Script, URB 4, pp. 69–70
- Audio Script, URB 4, pp. 73–77
- Vocabulary Video, DVD 1
- Fine Art Activities, URB 4, p. 87
- Fine Art Transp. 3, UTB 4

Practice
- Practice Games, URB 4, p. 31
- Video Activities, URB 4, pp. 51–52

Assess
- Reteaching Copymasters, URB 4, pp. 1–2

TECHNOLOGY TOOLS	
Teacher Tools	**Student Tools**
Power Presentations	@Home Tutor
EasyPlanner CD-ROM	ClassZone.com
	Cultura interactiva
	eEdition Online or CD-ROM

Vocabulario en contexto, pp. 222–223

OBJECTIVES
- Present and practice clothing vocabulary and seasons.
- **Recycle tener,** p. 100; after-school activities, pp. 32–33.

STANDARDS
• 1.1 Engage in conversation, Act. 4
• 1.2 Understand language, Act. 3
• 1.3 Present information, Act. 4

FOCUS AND MOTIVATE
❑ Telehistoria, escena 1, p. 222. Read the Cuando escuchas strategy.

TEACH
❑ Telehistoria, escena 1, p. 222. Direct students' attention to the photo and have them describe what Maribel and Enrique are wearing.

❑ Audio Program TXT CD 4, track 3. Listen to the audio for scene 1. Have students raise their hands each time they hear a target vocabulary word.

❑ Video Program DVD 1, Unit 4. Show the video for scene 1. Pause and ask personalized questions, such as: "¿Para qué necesitas tú un mapa?, ¿Necesitas comprar una chaqueta?"

❑ Telehistoria, escena 1, p. 222. Have students read the dialog out loud for correct pronunciation and intonation.

❑ Have a student read the También se dice box aloud.

PRACTICE AND APPLY
❑ Comprensión del episodio, Activity 3, p. 223. Listen to TXT CD 4, track 3.

❑ Review conjugation of **tener** and **tener** expressions. Ask students questions such as: "¿Cuántos años tienes?, ¿Tenemos clase los sábados?"

❑ Have students do Activity 4, p. 223 in pairs.

ASSESS AND RETEACH
❑ Para y piensa, p. 223.

❑ Vocabulary Production Quiz, On-level Assessment, p. 150.

IEP Modification   To ensure comprehension, pair students and have them practice and present the dialogue on p. 222.

OPTIONAL RESOURCES

Plan
- Best Practices Toolkit
- PE Answers, MSRB, Transp. 52–55
- Workbook Answers, UTB 4, Transp. 32–39
- Absent Student Copymasters, URB 4, p. 94

Present
- Warm-up Transp. 16, UTB 4
- Audio Script, URB 4, pp. 73–77
- Video Script, URB 4, pp. 69–70

Practice
- Video Activities, URB 4, pp. 53–54
- Practice Games, URB 4, p. 32

Assess
- Reteaching Copymasters, URB 4, pp. 1, 3, 11, 12

TECHNOLOGY TOOLS	
Teacher Tools	**Student Tools**
Power Presentations	@Home Tutor
EasyPlanner CD-ROM	ClassZone.com
Test Generator CD-ROM	eEdition Online or CD-ROM

Presentación y práctica de gramática 1, pp. 224–227

OBJECTIVES

- Present and practice **e → ie** stem-changing verbs.
- Have students use new verbs to discuss clothing.
- Demonstrate pronunciation of the letter c with **a, o, u.**

STANDARDS

- 1.1 Engage in conversation, Acts. 7, 9–10
- 1.2 Understand language, Act. 8, Pronunciación
- 1.3 Present information, Acts. 5–10
- 4.1 Compare languages

FOCUS AND MOTIVATE

- ❑ Write out the conjugation of **entender.** Say verb aloud as you write on the board.
- ❑ Ask students to guess when there is no stem change in the verb. **(entendemos, entendéis)**

TEACH

- ❑ Presentación de gramática, p. 224. Ask students questions with target verbs.
- ❑ Review the use of **querer** with infinitives by asking students personalized questions and questions based on the dialogue of the Telehistoria, scene 1: ¿Qué quieres hacer hoy?, ¿Quieres leer en voz alta ahora?, ¿Quiere Enrique comprar un sombrero?, ¿Quieren Enrique y Maribel ir a un restaurante?

PRACTICE AND APPLY

- ❑ Have students do Activity 5 individually and Activity 6 in pairs, p. 225.
- ❑ Expand Activity 6 by having students visit the Corte Inglés web site (or another Spanish clothing store such as Zara or Mango). Have them print out a catalog page and present to the class the items that they want to order, using the verbs **querer** and **pedir.**
- ❑ Activity 7, p. 226. Remind students to conjugate the verbs.
- ❑ Play TXT CD 4, track 4. Have students do Activity 8, p. 226.
- ❑ Pronunciación, p. 205. Listen to TXT CD 4, track 6 to practice pronunciation of the letter "c" when followed by "a", "o" or "u".
- ❑ Have students do Activity 9, p. 227 in pairs.
- ❑ Activity 10. Have students write complete sentence asnwers.

IEP Modification Ask students to generate other words with a hard "c" sound.

ASSESS AND RETEACH

- ❑ Para y piensa, p. 227.
- ❑ Homework: *Cuaderno,* pp. 154–156; *Cuaderno para hispanohablantes,* pp. 155–157.

IEP Modification Extend the deadline on homework assignments for students that need more time.

OPTIONAL RESOURCES

Plan
- Best Practices Toolkit
- PE Answers, MSRB, Transp. 52–55
- Workbook Answers, UTB 4, Transp. 32–39
- Absent Student Copymasters, URB 4, p. 95
- Easy Planner CD-ROM
- ClassZone.com

Present
- Warm-up Transp. 17, UTB 4
- Grammar Presentation Transp. 10, UTB 4
- Audio Script, URB 4, pp. 73–77

Practice
- Practice Games, URB 4, p. 33

Assess
- Reteaching Copymasters, URB 4, pp. 4–5

TECHNOLOGY TOOLS	
Teacher Tools	**Student Tools**
Power Presentations	@Home Tutor
EasyPlanner CD-ROM	ClassZone.com
Test Generator CD-ROM	eEdition Online or CD-ROM

Gramática en contexto, pp. 228–229

OBJECTIVES
- Present and practice **e → ie** stem-changing verbs.
- Practice new vocabulary in context.
- **Culture:** Surrealist art in Spain.

STANDARDS
- 1.1 Engage in conversation, Act. 12
- 1.2 Understand language, Act. 11
- 2.2 Products and perspectives, CC
- 4.2 Compare cultures, CC

FOCUS AND MOTIVATE
- ❑ Telehistoria escena 2, p. 228. Read the Cuando lees strategy.

TEACH
- ❑ Telehistoria escena 2, p. 228. Prepare students to watch the video by having them look at the photo and describe what is going on. Have them guess what will happen in the scene. To review vocabulary, use the photos on pp. 218–220.
- ❑ Telehistoria escena 2, p. 228. Have students read through the dialogue and identify all of the stem-changing verbs.
- ❑ Divide the class into two groups: the Maribel group and the Enrique group. Have them do the dialogue chorally, concentrating on correct pronunciation and intonation. Instructor will be the **Vendedora.**
- ❑ Video Program DVD 1, Unit 4. Show the video for scene 2.
- ❑ Audio Program TXT CD 4, track 5. Listen to audio for scene 2.

PRACTICE AND APPLY
- ❑ Comprensión del episodio, Activity 11, p. 229. Listen to TXT CD 4, track 5.
- ❑ Do Activity 12, p. 229 in pairs. Expansion: Have students explain their answers. Model: "Prefiero llevar pantalones cortos durante el verano…porque tengo calor."

IEP Modification   Give students who are reluctant to speak in Spanish the opportunity to contribute more to this class discussion as the material is presented in English.

ASSESS AND RETEACH
- ❑ Para y piensa, p. 229.
- ❑ Grammar Quiz 1, On-level Assessment, p. 151.

OPTIONAL RESOURCES

Plan
- Best Practices Toolkit
- PE Answers, MSRB, Transp. 52–55
- Workbook Answers, UTB 4, Transp. 32–39
- Absent Student Copymasters, URB 4, p. 96

Present
- Warm-up Transp. 17, UTB 4
- Audio Script, URB 4, pp. 73–77
- Video Script, URB 4, pp. 69–70

Practice
- Practice Games, URB 4, p. 34
- Video Activities, URB 4, pp. 55–56
- Fine Art Activities, URB 4, p. 86
- Fine Art Transp. 2, UTB 4

Assess
- Reteaching Copymasters, URB 4, pp. 4, 6

| TECHNOLOGY TOOLS ||
Teacher Tools	Student Tools
Power Presentations	@Home Tutor
EasyPlanner CD-ROM	ClassZone.com
Test Generator CD-ROM	eEdition Online or CD-ROM

Presentación y práctica de gramática 2, pp. 230–233

OBJECTIVES
- Present and practice direct object pronouns.
- Practice lesson vocabulary.

STANDARDS
- 1.1 Engage in conversation, Acts. 15–18
- 1.3 Present information, Acts. 13–18
- 2.1 Practices and perspectives, Act. 18
- 4.1 Compare languages
- 4.2 Compare cultures, Act. 18

FOCUS AND MOTIVATE
- ❑ Write the following sentences on the board: Compro el vestido., Quiero zapatos nuevos., Busco una chaqueta. Have students identify the direct object of each sentence. (vestido, zapatos, chaqueta)

TEACH
- ❑ Presentación de gramática, p. 230. Present use of direct object pronouns. Have students look at the sentences on the board (above) and then create a new sentence for each, replacing the direct object with a direct object pronoun. Model: "Compro el vestido. Lo compro."

PRACTICE AND APPLY
- ❑ Do Activities 13, 14, p. 231.
- ❑ Have students work in pairs to complete Activities 15–17.
- ❑ Activity 18, Comparación cultural, p. 233. Group students and have them read about and discuss climates in various Hispanic countries.

ASSESS AND RETEACH
- ❑ Para y piensa, p. 233.
- ❑ Homework: *Cuaderno*, pp. 157–159; *Cuaderno para hispanohablantes*, pp. 158–161.

OPTIONAL RESOURCES

Plan
- Best Practices Toolkit
- PE Answers, MSRB, Transp. 52–55
- Workbook Answers, UTB 4, Transp. 32–39
- Absent Student Copymasters, URB 4, p. 97

Present
- Warm-up Transp. 18, UTB 4
- Grammar Presentation Transp. 11, UTB 4

Practice
- Practice Games, URB 4, p. 35
- Audio Script, URB 4, pp. 73–77

Assess
- Reteaching Copymasters, URB 4, pp. 7–8

TECHNOLOGY TOOLS	
Teacher Tools	**Student Tools**
Power Presentations	@Home Tutor
EasyPlanner CD-ROM	ClassZone.com
Test Generator CD-ROM	eEdition Online or CD-ROM

Todo junto, Juegos y diversiones, pp. 234–237

OBJECTIVES

- Practice stem-changing verbs and clothing preferences.
- Review direct object pronouns.
- Review vocabulary by playing a game.

FOCUS AND MOTIVATE

❑ Have students summarize the two Telehistoria scenes from this lesson.

TEACH

❑ Video Program DVD 1, Unit 4. Show Telehistoria scenes 1 and 2 as a review before showing scene 3.

❑ Audio Program TXT CD 4, tracks 3 and 5. Listen to Telehistoria scenes 1 and 2 as a review before listening to scene 3 (TXT CD 4, track 7).

❑ Present reading and listening strategies, p. 234.

❑ Telehistoria completa, p. 234. Have students read the dialogue and identify all of the direct object pronouns. Ask them what nouns they replace.

IEP Modification   Prepare a brief True/False oral comprehension check based on the first two scenes of the *Telehistoria* to ensure that all students are following.

PRACTICE AND APPLY

❑ Comprensión de los episodios, p. 235. Listen to TXT CD 4, tracks 3, 5, and 7 to do Activities 19–20.

❑ Have students do Activity 21, p. 235 in pairs after reviewing the strategy.

❑ Have students do Activity 22, p. 236. Listen to CD 4, tracks 8 and 9. Expand Activity 22 and recycle numbers by having students tell the price of the clothes they are wearing, and what they would cost with a 10% discount coupon.

❑ Have students do Activity 23, p. 236. Expansion: Have students exchange poems and write helpful comments to each other.

❑ Have students play Pasa la bola to review vocabulary.

ASSESS AND RETEACH

❑ Para y piensa, p. 236.

❑ Grammar Quiz 2, On-level Assessment, p. 152.

❑ Homework: *Cuaderno*, pp. 160–161; *Cuaderno para hispanohablantes*, pp. 162–163.

OPTIONAL RESOURCES

Plan
- Best Practices Toolkit
- PE Answers, MSRB, Transp. 52–55
- Workbook Answers, UTB 4, Transp. 32–39
- Absent Student Copymasters, URB 4, p. 98

Present
- Warm-up Transp. 18, UTB 4
- Audio Script, URB 4, pp. 73–77
- Video Script, URB 4, pp. 69–70

Practice
- Learning Scenarios on Easy Planner
- Conversation cards on Easy Planner and ClassZone
- Video activities, URB 4, pp. 57–58
- Practice Games, URB 4, p. 36

Assess
- Reteaching Copymasters, URB 4, pp. 7, 9

TECHNOLOGY TOOLS	
Teacher Tools	**Student Tools**
Power Presentations	@Home Tutor
EasyPlanner CD-ROM	ClassZone.com
Test Generator CD-ROM	eEdition Online or CD-ROM

Lectura, Conexiones, pp. 238–240

OBJECTIVES

- Read and discuss a Spanish poem by Antonio Colinas.
- Discuss a poet's feelings about winter.
- Learn about the history of the Moors in Spain.

STANDARDS

- 1.2 Understand language
- 1.3 Present information
- 2.1 Practices and perspectives
- 3.1 Knowledge of other disciplines
- 3.2 Acquire information
- 4.1 Compare languages
- 4.2 Compare cultures

FOCUS AND MOTIVATE

- ❏ Have students locate the regions of León and Andalucía on the map of Spain, p. 214.
- ❏ Lectura, p. 238. Read the strategy aloud with students.

TEACH

- ❏ Have students read about the author, p. 238. Do a quick True/False comprehension check.
- ❏ Have students read the poem on p. 239 various times.
- ❏ *Las memorias del invierno* pp. 238–239. Listen to TXT CD 4, track 10. As they listen to the poem, have students follow along in their texts.

IEP Modification Have students identify words they do not know and make a list of them, along with their meanings, on the board for students to refer to as they read.

PRACTICE AND APPLY

- ❏ In groups, have students write a few lines describing a season where they live.
- ❏ Read Conexiones, p. 240 with students. Ask them to describe the photos.
- ❏ Assign projects 1, 2, 3 on p. 240. Have students work on Projects in small groups of 3–5 students.

ASSESS AND RETEACH

- ❏ Para y piensa, p. 239.
- ❏ Culture Quiz, On-level Assessment, p. 153.

OPTIONAL RESOURCES

Plan
- Best Practices Toolkit
- PE Answers, MSRB, Transp. 52–55
- Workbook Answers, UTB 4, Transp. 32–39
- Absent Student Copymasters, URB 4, p. 99

Present
- Warm-up Transp. 19, UTB 4

Practice
- Lecturas para todos pp. 32–36
- Lecturas para hispanohablantes
- Practice Games, URB 4, p. 37

TECHNOLOGY TOOLS	
Teacher Tools	**Student Tools**
Power Presentations	@Home Tutor
EasyPlanner CD-ROM	ClassZone.com
Test Generator CD-ROM	eEdition Online or CD-ROM

En resumen, Repaso de la lección, pp. 241–243

OBJECTIVES
- Review the lesson grammar and vocabulary.

STANDARDS
- 1.2 Understand language, Act. 1
- 1.3 Present information, Acts. 2–5
- 4.2 Compare cultures, Act. 5

FOCUS AND MOTIVATE
- ❏ Have students review the material on the **En resumen** page.

TEACH
- ❏ Have students review the vocabulary and grammar structures on p. 241. Do a quick oral drill to check for understanding. Ask for student volunteers to review the grammar points.

PRACTICE AND APPLY
- ❏ Do Repaso de la lección, Activity 1, p. 242. Play TXT CD 4, track 11. Do Repaso Activity 2, p. 242 and Activities 3 and 4, p. 243.
- ❏ Have students do Activity 5, p. 243 in groups and report the answers to the class.

IEP Modification   Leave time in class to ask and answer questions.

ASSESS AND RETEACH
- ❏ Homework: Study En resumen, p. 241; *Cuaderno*, pp. 162–173; *Cuaderno para hispanohablantes*, pp. 164–173.
- ❏ Lesson Test, On-level Assessment, pp. 154–160.

OPTIONAL RESOURCES

Plan
- Best Practices Toolkit
- PE Answers, MSRB, Transp. 52–55
- Workbook Answers, UTB 4, Transp. 32–39
- Absent Student Copymasters, URB 4, p. 100

Present
- Warm-up Transp. 19, UTB 4
- Audio Script, URB 4, pp. 73–77

Practice
- Practice Games, URB 4, p. 38
- Sing-along Audio CD

Assess
- Review Games Online
- Lesson Test, Modified Assessment, pp. 119–125
- Lesson Test, Pre-AP Assessment, pp. 119–125
- Lesson Test, Heritage Learners Assessment, pp. 125–131

TECHNOLOGY TOOLS	
Teacher Tools	**Student Tools**
Power Presentations	@Home Tutor
EasyPlanner CD-ROM	ClassZone.com
Test Generator CD-ROM	eEdition Online or CD-ROM
McDougal Littell Assessment System	

Lesson Opener,
Presentación y práctica de vocabulario, pp. 244–249

OBJECTIVES

- Introduce lesson theme: **¿Qué hacemos esta noche?**
- Present and practice vocabulary about places in town and items in a restaurant.
- **Recycle:** present tense of **-er** verbs, p. 168.

STANDARDS

- 1.1 Engage in conversation, Act. 2, PYP
- 1.2 Understand language
- 1.3 Present information, Acts. 1–2, PYP
- 2.2 Products and perspectives
- 4.1 Compare languages
- 4.2 Compare cultures

FOCUS AND MOTIVATE

- ❑ Lesson 2 Opener, pp. 244–245: Have students look at photos. Recycle clothing vocabulary and introduce the theme by asking: "¿Qué ropa llevan los chicos?, ¿Dónde están?, ¿Qué van a hacer?"
- ❑ Have students look at the photos on pp. 244–245 and make predictions about what they will learn.

TEACH

- ❑ Presentación de vocabulario pp. 246–248 paragraphs A–F. Have students take turns reading paragraphs A–F. Have students repeat the new words after you.
- ❑ Video Program DVD 1, Unit 4. Show Vocabulary Presentation video.
- ❑ Audio Program TXT CD 4, track 12. Ask students personalized questions using the target vocabulary.

PRACTICE AND APPLY

- ❑ Lesson 1 Opener, pp. 244–245. Read Comparación cultural. Have students view the photographs and respond to the ¿Qué ves? and Compara con tu mundo questions. Use the photo and TE margin notes to talk about Teatro de la comedia, p. 245.
- ❑ Listen to TXT CD 4, track 13 to do ¡A responder! Activity, p. 248.
- ❑ Pair students and have them write original sentences using the vocabulary words.
- ❑ Have students complete Activity 1 on p. 249.
- ❑ Have students work in pairs to complete Activity 2 on p. 249.

IEP Modification Be sure that when you pair and group students for activities you include a strong student to provide support and peer learning when possible.

ASSESS AND RETEACH

- ❑ Have students do Para y piensa, p. 249.
- ❑ Vocabulary Recognition Quiz, On-level Assessment, p. 166.
- ❑ Homework: *Cuaderno*, pp. 174–176. *Cuaderno para hispanohablantes*, pp. 174–177.

OPTIONAL RESOURCES

Plan
- Best Practices Toolkit
- Absent Student Copymasters, URB 4, p. 101
- PE Answers, MSRB, Transp. 56–59
- Workbook Answers, UTB 4, Transp. 40–47

Present
- Warm-up Transp. 20, UTB 4
- Vocabulary Transp. 8–9, UTB 4
- TPRS, pp. 50–56

- Video Script, URB 4, pp. 71–72
- Audio Script, URB 4, pp. 78–82
- Vocabulary Video, DVD 1

Practice
- Practice Games, URB 4, p. 39

Assess
- Reteaching Copymasters, URB 4, pp. 13, 14, 22

TECHNOLOGY TOOLS	
Teacher Tools	**Student Tools**
Power Presentations	@Home Tutor
EasyPlanner CD-ROM	ClassZone.com
	Cultura interactiva
	eEdition Online or CD-ROM

Vocabulario en contexto, pp. 250–251

OBJECTIVES

- Understand and practice using the vocabulary in context.
- Recycle the verb **ir,** p. 134.
- Practice **ir a** + infinitive to talk about what you are going to do.

STANDARDS
- 1.1 Engage in conversation, Act. 4
- 1.2 Understand language, Act. 3
- 1.3 Present information, Act. 4, PYP

FOCUS AND MOTIVATE

❏ Telehistoria escena 1, p. 250. Prepare students to watch the video by having them look at the photo and predict what will happen.

TEACH

❏ Present reading and listening strategies on p. 250.

❏ Video Program DVD 1, Unit 4. Show the video for scene 1.

❏ Audio Program TXT CD 4, track 14. Listen to the audio for scene 1. Have students raise their hands as they hear vocabulary words.

❏ Telehistoria escena 1, p. 250. Have students repeat the dialogue after you for correct pronunciation and intonation. Ask comprehension questions.

❏ Read and discuss with students the También se dice box, p. 250.

❏ Review Nota gramatical box, p. 251.

PRACTICE AND APPLY

❏ Group students and have them practice the dialogue and present it to the class.

❏ Comprensión del episodio, Activity 3, p. 251. Listen to TXT CD 4, track 14.

❏ Ask students a series of personalized questions with **ir a** + infinitive. Have students complete Activity 4, p. 251 in pairs.

IEP Modification   Have students write out the present tense conjugation for **ir.**

ASSESS AND RETEACH

❏ Para y piensa, p. 251.

❏ Vocabulary Production Quiz, On-level Assessment, p. 167.

OPTIONAL RESOURCES

Plan
- Best Practices Toolkit
- PE Answers, MSRB, Transp. 56–59
- Workbook Answers, UTB 4, Transp. 40–47
- Absent Student Copymasters, URB 4, p. 102

Present
- Warm-up Transp. 20, UTB 4
- Audio Script, URB 4, pp. 78–82
- Video Script, URB 4, pp. 71–72

Practice
- Video Activities, URB 4, pp. 61–62
- Practice Games, URB 4, p. 40

Assess
- Reteaching Copymasters, URB 4, pp. 13, 15, 22

TECHNOLOGY TOOLS	
Teacher Tools	**Student Tools**
Power Presentations	@Home Tutor
EasyPlanner CD-ROM	ClassZone.com
Test Generator CD-ROM	eEdition Online or CD-ROM

Presentación y práctica de gramática 1, pp. 252–255

OBJECTIVES

- Present and practice o → ue stem-changing verbs.
- Write about activities in town.
- Give excuses for things you cannot do.

STANDARDS

- 1.1 Engage in conversation, Acts. 8–10
- 1.3 Present information, Acts. 5–10, PYP
- 2.2 Products and perspectives, Act. 9
- 4.1 Compare languages
- 4.2 Compare cultures, Act. 9

FOCUS AND MOTIVATE

❑ Model stem-changing verbs by reciting a short paragraph: "Yo **vuelvo** a casa a las cinco pero mi hermana **vuelve** a las tres. Mis padres **vuelven** a casa a las siete. Y tú, ¿a qué hora **vuelves** a tu casa?" Put emphasis on the stem-changing verb and ask students to identify the infinitive (**volver**).

TEACH

❑ Presentación de gramática, p. 252. Review stem-changing verbs by asking students a series of questions with target verbs: **almorzar, poder, costar, dormir, encontrar, recordar.**

❑ Do Activity 5, p. 253, and follow up with a quick True/False comprehension check for extra practice.

PRACTICE AND APPLY

❑ Activitiy 6, p. 253. Have students write out the correct form of each verb.

❑ Have students do Activity 7, p. 254 in pairs. As an option for Expansión have students interview and write three extra sentences about each other.

❑ Have students do Activity 8, p. 254 in pairs. As a follow up have each student do a survey to find out how many of their classmates are planning to do the same activities.

❑ Have students study the Comparación cultural p. 255. in groups and write a brief summary of the most important points. Have them brainstorm answers to the Compara con tu mundo question. Each group will share their thoughts.

❑ Activity 10. Have students write out their answers and discuss them with partners or as a class.

IEP Modification Give students who are reluctant to speak in Spanish the opportunity to contribute more to this class discussion as the material is presented in English.

ASSESS AND RETEACH

❑ Para y piensa, p. 255.

❑ Homework: *Cuaderno*, pp. 177–179; *Cuaderno para hispanohablantes*, pp. 178–180.

OPTIONAL RESOURCES

Plan
- Best Practices Toolkit
- PE Answers, MSRB, Transp. 56–59
- Workbook Answers, UTB 4, Transp. 40–47
- Absent Student Copymasters, URB 4, p. 103
- Easy Planner CD-ROM
- ClassZone.com

Present
- Warm-up Transp. 21, UTB 4
- Grammar Presentation Transp. 12, UTB 4
- Audio Script, URB 4, pp. 78–82

Practice
- Practice Games, URB 4, p. 41

Assess
- Reteaching Copymasters, URB 4, pp. 16, 17

TECHNOLOGY TOOLS	
Teacher Tools	**Student Tools**
Power Presentations	@Home Tutor
EasyPlanner CD-ROM	ClassZone.com
Test Generator CD-ROM	eEdition Online or CD-ROM

Gramática en contexto, pp. 256–257

OBJECTIVES
- Identify **o → ue** stem-changing verbs in context.
- Talk about places around town and what you find there.

STANDARDS
- 1.1 Engage in conversation, Act. 12
- 1.2 Understand language, Act. 11
- 1.3 Present information, Act. 12, PYP

FOCUS AND MOTIVATE
- ❏ Telehistoria escena 2, p. 256. Present the reading and listening strategies.

TEACH
- ❏ Telehistoria escena 2, p. 256. Prepare students to watch the video by having them look at the photo and describe what is going on.
- ❏ As students read the dialogue, have them identify all of the stem-changing verbs.
- ❏ Audio Program TXT CD 4, track 15. Listen to the audio for scene 2.
- ❏ Have them repeat the dialogue after you for correct pronunciation and intonation.
- ❏ Video Program DVD 1, Unit 4. Show the video for scene 2.
- ❏ Have students anticipate what happens next using the verbs **poder, encontrar, querer,** and **costar.** Start by asking them: "¿Dónde está la camiseta?"

IEP Modification   Have student volunteers perform the dialogue in front of the class.

PRACTICE AND APPLY
- ❏ Do Activity 11, p. 257. Play TXT CD 4, track 15.
- ❏ Have students complete Activity 12, p. 257 in pairs. Expansion: Recycle previous vocabulary by adding places to the list, such as **supermercado, biblioteca, sala de clase.**

ASSESS AND RETEACH
- ❏ Para y piensa, p. 257.
- ❏ Grammar Quiz 1, On-level Assessment, p. 168.

OPTIONAL RESOURCES
Plan
- Best Practices Toolkit
- PE Answers, MSRB, Transp. 56–59
- Workbook Answers, UTB 4, Transp. 40–47
- Absent Student Copymasters, URB 4, p. 104

Present
- Warm-up Transp. 21, UTB 4
- Audio Script, URB 4, pp. 78–82
- Video Script, URB 4, pp. 71–72

Practice
- Practice Games, URB 4, p. 42
- Video Activities, URB 4, pp. 63–64

Assess
- Reteaching Copymasters, URB 4, pp. 16, 18

TECHNOLOGY TOOLS	
Teacher Tools	**Student Tools**
Power Presentations	@Home Tutor
EasyPlanner CD-ROM	ClassZone.com
Test Generator CD-ROM	eEdition Online or CD-ROM

Presentación y práctica de gramática 2, pp. 258–261

OBJECTIVES
- Present and practice **e → i** stem-changing verbs.
- Use new verbs to order from a menu.
- **Recycle:** direct object pronouns, p. 230; **tener** expressions, p. 223.

STANDARDS
- 1.1 Engage in conversation, Acts. 17–18
- 1.2 Understand language, Pronunciación, Act. 16
- 1.3 Present information, Acts. 11–12, 15–18, PYP
- 2.2 Products and perspectives, CC
- 4.1 Compare languages
- 4.2 Compare cultures, CC

FOCUS AND MOTIVATE
- ❏ Model stem-changing verbs by reciting a short paragraph: "Cuando salimos a comer mi padre siempre **pide** pollo, y mis hermanas **piden** pescado. Mi madre y yo **pedimos** el biftec. Y tú, ¿qué **pides**?" Bring in pictures of foods from magazines as prompts. Model a correct answer (Yo **pido** carne.)

TEACH
- ❏ Presentación de gramática, p. 258. Review e → i stem-changing verbs. Ask students questions with target verbs: **servir, pedir, repetir.**
- ❏ Review direct object pronouns with students, p. 230 before they complete Activity 14.

PRACTICE AND APPLY
- ❏ Have students complete Activities 13 and 14, p. 259.
- ❏ Pronunciación, p. 259. TXT CD 4, track 16. Have students repeat the words after you. Have them think of two more words that have a soft "c" sound. Review hard "c" sound with a, o, u.
- ❏ Activities 15, 17. Have students write their answers.
- ❏ Listen to TXT CD 4, track 17 and have students do Activity 16, p. 260.
- ❏ Review the verb **tener,** p. 223. Have students do Activity 18, p. 261.
- ❏ Group students for the Comparación cultural Activity, p. 261. Have the group write a brief description of the people in the original painting *Las meninas.*

IEP Modification Continue to model pronunciation of words with hard and soft "c." Write a list of words on the board and have students pronounce them. Write words with two c's to stress the difference: lección, sección.

ASSESS AND RETEACH
- ❏ Para y piensa, p. 261.
- ❏ Homework: *Cuaderno,* pp. 180–182. *Cuaderno para hispanohablantes,* pp. 181–184.

OPTIONAL RESOURCES
Plan
- Best Practices Toolkit
- PE Answers, MSRB, Transp. 56–59
- Workbook Answers, UTB 4, Transp. 40–47
- Absent Student Copymasters, URB 4, p. 105

Present
- Warm-up Transp. 22, UTB 4
- Fine Art Activities, URB 4, pp. 88–89

- Fine Art Transp. 4–5, UTB 4
- Grammar Presentation Transp. 13, UTB 4

Practice
- Practice Games, URB 4, p. 43
- Audio Script, URB 4, pp. 78–82

Assess
- Reteaching Copymasters, URB 4, pp. 19, 20, 23, 24

TECHNOLOGY TOOLS

Teacher Tools	Student Tools
Power Presentations	@Home Tutor
EasyPlanner CD-ROM	ClassZone.com
Test Generator CD-ROM	eEdition Online or CD-ROM

Todo junto, Juegos y diversiones, pp. 262–265

OBJECTIVES

- Integrate lesson content.
- Practice using and integrating lesson vocabulary and content.
- Review vocabulary by playing a game.

STANDARDS

- 1.1 Engage in conversation, Act. 21
- 1.2 Understand language, Acts. 19–20, 22
- 1.3 Present information, Acts. 19–20, 22–23, PYP
- 5.2 Life-long learners, Juegos y diversiones

FOCUS AND MOTIVATE

❑ Have students summarize the two Telehistoria scenes from this lesson.

TEACH

❑ Video Program DVD 1, Unit 4. Show Telehistoria scenes 1 and 2 as a review before showing scene 3.

❑ Audio Program Listen to Telehistoria scenes 1 and 2 as a review before listening to scene 3 (TXT CD 4, track 18).

❑ Present reading and listening strategies, p. 262. Have students give examples from the dialogue.

❑ Telehistoria completa, p. 262. Have the students read the dialogue out loud for correct pronunciation and intonation.

IEP Modification Have students read escena 3 out loud. Vary the roles. Repeat this until students can read with ease.

PRACTICE AND APPLY

❑ Comprensión de los episodios, p. 263. Listen to TXT CD 4, tracks 14, 15, and 18 to have students do Activities 19 and 20, pp. 263.

❑ Groups students for Activity 21, p. 263. Have them act out their original scene.

❑ Do Activity 22, p. 264. Play TXT CD 4, tracks 19, 20.

❑ Have students work in pairs to do Activity 23. As a variation, have them rate an excellent restaurant as well as a terrible fast-food restaurant. They should recycle comparatives (p. 196): **(más... que, menos... que, mejor que, peor que, tan(to)... como).**

❑ Have students play Cuatro rincones to review vocabulary.

ASSESS AND RETEACH

❑ Para y piensa, p. 264.

❑ Grammar Quiz 2, On-level Assessment, p. 169.

❑ Homework: *Cuaderno*, pp. 183–184; *Cuaderno para hispanohablantes*, pp. 185–186.

OPTIONAL RESOURCES

Plan
- Best Practices Toolkit
- PE Answers, MSRB, Transp. 56–59
- Workbook Answers, UTB 4, Transp. 40–47
- Absent Student Copymasters, URB 4, p. 106

Present
- Warm-up Transp. 22, UTB 4
- Audio Script, URB 4, pp. 78–82
- Video Script, URB 4, pp. 71–72

Practice
- Learning Scenarios on Easy Planner
- Conversation cards on Easy Planner and ClassZone
- Video activities, URB 4, pp. 65–66
- Practice Games, URB 4, p. 44

Assess
- Reteaching Copymasters, URB 4, pp. 19, 21

TECHNOLOGY TOOLS	
Teacher Tools	**Student Tools**
Power Presentations	@Home Tutor
EasyPlanner CD-ROM	ClassZone.com
Test Generator CD-ROM	eEdition Online or CD-ROM

Lectura cultural, Proyectos culturales, pp. 266–268

OBJECTIVES

- Read about weekend activities in Spain and Chile.
- Compare weekend activities in Spain, Chile, and the U.S.
- Teach about art and paintings from Spain and Chile.

STANDARDS

- 1.2 Understand language
- 1.3 Present information
- 2.1 Practices and perspectives
- 2.2 Products and perspectives
- 3.2 Acquire information
- 4.2 Compare cultures
- 5.1 Spanish in the community

FOCUS AND MOTIVATE

- ❏ Have students describe an ideal weekend. Be sure that they include at least two daytime and two evening activities. With whom do they typically spend their time on weekends?

- ❏ Ask two student volunteers to each draw a simple scene on the board. Have students interpret the scenes. What is the drawing of? How do they interpret the scenes?

TEACH

- ❏ *El fin de semana en España y* Chile pp. 266–267. Listen to TXT CD 4, track 21. Ask students to raise their hands each time an activity is mentioned that they participate in also.

- ❏ Have students describe the photos on pp. 266–267. To recycle previous vocabulary, ask them to describe what various people in the photos are wearing. Then, have them guess what season it is.

- ❏ Ask students to make original comparisons based on the photos.

PRACTICE AND APPLY

- ❏ Review Comparación cultural with students, p. 268. Remind students about the Focus and Motivate activity.

- ❏ Have students do Proyecto 1. Assign Proyecto 2 as homework. Expansion: have students bring in a picture of their favorite artwork to share with the class and describe in Spanish.

IEP Modification Extend the deadline on homework assignments for students that need more time.

ASSESS AND RETEACH

- ❏ Para y piensa, p. 267.
- ❏ Culture Quiz, On-level Assessment, p. 170.

OPTIONAL RESOURCES

Plan

- Best Practices Toolkit
- PE Answers, MSRB, Transp. 56–59
- Workbook Answers, UTB 4, Transp. 40–47
- Absent Student Copymasters, URB 4, p. 107

Present

- Warm-up Transp. 23, UTB 4

Practice

- Lecturas para todos pp. 37–41
- Lecturas para hispanohablantes
- Practice Games, URB 4, p. 45

TECHNOLOGY TOOLS	
Teacher Tools	**Student Tools**
Power Presentations	@Home Tutor
EasyPlanner CD-ROM	ClassZone.com
Test Generator CD-ROM	eEdition Online or CD-ROM

¡AVANCEMOS!
Unidad 4 Lección 2

En resumen, Repaso de la lección, pp. 269–271

OBJECTIVES

- Review lesson grammar and vocabulary.

STANDARDS
- 1.2 Understand language, Acts. 1, 3
- 1.3 Present information, Acts. 2, 4
- 4.2 Compare cultures, Act. 5

FOCUS AND MOTIVATE

❑ En resumen, p. 269. Review all vocabulary terms and grammar items.

❑ To recycle **ir a, pedir** and **poder,** ask students what they are going to do when they leave school today. Ask them what they order for lunch in the cafeteria. Ask them what they can do well.

TEACH

❑ En resumen. Review vocabulary and grammar structures on p. 269. Do a quick oral or written quiz. Show pictures and have students name the objects.

❑ En resumen. Assess which vocabulary terms need more practice and encourage students to form sentences with each.

❑ Do a quick True/False exercise: "Hay arroz en una ensalada. Mi postre favorito es el brócoli."

IEP Modification   Have students write out the conjugation of the verbs **poder, pedir** and **querer.** Draw their attention to the "boot" pattern.

PRACTICE AND APPLY

❑ Repaso de la lección, Activity 1, p. 270. Play TXT CD 4, track 22 as students complete the activity.

❑ Review **ir a** + infinitive and stem-changing verbs. Do Activities 2–4, pp. 270–271.

❑ Review Comparación cultural with students and have them complete Activity 5, p. 271.

ASSESS AND RETEACH

❑ Homework: Study En resumen, p. 269; *Cuaderno*, pp. 185–196; *Cuaderno para hispanohablantes*, pp. 187–196.

❑ Lesson Test, On-level Assessment, pp. 171–177.

OPTIONAL RESOURCES

Plan

- Best Practices Toolkit
- PE Answers, MSRB, Transp. 56–59
- Workbook Answers, UTB 4, Transp. 40–47
- Absent Student Copymasters, URB 4, p. 109

Present

- Warm-up Transp. 23, UTB 4
- Audio Script, URB 4, pp. 78–82

Practice

- Practice Games, URB 4, p. 46
- Sing-along Audio CD

Assess

- Review Games Online
- Lesson Test, Modified Assessment, pp. 131–137
- Lesson Test, Pre-AP Assessment, pp. 131–137
- Lesson Test, Heritage Learners Assessment, pp. 137–143

| TECHNOLOGY TOOLS ||
Teacher Tools	Student Tools
Power Presentations	@Home Tutor
EasyPlanner CD-ROM	ClassZone.com
Test Generator CD-ROM	eEdition Online or CD-ROM
McDougal Littell Assessment System	

Comparación cultural, Repaso inclusivo, pp. 272–275

OBJECTIVES
- Read three personal narratives about weekend activities in three different countries.
- Have students compare their favorite activities with one of the three students in the text.
- Cumulative review.

STANDARDS
- 1.1 Engage in conversation, Acts. 2–5
- 1.2 Understand language, Act. 1
- 1.3 Present information, Acts. 2–6
- 2.1 Practices and perspectives
- 2.2 Products and perspectives
- 4.2 Compare cultures

FOCUS AND MOTIVATE
- ❏ Have students read the title to the Comparación cultural spread and look at the photos to make predictions about the reading.
- ❏ Have students flip through the unit and share what they have learned.

TEACH
- ❏ Comparación cultural, pp. 272–273. Call on students to read the descriptions of Anita, Rodrigo, and Armando. Encourage them to note similarities between the three in language and theme.
- ❏ Audio Program TXT CD 4, track 23. Listen to Anita, Rodrigo, and Armando.
- ❏ Comparación cultural, pp. 272–273. Use the writing strategy to giude students in their own descriptions.
- ❏ Repaso inclusivo, pp. 274–275. Review the En resumen pages in Units 1–4 to prepare students for Activities 1–6.

PRACTICE AND APPLY
- ❏ Comparación cultural, pp. 272–273. Help students increase their cultural awareness by doing the Compara con tu mundo activity.
- ❏ Repaso inclusivo, pp. 274–275. Listen to TXT CD 4, track 24 to complete Activity 1.
- ❏ Repaso inclusivo, pp. 274–275. Complete Activities 2–6. Have students work in pairs/small groups to complete Activities 3, 4, and 5.

IEP Modification Be sure to include students of different abilities in each group. Encourage strong students to provide support to weaker students.

ASSESS AND RETEACH
- ❏ Homework: *Cuaderno*, pp. 197–199; *Cuaderno para hispanohablantes*, pp. 197–199.
- ❏ Unit Test, On-level Assessment, pp. 183–189.
- ❏ Midterm Test, On-level Assessment, pp. 195–204.

OPTIONAL RESOURCES
Plan
- Absent Student Copymasters, URB 4, pp. 110, 111

Present
- Audio Script, URB 4, pp. 78–82

Practice
- Situational Transp. and Copymasters, UTB 4, Transp. 14–15, pp. 1–2
- Family Involvement Activity, URB 4, p. 92
- ¡AvanzaCómics! SuperBruno y Nati, Episodio 2

Assess
- Unit Test, Modified Assessment, pp. 143–149
- Unit Test, Pre-AP Assessment, pp. 143–149
- Unit Test, Heritage Learners Assessment, pp. 149–155
- Midterm Test, Modified Assessment, pp. 155–164
- Midterm Test, Pre-AP Assessment, pp. 155–164
- Midterm Test, Heritage Learners Assessment, pp. 161–170

TECHNOLOGY TOOLS	
Teacher Tools	**Student Tools**
EasyPlanner CD-ROM	ClassZone.com
Test Generator CD-ROM	Cultura interactiva
McDougal Littell Assessment System	eEdition Online or CD-ROM

Lesson Opener, Parte 1 Repaso y Práctica de Vocabulario, pp. 1–5

OBJECTIVES
- Talk about activities
- Identify people and things
- What you like to do
- Describe others

FOCUS AND MOTIVATE
❑ Preliminary Lesson Opener, p. 1: Have students look at the photos, and describe what they see: **¿qué hay?/ ¿qué ves (ven)?, ¿de qué color es...? ¿dónde están los chicos?¿cuántos chicos hay?/¿cuántas chicas hay?/ ¿qué van a comer?/ ¿qué compran?/¿adónde van?** In pairs, have each other ask questions about what the kids in the photos are doing (**¿Qué hacen los chicos?**) or what they are going to do (**¿Qué van a hacer los chicos?**).

TEACH
❑ **Repaso: ¿Qué te gusta hacer?**, p. 2
❑ **Repaso: Mis amigos y yo**, p. 3.
❑ **¿Recuerdas?** Article agreement, p. 5

IEP Modification   Present major points orally and on overhead simultaneously.

PRACTICE AND APPLY
❑ Práctica de vocabulario, Activities 1–5, pp. 4–5. Have students work in pairs. Use reading, writing, and speaking skills listed next to the activity.

OPTIONAL RESOURCES
Plan
- Best Practices Toolkit
- PE Answers, MSRB, Transparencies 60–66

Present
- Warm-up Transp., MSRB, Transparency 20
- Audio Script, MSRB, pp. 55–56

- Vocabulary Transp., MSRB Transparencies 1–2

Practice
- Practice Pages, MSRB, pp. 10–11

Assess
- Diagnostic Test, MSRB, pp. 1–8

TECHNOLOGY TOOLS	
Teacher Tools	**Student Tools**
Power Presentations	@Home Tutor
EasyPlanner CD-ROM	ClassZone.com
	eEdition Online or CD-ROM

Práctica de Gramática, pp. 6–11

OBJECTIVES

- Identify people and things
- Tell where you are from
- Describe yourself and others
- Say what you and others like and don't like
- Talk about certain activities

STANDARDS

- 1.1 Engage in conversation, Acts. 9, 12–13, 17
- 1.2 Understand language, Acts. 6–18
- 1.3 Present information, Act. 13
- 4.1 Compare languages

FOCUS AND MOTIVATE

❑ Introduce yourself, someone else in class, or someone famous: who the person is, the person's name, where the person is from, describe the person, what the person likes and any **-ar** activities that person does or likes to do. Conversely, you may want to introduce someone without revealing person's name (identity) for student to guess that information based on everything else: **¿quién es?**

TEACH

❑ Repaso: Subject Pronouns and **ser,** p. 6

❑ ¿Recuerdas? Adjective agreement, p. 7

❑ Repaso: **Gustar** with Nouns and Infinitives, p. 8

❑ Repaso: Present tense of **-ar** verbs, p. 10

IEP Modification   Use color coding to illustrate grammar rules (e.g., the highlighted **n** at the end of **gustan** for showing contrast between the use of the plural and the singular forms).

PRACTICE AND APPLY

❑ Práctica de gramática, activities 6–9. Have students do activities 6, 7, and 9 in pairs. Use reading, writing, and speaking skills listed next to the activity.

❑ Práctica de gramática, activities 10–13. Have students do activities 10, 11, and 12 in pairs. Have students stand up to do activity 13. Use reading, writing, and speaking skills listed next to the activity.

❑ Práctica de gramática, activities 14–15. Play 1B TXT CD 1 track 1 to do actividad 15, p. 10

❑ Práctica de gramática, Activities 16–18, p. 11. Have students do activities 16–17 in pairs. Use reading, writing, and speaking skills listed next to the activity.

OPTIONAL RESOURCES

Plan
- Best Practices Toolkit
- PE Answers, MSRB, Transparencies 60–66

Present
- Warm-up Transp., MSRB, Transparency 20

- Audio Script, MSRB, pp. 55–56
- Grammar Transp., MSRB Transparencies 3–5

Practice
- Practice Pages, MSRB, pp. 12–17

TECHNOLOGY TOOLS	
Teacher Tools	**Student Tools**
Power Presentations	@Home Tutor
EasyPlanner CD-ROM	ClassZone.com
Test generator CD-ROM	eEdition Online or CD-ROM

OBJECTIVES

- Describe classes and classroom objects
- Talk about school schedules
- Say how you are feeling
- Say where things are located
- Tell time

> **STANDARDS**
> - 1.2 Understand language, Acts. 1–6
> - 1.3 Present information, Act. 6
> - 4.1 Compare languages

FOCUS AND MOTIVATE

❑ Turn the attention of the class to several target classroom objects. Have them identify some. Break down the class in small groups and set up a competition: **¿Cuántos objetos identifican?** The group that identifies the most wins.

TEACH

❑ Repaso: En la clase, p. 12

❑ Repaso: En la escuela, p. 13

❑ ¿Recuerdas?: Telling time, p. 14

❑ ¿Recuerdas?: Numbers with masculine and feminine forms, p. 15.

IEP Modification   Use verbal/visual mnemonic devices to assist in memory; let students design their own mnemonic devices and discuss value of this strategy.

PRACTICE AND APPLY

❑ Práctica de vocabulario, activities 1–6, pp. 14–15. Use reading, writing, and speaking skills listed next to the activity.

❑ Play 1B TXT CD 1 track 2 to do activity 3, p. 14

OPTIONAL RESOURCES

Plan
- Best Practices Toolkit
- PE Answers, MSRB, Transparencies 60–66

Present
- Warm-up Transp., MSRB, Transparency 21

- Audio Script, MSRB, pp. 55–56
- Vocabulary Transp., MSRB Transparencies 6–7

PRACTICE
- Practice Pages, MSRB, pp. 18–19

TECHNOLOGY TOOLS	
Teacher Tools	**Student Tools**
Power Presentations	@Home Tutor
EasyPlanner CD-ROM	ClassZone.com
Test generator CD-ROM	eEdition Online or CD-ROM

Práctica de Gramática, pp. 16–19

OBJECTIVES

- Say what you have and what you have to do
- Say how you are and where you are
- Say where you are going

STANDARDS

- 1.1 Engage in conversation, Acts. 10, 14
- 1.2 Understand language, Acts. 7–14
- 1.3 Present information, Acts. 10, 12
- 4.1 Compare languages

FOCUS AND MOTIVATE

❑ Have students say something that they have that they like a lot.

TEACH

❑ Repaso: The Verb **tener,** p. 16.
❑ Repaso: The Verb **estar,** p. 18.
❑ ¿Recuerdas? Article contraction with the preposition **de,** p. 18
❑ Repaso: The Verb **ir,** p. 19.
❑ ¿Recuerdas? Article contraction with the preposition **a,** p. 19.

PRACTICE AND APPLY

❑ Práctica, Activities 7–10, pp. 16–17. Have students stand up to do activity 10. Use reading, writing, and speaking skills listed next to the activity.

❑ Práctica, Activities 11–12, p. 18. Use reading, writing, and speaking skills listed next to the activity.

❑ Práctica, Activities 13–14, p. 19. Have students do activity 14 in pairs. Use reading, writing, and speaking skills listed next to the activity.

IEP Modification Pair students with good role models in pair work so that they can learn by peer example.

OPTIONAL RESOURCES

Plan

- Best Practices Toolkit
- PE Answers, MSRB, Transparencies 60–66

Present

- Warm-up Transp., MSRB, Transparency 21

- Audio Script, MSRB, pp. 55–56
- Grammar Transp., MSRB Transparencies 8–10

Practice

- Practice Pages, MSRB, pp. 20–25

TECHNOLOGY TOOLS	
Teacher Tools	**Student Tools**
Power Presentations	@Home Tutor
EasyPlanner CD-ROM	ClassZone.com
Test generator CD-ROM	eEdition Online or CD-ROM

Parte 3: Comer en Familia, pp. 20–24

OBJECTIVES
- Talk about foods and beverages
- Talk about relatives
- Ask questions with interrogative words
- Express possession
- Give dates
- Make comparisons

STANDARDS
- 1.1 Engage in conversation, Act. 7
- 1.2 Understand language, Acts. 1–8
- 4.1 Compare languages

FOCUS AND MOTIVATE
- ❏ Talk to the class about the foods and beverages that you usually (like to) have for breakfast and lunch
- ❏ Talk to the class about your relatives (siblings, parents, aunts, uncles, cousins, grandparents) and pets

TEACH
- ❏ Repaso: El desayuno
- ❏ Repaso: El almuerzo
- ❏ Repaso: La familia
- ❏ ¿Recuerdas? Possessive adjectives
- ❏ ¿Recuerdas? Give dates
- ❏ ¿Recuerdas? Expressions to compare

IEP Modification Develop a routine where the class slowly repeats a new multisyllabic vocabulary word after you say it and then says the word slowly syllable by syllable as they tap out each syllable.

PRACTICE AND APPLY
- ❏ Práctica, Activities 1–7, pp. 22–24. Have students play 1B TXT CD 1 track 3 to do activity 3. Have students work in pairs on activity 7. Use reading, writing, and speaking skills listed next to the activity.

OPTIONAL RESOURCES
Plan
- Best Practices Toolkit
- PE Answers, MSRB, Transparencies 60–66

Present
- Warm-up Transp., MSRB, Transparency 22

- Audio Script, MSRB, pp. 55–56
- Vocabulary Transp., MSRB Transparencies 11–12

Practice
- Practice Pages, MSRB, pp. 26–27

TECHNOLOGY TOOLS

Teacher Tools	Student Tools
Power Presentations	@Home Tutor
EasyPlanner CD-ROM	ClassZone.com
Test generator CD-ROM	eEdition Online or CD-ROM

Práctica de Gramática, pp. 25–27

OBJECTIVES
- Talk about doing certain things

STANDARDS
- 1.1 Engage in conversation, Acts. 7, 11
- 1.2 Understand language, Acts. 6–13
- 4.1 Compare languages

FOCUS AND MOTIVATE
❑ Tell students some of the things that you like to do (**-er** and **-ir** verbs) and when/where you do (**hacer**) certain things.

TEACH
❑ Repaso: Present Tense of **-er** and **-ir** Verbs, p. 25
❑ ¿Recuerdas? The Verb **hacer**, p. 26
❑ Repaso: Stem-Changing Verbs: **e ⟶ ie**, p. 27

PRACTICE AND APPLY
❑ Práctica, Activities 8–11, pp. 25–26. Have students work in pairs on activity 11. Use reading, writing, and speaking skills listed next to the activity.

❑ Práctica, Activities 12 and 13, p. 27. Use reading, writing, and speaking skills listed next to the activity.

IEP Modification   Use the modelos for the activities so that students have a clear understanding of what they are expected to do.

OPTIONAL RESOURCES
Plan
- Best Practices Toolkit
- PE Answers, MSRB, Transparencies 60–66

Present
- Warm-up Transp., MSRB, Transparency 22

- Audio Script, MSRB, pp. 55–56
- Grammar Transp., MSRB Transparencies 13–14

Practice
- Practice Pages, MSRB, pp. 28–30

TECHNOLOGY TOOLS	
Teacher Tools	**Student Tools**
Power Presentations	@Home Tutor
EasyPlanner CD-ROM	ClassZone.com
Test generator CD-ROM	eEdition Online or CD-ROM

Parte 4: En el centro, pp. 28–31

OBJECTIVES

- Talk about what clothes you want to buy
- Say what you wear in different seasons
- Order from a menu
- Describe places and events in town
- Talk about types of transportation
- Say what you are going to do

STANDARDS

- 1.1 Engage in conversation, Act. 5
- 1.2 Understand language, Acts. 1–6
- 1.3 Present information, Act. 5

FOCUS AND MOTIVATE

❏ Describe what you are wearing today and what some of the students are wearing Then break down your class in small groups to have them talk about what classmates and teacher are wearing today.

TEACH

❏ Repaso: En la tienda de ropa, p. 28

❏ Repaso: En el restaurante, p. 29

❏ ¿Recuerdas? **Ir a** + infinitive, p. 30

PRACTICE AND APPLY

❏ Práctica, Activities 1–6, pp. 30–31. Play 1B TXT CD 1 track 4 to do activity 3. Have students stand up to do activity 5. Use reading, writing, and speaking skills listed next to the activity.

IEP Modification   Give active students roles such as rearranging chairs. This way they learn the importance of responsible contributions to the classroom as a whole and are less restless.

OPTIONAL RESOURCES

Plan

- Best Practices Toolkit
- PE Answers, MSRB, Transparencies 60–66

Present

- Warm-up Transp., MSRB, Transparency 23

- Audio Script, MSRB, pp. 55–56
- Vocabulary Transp., MSRB Transparencies 15–16

Practice

- Practice Pages, MSRB, pp. 31–32

TECHNOLOGY TOOLS	
Teacher Tools	**Student Tools**
Power Presentations	@Home Tutor
EasyPlanner CD-ROM	ClassZone.com
Test generator CD-ROM	eEdition Online or CD-ROM

Práctica de Gramática, Repaso de Partes 1 a 4, pp. 32–37

OBJECTIVES

- Refer to something already mentioned using direct object pronouns
- Express being able to do something
- Talk about certain activities
- Order at a restaurant

STANDARDS

- 1.1 Engage in conversation, Acts. 9–10, 15, 1–5
- 1.2 Understand language, Acts. 7–15
- 1.3 Present information, Acts. 10, 15
- 4.1 Compare languages

FOCUS AND MOTIVATE

❑ Put something on the desk and say what you are doing. Then repeat it replacing the name of the object(s) that you put with the correct direct object pronoun. Break down class in pairs and have them do the same; partners will say what each other are doing (**Pones x en el escritorio ⟶ Lo(s)/La(s) pones en el escritorio**).

TEACH

❑ Repaso: Direct object pronouns, p. 32
❑ Repaso: Stem-Changing Verbs: **o ⟶ ue,** p. 34
❑ Repaso: Stem-Changing Verbs: **e ⟶ i,** p. 35

IEP Modification   Task-analyze the direct-object pronoun concept to be reviewed and talk students through the sequence of steps needed to master the concept. Have written samples to show.

PRACTICE AND APPLY

❑ Práctica, Activities 7–11, pp. 32–33. Have students do activity 9 in pairs. Have students stand up to do survey activity 10. Use reading, writing, and speaking skills listed next to the activity.

❑ Repaso activities 1–5, pp. 36–37. Play 1B TXT CD 1 track 5 to do activity 1.

OPTIONAL RESOURCES

Plan
- Best Practices Toolkit
- PE Answers, MSRB, Transparencies 60–66

Present
- Warm-up Transp., MSRB, Transparency 23
- Audio Script, MSRB, pp. 55–56

- Grammar Transp., MSRB Transparencies 17–19

Practice
- Practice Pages, MSRB, pp. 33–36

Assess
- Antes de avanzar Test, MSRB, pp. 41–47

TECHNOLOGY TOOLS	
Teacher Tools	**Student Tools**
Power Presentations	@Home Tutor
EasyPlanner CD-ROM	ClassZone.com
Test generator CD-ROM	eEdition Online or CD-ROM
McDougal Littell Assessment System	

Unit and Lesson Opener,
Presentación y práctica de vocabulario, pp. 38–45

OBJECTIVES

- Introduce lesson theme: **Vivimos aquí.**
- Present vocabulary: rooms of a house, furniture, household items
- **Recycle:** stem-changing verbs: **o → ue,** p. 34.

STANDARDS

- 1.2 Understand language
- 1.3 Present information, Acts. 1–2, PYP
- 2.2 Products and perspectives
- 4.2 Compare cultures, CC

FOCUS AND MOTIVATE

❏ Unit and Lesson Opener, pp. 38–41. Introduce students to the culture of Ecuador and the lesson theme of talking about houses and household items.

TEACH

❏ Presentación de vocabulario, pp. 42–44, paragraphs A–E. Read the paragraphs.

❏ Video Program DVD 2, Unit 5. Show Vocabulary Presentation video.

❏ Audio Program TXT CD 5, track 1. Play Vocabulary Presentation audio.

IEP Modification Have students repeat after you the boldfaced vocabulary words.

PRACTICE AND APPLY

❏ Lesson Opener, pp. 40–41: Read Comparación cultural. Ask students to respond to ¿Qué ves? questions based on the photo.

❏ Listen to 1B TXT CD 1, track 6 and do ¡A responder! activity, p. 44.

❏ Assign activities 1 and 2 on p. 45 to practice new vocabulary while recycling stem-changing verbs: **o → ue.**

ASSESS AND RETEACH

❏ Para y piensa, p. 45. Have students name three items that can be found in la **sala, el cuarto,** and other rooms.

❏ Vocabulary Recognition Quiz, On-level Assessment, p. 210.

❏ Homework: *Cuaderno,* pp. 1–3; *Cuaderno para hispanohablantes,* pp. 1–4.

OPTIONAL RESOURCES

Plan
- Family Letter, URB 5, p. 91
- Family letters in Haitian Creole and Spanish on ClassZone.com
- Best Practices Toolkit
- Absent Student Copymasters, URB 5, p. 93
- PE Answers, MSRB, Transp. 67–70
- Workbook Answers, UTB 5, Transp. 32–39

Present
- Warm-up Transp. 16, UTB 5
- Atlas Map, UTB 1, Transp. 5
- Map Transp. 1, UTB 5
- Map-Culture Activities, URB 5, pp. 83–84
- Música del mundo hispano
- Fine Art Activities, URB 5, pp. 87–89

- Fine Art Transp. 3–5, UTB 5
- Vocabulary Transp. 6–7, UTB 5
- TPRS, pp. 57–63
- Video Script, URB 5, pp. 69–70
- Audio Script, URB 5, pp. 73–77
- Vocabulary Video, DVD 2

Practice
- Practice Games, URB 5, p. 31
- Video Activities, URB 5, pp. 51–52

Assess
- Reteaching Copymasters, URB 5, pp. 1, 2, 10

TECHNOLOGY TOOLS	
Teacher Tools	**Student Tools**
Power Presentations	@Home Tutor
EasyPlanner CD-ROM	ClassZone.com
	Cultura interactiva
	eEdition Online or CD-ROM

Vocabulario en contexto, pp. 46–47

OBJECTIVES

- Understand and practice activity vocabulary in context.
- Practice using **tener** referring to places or things in a home or apartment

STANDARDS

- 1.1 Engage in conversation, Act. 4
- 1.2 Understand language, Act. 3
- 1.3 Present information, Acts. 4–5, PYP

FOCUS AND MOTIVATE

❑ Telehistoria escena 1, p. 46. Read the Cuando lees strategy.

TEACH

❑ Telehistoria escena 1, p. 46. Direct students' attention to the photo(s) and have them guess what is happening in the scene.

❑ Video Program DVD 2, Unit 5. Show the video for scene 1.

❑ Audio Program TXT CD 5, track 3. Play audio for scene 1.

IEP Modification Go over the También se dice and ask heritage learners which word(s) they use to say "bedroom."

PRACTICE AND APPLY

❑ **Comprensión del episodio,** Activity 3, p. 46. Play TXT CD 5 track 3. Call on students to give the answers.

ASSESS AND RETEACH

❑ Para y piensa, p. 47. Have students name the different items for different rooms.

❑ Vocabulary Production Quiz, On-level Assessment, p. 211.

OPTIONAL RESOURCES

Plan

- Best Practices Toolkit
- PE Answers, MSRB, Transp. 67–70
- Workbook Answers, UTB 5, Transp. 32–39
- Absent Student Copymasters, URB 5, p. 94

Present

- Warm-up Transp. 16, UTB 5
- Audio Script, URB 5, pp. 73–77
- Video Script, URB 5, pp. 69–70

Practice

- Video Activities, URB 5, pp. 53–54
- Practice Games, URB 5, p. 32

Assess

- Reteaching Copymasters, URB 5, pp. 1, 3

TECHNOLOGY TOOLS	
Teacher Tools	**Student Tools**
Power Presentations	@Home Tutor
EasyPlanner CD-ROM	ClassZone.com
Test Generator CD-ROM	eEdition Online or CD-ROM

Presentación y práctica de gramática 1, pp. 48–51

OBJECTIVES
- Present and practice the different uses of **ser** and **estar.**
- Use new verbs to discuss plans with friends.
- **Recycle:** location words, p. 13 and colors, p. 28.

STANDARDS
- 1.1 Engage in conversation, Act. 10
- 1.2 Understand language, Act. 8
- 1.3 Present information, Acts. 6–12
- 4.1 Compare languages
- 4.2 Compare cultures, Act. 11

FOCUS AND MOTIVATE
☐ Presentación de gramática, p. 48. Briefly review **ser** (p. 6) and **estar** (p. 18) with the students.

TEACH
☐ Presentación de gramática, p. 48. Write the following sentences on the board: Roberta _____ mi amiga. Mi calculadora _____ en su mochila. Nosotros no _____ bien. Ask students to explain which verb, ser or estar, would be appropriate in that sentence, and to give the correct conjugation.

☐ Comparación cultural, p. 51, Activity 11. Ask students to describe the homes portrayed in Oswaldo Guayasamín's painting, Canoas y casas en el suburbio.

IEP Modification Ask English learners how they express "to be" in their language. Does it change depending on the context, as in Spanish?

PRACTICE AND APPLY
☐ Activities 6, 7, p. 49. Have students write out their answers.

☐ Activity 8, p. 49. Play 1B TXT CD 1, track 7. Call on students to give the answers.

☐ Activities 9, 12, pp. 50–51. Have students write their answers or work in pairs.

☐ Activity 10, p. 50. Have students work in groups of three.

☐ Activity 11, p. 51. Ask students to draw a picture of their home that they are describing.

ASSESS AND RETEACH
☐ Para y piensa, p. 51. Have students complete sentences with **ser** or **estar.**

☐ Homework: *Cuaderno*, pp. 4–6; *Cuaderno para hispanohablantes*, pp. 5–7.

OPTIONAL RESOURCES

Plan
- Best Practices Toolkit
- PE Answers, MSRB, Transp. 67–70
- Workbook Answers, UTB 5, Transp. 32–39
- Absent Student Copymasters, URB 5, p. 95
- Easy Planner CD-ROM
- ClassZone.com

Present
- Warm-up Transp. 17, UTB 5
- Grammar Presentation Transp. 10, UTB 5

- Fine Art Activities, URB 5, p. 86
- Fine Art Transp. 2, UTB 5
- Audio Script, URB 5, pp. 73–77

Practice
- Practice Games, URB 5, p. 33

Assess
- Reteaching Copymasters, URB 5, pp. 4, 5, 11, 12

TECHNOLOGY TOOLS	
Teacher Tools	**Student Tools**
Power Presentations	@Home Tutor
EasyPlanner CD-ROM	ClassZone.com
Test Generator CD-ROM	eEdition Online or CD-ROM

Gramática en contexto, pp. 52–53

OBJECTIVES

- Practice **ser** and **estar** and new vocabulary in context.

FOCUS AND MOTIVATE

- ❏ Telehistoria escena 2, p. 52. Read the Cuando escuchas strategy.

STANDARDS
- 1.1 Engage in conversation, Act. 15
- 1.2 Understand language, Act. 13
- 1.3 Present information, Acts. 14–15

TEACH

- ❏ Audio Program TXT CD 5, track 5. Play the audio for scene 2. Ask students to raise their hands each time they hear **ser** or **estar** being used.
- ❏ Video Program DVD 2, Unit 5. Show the video for scene 2.
- ❏ Telehistoria escena 2, p. 52. Have students read the dialog out loud for correct pronunciation and intonation. Point out where and how **ser** and **estar** are being used in the dialogue.

PRACTICE AND APPLY

- ❏ Comprensión del episodio, Activity 13, p. 53. Listen to TXT CD 5, track 5. Call on students to give the answers.
- ❏ Activity 14, p. 53. Have students write their descriptions.
- ❏ Activity 15, p. 53. Have students switch roles so that they both are able to describe their bedrooms.

IEP Modification Ask various students some of the organizing questions from Activity 14 (**¿Quién es una persona importante en tu vida? ¿Cómo es?**) to model correct sentence formation before students begin writing.

ASSESS AND RETEACH

- ❏ Para y piensa, p. 53. Have students choose the correct verb.
- ❏ Grammar Quiz 1, On-level Assessment, p. 212.

OPTIONAL RESOURCES

Plan
- Best Practices Toolkit
- PE Answers, MSRB, Transp. 67–70
- Workbook Answers, UTB 5, Transp. 32–39
- Absent Student Copymasters, URB 5, p. 96

Present
- Warm-up Transp. 17, UTB 5
- Audio Script, URB 5, pp. 73–77
- Video Script, URB 5, pp. 69–70

Practice
- Practice Games, URB 5, p. 34
- Video Activities, URB 5, pp. 55–56

Assess
- Reteaching Copymasters, URB 5, pp. 4, 6

TECHNOLOGY TOOLS	
Teacher Tools	**Student Tools**
Power Presentations	@Home Tutor
EasyPlanner CD-ROM	ClassZone.com
Test Generator CD-ROM	eEdition Online or CD-ROM

Presentación y práctica de gramática 2, pp. 54–57

OBJECTIVES
- Present and practice using ordinal numbers.
- **Recycle:** clothes, p. 28.
- Practice stressing syllables in Spanish.

FOCUS AND MOTIVATE
❑ Presentación de gramática, p. 54. Introduce ordinal numbers. Review noun-adjective agreement.

STANDARDS
- 1.1 Engage in conversation, Acts.18–19
- 1.3 Present information, Acts. 16–20
- 4.1 Compare languages
- 4.2 Compare cultures, CC

TEACH
❑ Presentación de gramática, p. 54. Have students repeat after you the ordinal numbers in rising and descending order.

❑ Comparación cultural, p. 57. Ask students to compare and contrast the two geographical sites mentioned.

❑ Pronunciación, p. 56. Use TXT CD 5, track 6 to teach what syllables are stressed in Spanish words.

IEP Modification   Give students examples of words they have not yet learned that are cognates (**la cámara digital, el tenis, los artículos, un momento**) and have them say the words correctly, based on the rules of accentuation they have just learned.

PRACTICE AND APPLY
❑ Activities 16, 17, p. 55. Have students write their answers.

❑ Activities 18 and 19, pp. 55–56. Have students perform these activities in pairs. Then call on students to ask and answer questions aloud.

❑ Pronunciación, p. 56. Have students give words they know that have written accents.

ASSESS AND RETEACH
❑ Para y piensa, p. 57. Have students do translations from English to Spanish of ordinal numbers.

❑ Homework: *Cuaderno*, pp. 7–9; *Cuaderno para hispanohablantes*, pp. 8–11.

OPTIONAL RESOURCES
Plan
- Best Practices Toolkit
- PE Answers, MSRB, Transp. 67–70
- Workbook Answers, UTB 5, Transp. 32–39
- Absent Student Copymasters, URB 5, p. 97

Present
- Warm-up Transp. 18, UTB 5
- Grammar Presentation Transp. 11, UTB 5

Practice
- Practice Games, URB 5, p. 35
- Audio Script, URB 5, pp. 73–77

Assess
- Reteaching Copymasters, URB 5, pp. 7, 8, 12

TECHNOLOGY TOOLS	
Teacher Tools	**Student Tools**
Power Presentations	@Home Tutor
EasyPlanner CD-ROM	ClassZone.com
Test Generator CD-ROM	eEdition Online or CD-ROM

Todo junto, Juegos y diversiones, pp. 58–61

OBJECTIVES

- Integrate lesson content.
- Practice using and integrating lesson vocabulary and grammar.
- Review vocabulary by playing a game.

STANDARDS

- 1.1 Engage in conversation, Act. 23
- 1.2 Understand language, Acts. 21, 22, 24
- 1.3 Present information, Acts. 22–25, PYP
- 5.2 Life-long learners, Juegos y diversiones

FOCUS AND MOTIVATE

- ☐ Todo junto, p. 58. Do the reading or listening strategies prior to reading the dialogue, listening to the audio CD, or watching the DVD.

TEACH

- ☐ Video Program DVD 2, Unit 5. Show Telehistoria scenes 1 and 2 as a review before showing scene 3.
- ☐ Audio Program TXT CD 5 tracks 3 and 5. Play Telehistoria scenes 1 and 2 as a review before listening to scene 3 (TXT CD 5 track 7).
- ☐ Telehistoria completa, p. 58. Have students read the dialogue aloud for correct pronunciation and intonation.

IEP Modification Ask groups of students to write a summary of escena 3, then re-create the scene in their own words.

PRACTICE AND APPLY

- ☐ Comprensión de los episodios, p. 59. Listen to TXT CD 5 tracks 3, 5, and 7 to do Activities 21 and 22.
- ☐ Activity 23, p. 59. Have students switch roles so that they each describe their dream homes.
- ☐ Activity 24, p. 60. Audio program: 1B TXT CD 1 tracks 8, 9. Practice using reading, writing, listening, and speaking skills.
- ☐ Juegos y diversiones, p. 61. Have students play ¡Dibújalo!

ASSESS AND RETEACH

- ☐ Para y piensa, p. 60. Have students do the activity. Ask them to form other similar sentences using other household items and ordinals.
- ☐ Grammar Quiz 2, On-level Assessment, p. 213.
- ☐ Homework: *Cuaderno*, pp. 10–11; *Cuaderno para hispanohablantes*, pp. 12–13.

OPTIONAL RESOURCES

Plan
- Best Practices Toolkit
- PE Answers, MSRB, Transp. 67–70
- Workbook Answers, UTB 5, Transp. 32–39
- Absent Student Copymasters, URB 5, p. 98

Present
- Warm-up Transp. 18, UTB 5
- Audio Script, URB 5, pp. 73–77
- Video Script, URB 5, pp. 69–70

Practice
- Learning Scenarios on Easy Planner
- Conversation cards on Easy Planner and ClassZone
- Video activities, URB 5, pp. 57–58
- Practice Games, URB 5, p. 36

Assess
- Reteaching Copymasters, URB 5, pp. 7, 9

TECHNOLOGY TOOLS	
Teacher Tools	**Student Tools**
Power Presentations	@Home Tutor
EasyPlanner CD-ROM	ClassZone.com
Test Generator CD-ROM	eEdition Online or CD-ROM

Lectura/Conexiones, pp. 62–64

OBJECTIVES
- Learn about real estate in Ecuador.
- Compare houses and apartments for sale.
- Learn about an Inca settlement.

STANDARDS
- 1.2 Understand language
- 1.3 Present information
- 2.1 Practices and perspectives
- 2.2 Products and perspectives
- 3.1 Knowledge of other disciplines
- 4.2 Compare cultures

FOCUS AND MOTIVATE
- ❏ Lectura, pp. 62–63. Have students scan both home brochures briefly to find major differences in the two homes.
- ❏ Conexiones, p. 64. Introduce background information on the Incan empire.

TEACH
- ❏ Lectura, Vivir en Ecuador, pp. 62–63. Play TXT CD 5, track 10 as students follow along.
- ❏ Conexiones, p. 64. Talk about how the pictures reflect the descriptions of the Incan buildings in the text.

PRACTICE AND APPLY
- ❏ Lectura, Vivir en Ecuador, pp. 62–63. Have students answer the ¿Comprendiste? questions in Spanish, as well as do the ¿Y tú? activity with a partner.
- ❏ Conexiones, p. 64. Assign each Proyecto to a group of students. Have the groups present what they have learned to the class.

IEP Modification   Ask students to create an advertisement for a real or imaginary apartment building, using the ads from the Lectura as a model.

ASSESS AND RETEACH
- ❏ Para y piensa, p. 63. Have students answer the questions.
- ❏ Culture Quiz, On-level Assessment, p. 214.

OPTIONAL RESOURCES
Plan
- Best Practices Toolkit
- PE Answers, MSRB, Transp. 67–70
- Workbook Answers, UTB 5, Transp. 32–39
- Absent Student Copymasters, URB 5, p. 99

Present
- Warm-up Transp. 19, UTB 5

Practice
- Lecturas para todos, pp. 42–46
- Lecturas para hispanohablantes
- Practice Games, URB 5, p. 37

TECHNOLOGY TOOLS	
Teacher Tools	**Student Tools**
Power Presentations	@Home Tutor
EasyPlanner CD-ROM	ClassZone.com
Test Generator CD-ROM	eEdition Online or CD-ROM

En resumen, Repaso de la lección, pp. 65–67

OBJECTIVES

- Review lesson grammar and vocabulary.

FOCUS AND MOTIVATE

❑ En resumen, p. 65. Review all vocabulary terms andgrammar items.

❑ Repaso de la lección, pp. 66–67. Review the information in ¡Llegada! Do a quick oral review of **ser** or **estar**, ordinal numbers, and vocabulary.

TEACH

❑ En resumen, p.65. Assess which vocabulary terms need more practice and encourage students to form sentences with each.

❑ Repaso de la lección, pp. 66–67. Point out the pages students can review before doing each activity.

PRACTICE AND APPLY

❑ Repaso de la lección, Activity 1, p. 66. Play Audio Program 1B TXT CD 1 track 10 while they do Activity 1.

❑ Complete Activities 2–5, pp. 66–67.

IEP Modification Instruct students to answer the items in Activity 5 in Spanish.

ASSESS AND RETEACH

❑ Homework: Study En resumen, p. 65; *Cuaderno*, pp. 12–23; *Cuaderno para hispanohablantes*, pp. 14–23.

❑ Lesson Test, On-level Assessment, pp. 215–221.

OPTIONAL RESOURCES

Plan
- Best Practices Toolkit
- PE Answers, MSRB, Transp. 67–70
- Workbook Answers, UTB 5, Transp. 32–39
- Absent Student Copymasters, URB 5, p. 100

Present
- Warm-up Transp. 19, UTB 5
- Audio Script, URB 5, pp. 73–77

Practice
- Practice Games, URB 5, p. 38
- Sing-along Audio CD

Assess
- Review Games Online
- Lesson Test, Modified Assessment, pp. 170–176
- Lesson Test, Pre-AP Assessment, pp. 170–176
- Lesson Test, Heritage Learners Assessment, pp. 176–182

TECHNOLOGY TOOLS	
Teacher Tools	**Student Tools**
Power Presentations	@Home Tutor
EasyPlanner CD-ROM	ClassZone.com
Test Generator CD-ROM	eEdition Online or CD-ROM
McDougal Littell Assessment System	

Lesson Opener,
Presentación y práctica de vocabulario, pp. 68–73

OBJECTIVES

- Introduce lesson theme: **Una fiesta en casa.**
- **Culture:** learn how family parties are celebrated in different countries.
- Present and practice vocabulary: household chores, party activities.

STANDARDS

- 1.2 Understand language
- 1.3 Present information, Acts. 1–2, PYP
- 2.2 Products and perspectives
- 4.2 Compare cultures

FOCUS AND MOTIVATE

❑ Introduce students to the culture of Ecuador and the lesson theme of planning a party and talking about chores, pp. 68–69.

TEACH

❑ Presentación de vocabulario, pp. 70–72, paragraphs A–E. Read the paragraphs.
❑ Video Program DVD 2, Unit 5. Show Vocabulary Presentation video.
❑ Audio Program TXT CD 5, track 12. Play Vocabulary Presentation audio.

PRACTICE AND APPLY

❑ Lesson 1 Opener, pp. 68–69. Read Comparación cultural. Have students view the photographs and respond to the ¿Qué ves? questions.
❑ Use the ¡A responder! activity (1B TXT CD 1, Track 11) on p. 72 to check recognition of new vocabulary.
❑ Assign Activities 1 and 2 on p. 73.

IEP Modification   Hold up pictures of certain household items (bed, plates, broom, etc.). The students will then guess the chore that the item symbolizes.

ASSESS AND RETEACH

❑ Para y piensa, p. 73. Ask students to talk about the things they do before a party.
❑ Vocabulary Recognition Quiz, On-level Assessment, p. 227.
❑ Homework: *Cuaderno*, pp. 24–26; *Cuaderno para hispanohablantes*, pp. 24–27.

OPTIONAL RESOURCES

Plan
- Best Practices Toolkit
- Absent Student Copymasters, URB 5, p. 101
- PE Answers, MSRB, Transp. 71–74
- Workbook Answers, UTB 5, Transp. 40–47

Present
- Warm-up Transp. 20, UTB 5
- Vocabulary Transp. 8–9, UTB 5
- TPRS, pp. 64–70

- Video Script, URB 5, pp. 71–72
- Audio Script, URB 5, pp. 78–82
- Vocabulary Video, DVD 2

Practice
- Practice Games, URB 5, p. 39
- Video Activities, URB 5, pp. 59–60

Assess
- Reteaching Copymasters, URB 5, pp. 13–14

TECHNOLOGY TOOLS	
Teacher Tools	**Student Tools**
Power Presentations	@Home Tutor
EasyPlanner CD-ROM	ClassZone.com
	Cultura interactiva
	eEdition Online or CD-ROM

Vocabulario en contexto, pp. 74–75

OBJECTIVES

- Understand and practice activity vocabulary in context.
- **Recycle: tener que,** p. 16.

STANDARDS
- 1.1 Engage in conversation, Act. 4
- 1.2 Understand language, Act. 3
- 1.3 Present information, Act. 4, PYP

FOCUS AND MOTIVATE

❏ Telehistoria escena 1, p. 74. Read the Cuando lees strategy.

TEACH

❏ Telehistoria escena 1, p. 74. Direct students' attention to the photo(s) and have them guess what is happening in the scene.

❏ Video Program DVD 2, Unit 5. Show the video for scene 1.

❏ Audio Program TXT CD 5, track 14. Play the audio for scene 1.

IEP Modification   Have students write a brief narrative about the Telehistoria characters and their chores, based on the photos in Activity 4.

PRACTICE AND APPLY

❏ **Comprensión del episodio,** Activity 3, p. 75. Play TXT CD 5 track 14. Call on students to give the answers.

❏ Activity 4, Recycle: Review **tener que,** p. 16.

ASSESS AND RETEACH

❏ Para y piensa, p. 75. Have students complete sentences.

❏ Vocabulary Production Quiz, On-level Assessment, p. 228.

OPTIONAL RESOURCES

Plan
- Best Practices Toolkit
- PE Answers, MSRB, Transp. 71–74
- Workbook Answers, UTB 5, Transp. 40–47
- Absent Student Copymasters, URB 5, p. 102

Present
- Warm-up Transp. 20, UTB 5
- Audio Script, URB 5, pp. 78–82
- Video Script, URB 5, pp. 71–72

Practice
- Video Activities, URB 5, pp. 61–62
- Practice Games, URB 5, p. 40

Assess
- Reteaching Copymasters, URB 5, pp. 13, 15, 22

TECHNOLOGY TOOLS	
Teacher Tools	**Student Tools**
Power Presentations	@Home Tutor
EasyPlanner CD-ROM	ClassZone.com
Test Generator CD-ROM	eEdition Online or CD-ROM

Presentación y práctica de gramática 1, pp. 76–79

OBJECTIVES

- Present and practice more irregular verbs.
- Review lesson vocabulary.
- **Recycle:** interrogative words, p. 20.
- Pronunciation: Compare pronunciation of the letters **b** and **v**.

FOCUS AND MOTIVATE

- ❏ Presentación de gramática, p. 76. Introduce the conjugations of the verbs **decir, venir, dar, poner, salir,** and **traer.**

TEACH

- ❏ Presentación de gramática, p. 76. Emphasize why these verbs are considered irregular, and which forms, if any, of these verbs are regular.
- ❏ Comparación cultural, p. 77. Write a list on the board of all the activities that *quiteños* do during Fiestas de Quito.
- ❏ Pronunciación, p. 79. Play TXT CD 5, track 16.

IEP Modification   Have students create a poster for Fiestas de Quito, based on the information they learned in Activity 6.

PRACTICE AND APPLY

- ❏ Práctica de gramática, pp. 77–78. Have students write their answers to Activities 5–7.
- ❏ Have students do activities 8 and 9 in pairs. Call on students to ask and answer questions aloud.
- ❏ Activity 9, p. 79. Recycle: Review interrogative words, p. 20.
- ❏ Pronunciación, p. 79. Say a list of words containing either **b** or **v** aloud, and have the students guess which letter is in the word.

ASSESS AND RETEACH

- ❏ Para y piensa, p. 79. Have students complete sentences with irregular verbs.
- ❏ Homework: *Cuaderno*, pp. 27–29; *Cuaderno para hispanohablantes*, pp. 28–30.

OPTIONAL RESOURCES

Plan
- Best Practices Toolkit
- PE Answers, MSRB, Transp. 71–74
- Workbook Answers, UTB 5, Transp. 40–47
- Absent Student Copymasters, URB 5, p. 103
- Easy Planner CD-ROM
- ClassZone.com

Present
- Warm-up Transp. 21, UTB 5
- Grammar Presentation Transp. 12, UTB 5
- Audio Script, URB 5, pp. 78–82

Practice
- Practice Games, URB 5, p. 41

Assess
- Reteaching Copymasters, URB 5, pp. 16–17

TECHNOLOGY TOOLS

Teacher Tools	Student Tools
Power Presentations	@Home Tutor
EasyPlanner CD-ROM	ClassZone.com
Test Generator CD-ROM	eEdition Online or CD-ROM

Gramática en contexto, pp. 80–81

OBJECTIVES
- Practice irregular verbs and lesson vocabulary in context.
- **Recycle:** expressions of frequency.

STANDARDS
- 1.1 Engage in conversation, Act. 11
- 1.2 Understand language, Act. 10
- 1.3 Present information, Acts. 11–12

FOCUS AND MOTIVATE
- ❏ Telehistoria escena 2, p. 80. Read the Cuando escuchas strategy.

TEACH
- ❏ Audio Program TXT CD 5, track 15. Play the audio for scene 2.
- ❏ Video Program DVD 2, Unit 5. Show the video for scene 2.
- ❏ Telehistoria escena 2, p. 80. Direct students' attention to the photo(s) and have them guess what is happening in the scene.

PRACTICE AND APPLY
- ❏ Activity 10. Have students answer the questions based on the Telehistoria.
- ❏ Activity 11, p. 81. Recycle: Review expressions of frequency, p. 13.
- ❏ Activity 12, p. 81. After students write their answers, ask the questions aloud and have the students say what they wrote.

IEP Modification Have students find the other irregular verbs in the script, and say how the forms are similar to the irregular verbs they just learned.

ASSESS AND RETEACH
- ❏ Para y piensa, p. 81. Have students complete sentences with **venir, traer,** or **decir.**
- ❏ Grammar Quiz 1, On-level Assessment, p. 229.

OPTIONAL RESOURCES

Plan
- Best Practices Toolkit
- PE Answers, MSRB, Transp. 71–74
- Workbook Answers, UTB 5, Transp. 40–47
- Absent Student Copymasters, URB 5, p. 104

Present
- Warm-up Transp. 21, UTB 5
- Audio Script, URB 5, pp. 78–82
- Video Script, URB 5, pp. 71–72

Practice
- Practice Games, URB 5, p. 42
- Video Activities, URB 5, pp. 63–64

Assess
- Reteaching Copymasters, URB 5, pp. 16, 18, 23

TECHNOLOGY TOOLS	
Teacher Tools	**Student Tools**
Power Presentations	@Home Tutor
EasyPlanner CD-ROM	ClassZone.com
Test Generator CD-ROM	eEdition Online or CD-ROM

Presentación y práctica de gramática 2, pp. 82–85

OBJECTIVES

- Present and practice affirmative **tú** commands.
- **Recycle:** direct object pronouns, p. 32.

FOCUS AND MOTIVATE

- ❑ Presentación de gramática, p. 82. Introduce affirmative **tú** commands.
- ❑ Nota gramatical, p. 84. Introduce **acabar de** + infinitive.

STANDARDS
- 1.1 Engage in conversation, Acts. 14, 17
- 1.2 Understand language, Act. 15
- 1.3 Present information, Acts. 13–18, PYP
- 2.2 Products and perspectives, CC
- 4.1 Compare languages
- 4.2 Compare cultures, CC

TEACH

- ❑ Presentación de gramática, p. 82. Have the students repeat after you the irregular commands.
- ❑ Presentación de gramática, p. 82. Demonstrate where the stress falls on commands with a direct object pronoun attached.
- ❑ Nota gramatical, p. 84. Give examples of **acabar de** + infinitive with different subject pronouns and infinitives.
- ❑ Comparación cultural, p. 85. Discuss what designs are found in the picture of the Otavalos' textiles.

IEP Modification   Have students invent a chant or acronym to help the remember the eight irregular affirmative tú commands.

PRACTICE AND APPLY

- ❑ Activity 14, p. 83. Recycle: Review direct object pronouns, p. 32.
- ❑ Activity 15, p. 83. Audio program: 1B TXT CD 1 track 12.
- ❑ Have students work in pairs to complete Activities 14, 16, 17.

ASSESS AND RETEACH

- ❑ Para y piensa, p. 85. Ask students to give **tú** commands of the verbs in the exercise. Have extra verbs to keep practicing.
- ❑ Homework: *Cuaderno*, pp. 30–32; *Cuaderno para hispanohablantes*, pp. 31–34.

OPTIONAL RESOURCES

Plan
- Best Practices Toolkit
- PE Answers, MSRB, Transp. 71–74
- Workbook Answers, UTB 5, Transp. 40–47
- Absent Student Copymasters, URB 5, p. 105

Present
- Warm-up Transp. 22, UTB 5
- Grammar Presentation Transp. 13, UTB 5

Practice
- Practice Games, URB 5, p. 43
- Audio Script, URB 5, pp. 78–82

Assess
- Reteaching Copymasters, URB 5, pp. 19, 20, 24

TECHNOLOGY TOOLS	
Teacher Tools	**Student Tools**
Power Presentations	@Home Tutor
EasyPlanner CD-ROM	ClassZone.com
Test Generator CD-ROM	eEdition Online or CD-ROM

Todo junto, Juegos y Diversiones, pp. 86–89

OBJECTIVES

- Integrate lesson content.
- Practice using and integrating lesson vocabulary and grammar.
- Review vocabulary by playing a game.

STANDARDS

- 1.1 Engage in conversation, Acts. 21–22
- 1.2 Understand language, Acts. 19–20, 22
- 1.3 Present information, Acts. 18, 23–24, PYP
- 5.2 Life-long learners, Juegos y diversiones

FOCUS AND MOTIVATE

❑ Telehistoria completa, p. 86. Do the reading or listening strategies prior to reading the dialogue, listening to the audio CD, or watching the DVD.

TEACH

❑ Video Program DVD 2, Unit 5. Show Telehistoria scenes 1 and 2 as a review before showing scene 3.

❑ Audio Program TXT CD 5 tracks 14 and 15. Play Telehistoria scenes 1 and 2 as a review before listening to scene 3 (TXT CD 5 track 16).

❑ Telehistoria completa, p. 86. Have students read the dialog out loud for correct pronunciation and intonation.

IEP Modification   Help students prepare for Activity 23 by having them create a chart listing the rooms in their house and the chores that need to be done in each.

PRACTICE AND APPLY

❑ Comprensión de los episodios, p. 87. Play TXT CD 5 tracks 14, 15, and 16 to do Activities 19 and 20.

❑ Activity 22, p. 88. Audio program: 1B TXT CD 1 tracks 13, 14. Practice using reading, writing, listening, speaking skills.

❑ Have students play Mímica to review vocabulary.

ASSESS AND RETEACH

❑ Para y piensa, p. 88. Pair students and have them give each other different commands for chores at home or things to do at school.

❑ Grammar Quiz 2, On-level Assessment, p. 230.

❑ Homework: *Cuaderno*, pp. 33–34; *Cuaderno para hispanohablantes*, pp. 35–36.

OPTIONAL RESOURCES

Plan

- Best Practices Toolkit
- PE Answers, MSRB, Transp. 71–74
- Workbook Answers, UTB 5, Transp. 40–47
- Absent Student Copymasters, URB 5, p. 106

Present

- Warm-up Transp. 22, UTB 5
- Audio Script, URB 5, pp. 78–82
- Video Script, URB 5, pp. 71–72

Practice

- Learning Scenarios on Easy Planner
- Conversation cards on Easy Planner and ClassZone
- Video activities, URB 5, pp. 65–66
- Practice Games, URB 5, p. 44

Assess

- Reteaching Copymasters, URB 5, pp. 19, 21

TECHNOLOGY TOOLS	
Teacher Tools	**Student Tools**
Power Presentations	@Home Tutor
EasyPlanner CD-ROM	ClassZone.com
Test Generator CD-ROM	eEdition Online or CD-ROM

Lectura/Proyectos culturales, pp. 90–92

OBJECTIVES

- Read about folk dances in **Ecuador** and **Panamá**.
- Learn about the origins of the **sanjuanito** and **tamborino** and compare their music and costumes.
- Learn about tapestries of **Ecuador** and the **molas** of **Panamá**.

STANDARDS

- 1.2 Understand language
- 1.3 Present information, PYP
- 2.1 Practices and perspectives, PYP
- 2.2 Products and perspectives
- 4.2 Compare cultures, PYP

FOCUS AND MOTIVATE

- ❑ Lectura cultural, pp. 90–91. Have students read the Leer strategy and think about what they will draw as they read.

TEACH

- ❑ Lectura cultural, Bailes folklóricos de Ecuador y Panamá, pp. 90–91. Play Audio Program TXT CD 5, track 21. Play the audio as students follow along.
- ❑ Proyectos, p. 92. Discuss with students what the tapestries and the **molas** tell about the Otavalan and Kuna cultures.

PRACTICE AND APPLY

- ❑ Lectura cultural, Bailes folklóricos de Ecuador y Panamá, pp. 90–91. Call on students to answer the ¿Comprendiste? questions aloud. The ¿Y tú? questions can be answered with a partner.
- ❑ Proyectos culturales, p. 92. Split the class into two groups and have each group do one of the Proyectos. Then have students explain why they decorated their tapestries or molas the way they did.

IEP Modification   Ask students describe the traditional dances in their own or their parents' countries of origin.

ASSESS AND RETEACH

- ❑ Para y piensa, p. 91. Have students answer ¿Comprendiste? questions. Group students to do ¿Y tú?
- ❑ Culture Quiz, On-level Assessment, p. 231.

OPTIONAL RESOURCES

Plan

- Best Practices Toolkit
- PE Answers, MSRB, Transp. 71–74
- Workbook Answers, UTB 5, Transp. 40–47
- Absent Student Copymasters, URB 5, pp. 107–108

Present

- Warm-up Transp. 23, UTB 5

Practice

- Lecturas para todos, pp. 47–51
- Lecturas para hispanohablantes
- Practice Games, URB 5, p. 45

TECHNOLOGY TOOLS	
Teacher Tools	**Student Tools**
Power Presentations	@Home Tutor
EasyPlanner CD-ROM	ClassZone.com
Test Generator CD-ROM	eEdition Online or CD-ROM

En resumen, Repaso de la lección, pp. 93–95

OBJECTIVES
- Review lesson grammar and vocabulary.

FOCUS AND MOTIVATE
❑ En resumen, p. 93. Review all vocabulary terms and grammar items.

❑ Repaso de la lección, pp. 94–95. Review the information in ¡Llegada! Do a quick oral review of irregular verbs, affirmative tú commands, and vocabulary.

TEACH
❑ En resumen, p. 93. Assess which vocabulary terms need more practice and encourage students to form sentences with each.

❑ Point out the pages students can review before doing each activity.

PRACTICE AND APPLY
❑ Activity 1, p. 94. Play Audio Program 1B TXT CD 1 track 15 while they do Activity 1.

❑ Complete Activities 2–5, pp. 94–95.

IEP Modification Instruct students to answer the items in Activity 5 in Spanish.

ASSESS AND RETEACH
❑ Homework: Study En resumen, p. 93; *Cuaderno*, pp. 35–46; *Cuaderno para hispanohablantes*, pp. 37–46.

❑ Lesson Test, On-level Assessment, pp. 232–238.

OPTIONAL RESOURCES

Plan
- Best Practices Toolkit
- PE Answers, MSRB, Transp. 71–74
- Workbook Answers, UTB 5, Transp. 40–47
- Absent Student Copymasters, URB 5, p. 109

Present
- Warm-up Transp. 23, UTB 5
- Audio Script, URB 5, pp. 78–82

Practice
- Practice Games, URB 5, p. 46
- Sing-along Audio CD

Assess
- Review Games Online
- Lesson Test, Modified Assessment, pp. 182–188
- Lesson Test, Pre-AP Assessment, pp. 182–188
- Lesson Test, Heritage Learners Assessment, pp. 188–194

TECHNOLOGY TOOLS	
Teacher Tools	**Student Tools**
Power Presentations	@Home Tutor
EasyPlanner CD-ROM	ClassZone.com
Test Generator CD-ROM	eEdition Online or CD-ROM
McDougal Littell Assessment System	

Comparación cultural, Repaso inclusivo, pp. 96–99

OBJECTIVES

- Read what three teens have to say about celebrations in their countries.
- Compare your family celebrations with those in Panama, Argentina, and Ecuador.
- Cumulative review.

STANDARDS
- 1.2 Understand language
- 1.3 Present information
- 2.1 Practices and perspectives
- 4.2 Compare cultures

FOCUS AND MOTIVATE

❑ Comparación cultural, ¡Así celebramos!, pp. 96–97. Have students read about celebrations in Panama, Argentina, and Ecuador.

❑ Repaso inclusivo, pp. 98–99. Choose certain activities for your students to complete.

TEACH

❑ Comparación cultural, ¡Así celebramos!, pp. 96–97. Call on students to read the descriptions of María Elena, Carla, and Daniel. Encourage them to note similarities between the three in language and theme.

❑ Audio Program TXT CD 5 track 23. Listen to María Elena, Carla, and Daniel.

❑ Comparación cultural, pp. 96–97. Use the writing strategy to guide students in their own descriptions.

❑ Repaso inclusivo, pp. 98–99. Review the En resumen pages in Units 1, 2, 3, 4, and 5 to prepare students for Activities 1–6.

IEP Modification   When going over Activity 4, explain what yard sales are to English learners who may not be familiar with the terms.

PRACTICE AND APPLY

❑ Comparación cultural, ¡Así celebramos!, pp. 96–97. Help students increase their cultural awareness by doing the **Compara con tu mundo** activity.

❑ Repaso inclusivo, pp. 98–99. Play Audio Program TXT CD 5 track 24 to complete Activity 1.

❑ Repaso inclusivo, pp. 98–99. Complete Activities 2–6.

ASSESS AND RETEACH

❑ Homework: *Cuaderno*, pp. 47–49; *Cuaderno para hispanohablantes*, pp. 47–49.

❑ Unit Test, On-level Assessment, pp. 244–250.

OPTIONAL RESOURCES

Plan
- Absent Student Copymasters, URB 5, pp. 110–111

Present
- Audio Script, URB 5, pp. 78–82

Practice
- Situational Transp. and Copymasters, UTB 5, Transp. 14–15, pp. 1–2
- Family Involvement Activity, URB 5, p. 92
- ¡AvanzaCómics! SuperBruno y Nati, Episodio 2

Assess
- Unit Test, Modified Assessment, pp. 194–200
- Unit Test, Pre-AP Assessment, pp. 194–200
- Unit Test, Heritage Learners Assessment, pp. 200–206

TECHNOLOGY TOOLS	
Teacher Tools	**Student Tools**
EasyPlanner CD-ROM	ClassZone.com
Test Generator CD-ROM	Cultura interactiva
McDougal Littell Assessment System	eEdition Online or CD-ROM

Unit and Lesson Opener,
Presentación y práctica de vocabulario, pp. 100–107

OBJECTIVES
- Introduce lesson theme: **¿Cuál es tu deporte favorito?**
- Present and practice vocabulary: sports, places where sports are played, sports equipment.
- **Recycle:** numbers from 200 to 1,000,000, p. 21.

STANDARDS
- 1.2 Understand language, Act. 1
- 1.3 Present information, Act. 2
- 4.2 Compare cultures

FOCUS AND MOTIVATE
- ❑ Unit Opener, pp. 100–101: Introduce students to the culture of the Dominican Republic and the lesson theme of keeping healthy.

- ❑ Lesson Opener, pp. 102–103: Read Comparación cultural. Ask students to respond to "¿Qué ves?" questions based on the photo.

TEACH
- ❑ Presentación de vocabulario: Read A–D on pp. 104–106. Ask students to repeat the sports-related vocabulary after you.
- ❑ View Vocabulary Video, DVD 2.

IEP Modification Ask students what they wear to play sports by giving them a choice: e.g., "¿Llevas chaqueta o camiseta para correr?" or "¿Llevas pantalones largos o pantalones cortos para jugar al fútbol?"

PRACTICE AND APPLY
- ❑ Use the ¡A responder! activity (1B TXT CD 1, Track 16) on p. 106 to check comprehension of new vocabulary.
- ❑ Assign activities 1 and 2 on p. 107 to identify sports equipment and to review numbers from Unit 3.

ASSESS AND RETEACH
- ❑ Para y piensa, p. 107. Have students say sports-related items.
- ❑ Vocabulary Recognition Quiz, On-level Assessment, p. 256.
- ❑ Homework: *Cuaderno*, pp. 50–52; *Cuaderno para hispanohablantes*, pp. 50–53.

OPTIONAL RESOURCES
Plan
- Family Letter, URB 6, p. 91
- Family letters in Haitian Creole and Spanish on ClassZone.com
- Best Practices Toolkit
- Absent Student Copymasters, URB 6, p. 93
- PE Answers, MSRB, Transp. 75–78
- Workbook Answers, UTB 6, Transp. 32–39

Present
- Warm-up Transp. 16, UTB 6
- Atlas Map, UTB 1, Transp. 4
- Map Transp. 1, UTB 6
- Map-Culture Activities, URB 6, pp. 83–84
- Música del mundo hispano

- Fine Art Activities, URB 6, pp. 87, 89
- Fine Art Transp. 3, 5, UTB 6
- Vocabulary Transp. 6–7, UTB 6
- TPRS, pp. 71–77
- Video Script, URB 6, pp. 69–70
- Audio Script, URB 6, pp. 73–77
- Vocabulary Video, DVD 2

Practice
- Practice Games, URB 6, p. 31
- Video Activities, URB 6, pp. 51–52

Assess
- Reteaching Copymasters, URB 6, pp. 1, 2, 10

TECHNOLOGY TOOLS	
Teacher Tools	**Student Tools**
Power Presentations	@Home Tutor
EasyPlanner CD-ROM	ClassZone.com
Test Generator CD-ROM	Cultura interactiva
	eEdition Online or CD-ROM

Vocabulario en contexto, pp. 108–109

OBJECTIVES

- Understand and practice activity vocabulary in context.
- **Recycle: gustar** with nouns, p. 8.

STANDARDS
- 1.1 Engage in conversation, Act. 4
- 1.2 Understand language, Act. 3

FOCUS AND MOTIVATE

❏ Telehistoria escena 1, p. 108: Have students look at the picture and describe the scene. Ask them to try and guess what conversation the kids are having.

TEACH

❏ Telehistoria escena 1, p. 108: Strategies. Have students do the reading strategy as a class before listening to or watching the video.

❏ View Telehistoria escena 1, Video program, DVD 2.

❏ Tell students that not all Spanish speakers use the same words for a given item. Present También se dice and ask: "¿Cómo se dice **piscina** en México? ¿Cómo se dice en Argentina?"

PRACTICE AND APPLY

❏ Have students complete Activity 3, *Comprensión del episodio* on p. 109 (TXT CD 6, Track 3, if not viewing video).

❏ Pair students up to do Activity 4, p. 109.

IEP Modification   Put students in pairs and have them create an original dialogue about sports using the vocabulary from the lesson. Several groups can present their dialogue to the class, time permitting.

ASSESS AND RETEACH

❏ Para y piensa, p. 109. Have students find the correct vocabulary words.

❏ Vocabulary Production Quiz, On-level Assessment, p. 257.

OPTIONAL RESOURCES

Plan
- Best Practices Toolkit
- PE Answers, MSRB, Transp. 75–78
- Workbook Answers, UTB 6, Transp. 32–39
- Absent Student Copymasters, URB 6, p. 94

Present
- Warm-up Transp. 16, UTB 6
- Audio Script, URB 6, pp. 73–77
- Video Script, URB 6, pp. 69–70

Practice
- Video Activities, URB 6, pp. 53–54
- Practice Games, URB 6, p. 32

Assess
- Reteaching Copymasters, URB 6, pp. 1, 3, 11

TECHNOLOGY TOOLS	
Teacher Tools	**Student Tools**
Power Presentations	@Home Tutor
EasyPlanner CD-ROM	ClassZone.com
Test Generator CD-ROM	eEdition Online or CD-ROM

Presentación y práctica de gramática 1, pp. 110–113

OBJECTIVES

- Present and practice the verb **jugar.**
- **Culture:** Find out how professional athletes support their home countries.
- **Recycle:** comparatives, p. 24.

STANDARDS

- 1.1 Engage in conversation, Acts. 7–11
- 1.3 Present information, Acts. 7–11, PYP
- 2.1 Practices and perspectives, Act. 8
- 4.2 Compare cultures, Act. 8

FOCUS AND MOTIVATE

❑ Presentación de gramática, p. 110: Start by brainstorming with students a list of sports and games that they enjoy.

IEP Modification Ask Heritage Learners to expand on the list of sports and games, especially those that are common in or specific to the Spanish-speaking world (e.g. **la lotería mexicana**).

TEACH

❑ Presentación de gramática, p. 110: Remind students that they have already learned **o → ue** stem-changing verbs in Unit 4. Review the verbs **encontrar** and **almorzar** before presenting the conjugation of **jugar.** Point out that students learned the phrase **jugar al fútbol** in Unit 1.

❑ Presentación de gramática, p. 110. Write on the board **jugar al _____**, then say: "Yo juego al fútbol. Y tú, ¿juegas al fútbol?" Expand question by using **¿dónde?** and **¿cuándo?.**

❑ Comparación cultural, p. 112: Discuss as a class the Compara con tu mundo question before pairing students off for Activity 7.

PRACTICE AND APPLY

❑ Do as a class Activity 5, p. 111. Ask individual students to read the sentences aloud.

❑ Play the audio (1B TXT CD 1 track 17) while students complete Activity 6, p. 111.

ASSESS AND RETEACH

❑ Para y piensa, p. 113. Have students talk about who plays what sport, using jugar.

❑ Homework: *Cuaderno*, pp. 53–55; *Cuaderno para hispanohablantes*, pp. 54–56.

OPTIONAL RESOURCES

Plan
- Best Practices Toolkit
- PE Answers, MSRB, Transp. 75–78
- Workbook Answers, UTB 6, Transp. 32–39
- Absent Student Copymasters, URB 6, p. 95
- Easy Planner CD-ROM
- ClassZone.com

Present
- Warm-up Transp. 17, UTB 6
- Grammar Presentation Transp. 10, UTB 6
- Audio Script, URB 6, pp. 73–77

Practice
- Practice Games, URB 6, p. 33

Assess
- Reteaching Copymasters, URB 6, pp. 4, 5, 12

TECHNOLOGY TOOLS	
Teacher Tools	**Student Tools**
Power Presentations	@Home Tutor
EasyPlanner CD-ROM	ClassZone.com
Test Generator CD-ROM	eEdition Online or CD-ROM

¡AVANCEMOS!
Unidad 6 Lección 1

Gramática en contexto, pp. 114–115

OBJECTIVES

- Practice **jugar** and lesson vocabulary in context.
- Practice pronunciation of the letter g before **a, o, u.**

STANDARDS
- 1.1 Engage in conversation, Act. 13
- 1.2 Understand language, Act. 12, PYP
- 4.1 Compare languages, Pronunciación

FOCUS AND MOTIVATE

- ❏ Telehistoria escena 2, p. 114: Have students describe the picture and guess why the kids are at the sporting goods store.

TEACH

- ❏ Telehistoria escena 2, p. 114: Have students make a list of the suggested gifts as they listen/watch.
- ❏ View Telehistoria escena 2, Video program, DVD 2.
- ❏ Use TXT CD 6, Track 6 to practice the pronunciation of the letter **g** before **a, o, u,** and consonants. Have students repeat the sample sentence after you.

IEP Modification   Point out that in English this rule is also true. Give some examples of English words that demonstrate this: Gregory gladly plays the guitar at the gas station in August.

PRACTICE AND APPLY

- ❏ Have students complete Activity 12, *Comprensión del episodio* on p. 115 (TXT CD 6, Track 5, if not viewing video).
- ❏ Pair students up to do Activity 13, p. 115.

ASSESS AND RETEACH

- ❏ Para y piensa, p. 115. Have students complete the sentences with the appropriate form of the verb **jugar.**
- ❏ Grammar Quiz 1, On-level Assessment, p. 258.

OPTIONAL RESOURCES

Plan
- Best Practices Toolkit
- PE Answers, MSRB, Transp. 75–78
- Workbook Answers, UTB 6, Transp. 32–39
- Absent Student Copymasters, URB 6, p. 96

Present
- Warm-up Transp. 17, UTB 6
- Audio Script, URB 6, pp. 73–77
- Video Script, URB 6, pp. 69–70

Practice
- Practice Games, URB 6, p. 34
- Video Activities, URB 6, pp. 55–56

Assess
- Reteaching Copymasters, URB 6, pp. 4, 6

TECHNOLOGY TOOLS	
Teacher Tools	**Student Tools**
Power Presentations	@Home Tutor
EasyPlanner CD-ROM	ClassZone.com
Test Generator CD-ROM	eEdition Online or CD-ROM

Presentación y práctica de gramática 2, pp. 116–119

OBJECTIVES

- Present and practice **saber** and **conocer**.
- Practice lesson vocabulary: sports.
- Practice the personal **a** after verbs **like conocer**.

STANDARDS
- 1.1 Engage in conversation, Acts. 16–17, 19
- 1.3 Present information, Acts. 14–19, CC, PYP
- 4.1 Compare languages
- 4.2 Compare cultures, CC

FOCUS AND MOTIVATE

- ❏ Presentación de gramática, p. 116: Introduce verbs **saber** and **conocer.**

TEACH

- ❏ Presentación de gramática, p. 116: Point out that **saber que** followed by a complete sentence is a way of stating a fact that is known: "**Sé que** te gusta la pizza".
- ❏ Nota gramatical, p. 117. Present students with several examples using veo with objects and people in the classroom: "Veo un pizarrón. Veo a 10 estudiantes." Ask them to identify what's different about the statements and make a guess as to the rule.
- ❏ Comparación cultural, p. 119: Discuss the painting and Compara con tu mundo question as a class.

IEP Modification   Expand on the definition of **conocer** to include other items that one might be familiar with (e.g. a book or movie). Draw two columns on the board labeled **saber** and **conocer,** and ask students to make statements that fit into each column.

PRACTICE AND APPLY

- ❏ Do Activity 14, p. 117 as a class.
- ❏ Practice **saber, conocer** and personal **a** in Activity 15, p. 117.
- ❏ Group students together to do Activities 16, 17.
- ❏ Assign Activity 18.

ASSESS AND RETEACH

- ❏ Para y piensa, p. 119. Have students explain why they used a certain verb form.
- ❏ Homework: *Cuaderno*, pp. 56–58; *Cuaderno para hispanohablantes*, pp. 57–60.

OPTIONAL RESOURCES

Plan
- Best Practices Toolkit
- PE Answers, MSRB, Transp. 75–78
- Workbook Answers, UTB 6, Transp. 32–39
- Absent Student Copymasters, URB 6, p. 97

Present
- Warm-up Transp. 18, UTB 6
- Fine Art Activities, URB 6, p. 86

- Fine Art Transp. 2, UTB 6
- Grammar Presentation Transp. 11, UTB 6

Practice
- Practice Games, URB 6, p. 35
- Audio Script, URB 6, pp. 73–77

Assess
- Reteaching Copymasters, URB 6, pp. 7, 8

TECHNOLOGY TOOLS	
Teacher Tools	**Student Tools**
Power Presentations	@Home Tutor
EasyPlanner CD-ROM	ClassZone.com
Test Generator CD-ROM	eEdition Online or CD-ROM

Todo junto, Juegos y diversiones, pp. 120–123

OBJECTIVES

- Integrate lesson content.
- Practice using and integrating lesson vocabulary and grammar.
- Review sports vocabulary by playing a game.

STANDARDS
- 1.1 Engage in conversation, Acts. 22, 23
- 1.2 Understand language, Acts. 20–21, 23
- 1.3 Present information, Act. 22–24, PYP
- 5.2 Life-long learners, Juegos y diversiones

FOCUS AND MOTIVATE

❑ Telehistoria completa, p. 120: Look at the photos from Escena 1 and 2. Then look at the two photos for the final scene and ask students for predictions about what will happen.

TEACH

❑ Telehistoria completa, p. 120: Strategies. Use the listening strategy to focus students while playing the video or audio.

❑ Telehistoria completa, p. 120. Read the Resumen sections for Escena 1 and 2 before proceeding to Escena 3.

❑ Telehistoria completa, p. 120, Escena 3. Play Escena 3 on Video Program, DVD 2; replay Escena 1 and 2 to review entire story. After playing, you may want to pair students up to play the roles of Isabel and Mario in Episodio 3. Circulate and help with pronunciation and emphasis.

IEP Modification Have students retell the incidents from all three scenes in their own words. Ask them to imagine how the story might continue.

PRACTICE AND APPLY

❑ Do Activities 20 and 21, *Comprensión de los episodios*, p. 316. Use Audio Program, TXT CD 6 tracks 3, 5, and 7 if not viewing video.

❑ Group students together to do Activity 22, p. 121. If you have a tape recorder, circulate it so students can record their ads. Otherwise, have groups present them before the class.

❑ Activity 23, Integración, p. 122: use Audio Program. 1B TXT CD 1, tracks 18 and 19. Use a language lab if available, or do as a small group activity.

❑ Assign Activity 24.

❑ Have students play Memoria to review vocabulary.

ASSESS AND RETEACH

❑ Para y piensa, p. 122. Ask students to create similar sentences using both **saber** and **conocer**.

❑ Grammar Quiz 2, On-level Assessment, p. 259.

❑ Homework: *Cuaderno*, pp. 59–60; *Cuaderno para hispanohablantes*, pp. 61–62.

OPTIONAL RESOURCES

Plan
- Best Practices Toolkit
- PE Answers, MSRB, Transp. 75–78
- Workbook Answers, UTB 6, Transp. 32–39
- Absent Student Copymasters, URB 6, p. 98

Present
- Warm-up Transp. 18, UTB 6
- Audio Script, URB 6, pp. 73–77
- Video Script, URB 6, pp. 69–70

Practice
- Learning Scenarios on Easy Planner
- Conversation cards on Easy Planner and ClassZone
- Video activities, URB 6, pp. 57–58
- Practice Games, URB 6, p. 36

Assess
- Reteaching Copymasters, URB 6, pp. 7, 9

TECHNOLOGY TOOLS	
Teacher Tools	**Student Tools**
Power Presentations	@Home Tutor
EasyPlanner CD-ROM	ClassZone.com
Test Generator CD-ROM	eEdition Online or CD-ROM

Lectura/Conexiones, pp. 124–126

STANDARDS
- 1.2 Understand language
- 1.3 Present information
- 2.1 Practices and perspectives
- 2.2 Products and perspectives
- 3.1 Knowledge of other disciplines
- 3.2 Acquire information
- 4.2 Compare cultures

OBJECTIVES
- Read about a sports club in the Dominican Republic.
- Compare sports facilities in the Dominican Republic and the U.S.
- Learn about the Dominican flag.

FOCUS AND MOTIVATE
❑ Lectura, pp. 124–125: Have students scan the photos and note what kinds of activities the facility offers.

❑ Conexiones, p. 126: Ask students to look at the flag and note the similarities and differences to their own flag.

TEACH
❑ Lectura, pp. 124–125: Play Audio Program, TXT CD track 10 as the students follow along in the brochures.

❑ Conexiones, p. 126: Go over the reading and discuss the Dominican flag. Ask students to research in the library or on the Internet to learn more about its symbolism.

IEP Modification Pair students together to create a dialogue between a potential customer and a representative from the health club using the information provided in the brochure.

PRACTICE AND APPLY
❑ Lectura, pp. 124–125: Ask students to do the reading strategy as they read. Expansion: afterwards, students can use a mind map like this to describe a gym they know or their school's health and fitness facilities.

❑ Conexiones, p. 126, Proyectos 1, 2, 3. Allow students to pick the project that interests them the most.

ASSESS AND RETEACH
❑ Para y piensa, p. 122. Have students review the brochure information before answering the questions.

❑ Culture Quiz, On-level Assessment, p. 260.

OPTIONAL RESOURCES

Plan
- Best Practices Toolkit
- PE Answers, MSRB, Transp. 75–78
- Workbook Answers, UTB 6, Transp. 32–39
- Absent Student Copymasters, URB 6, p. 99

Present
- Warm-up Transp. 19, UTB 6

Practice
- Lecturas para todos, pp. 52–56
- Lecturas para hispanohablantes
- Practice Games, URB 6, p. 37

TECHNOLOGY TOOLS	
Teacher Tools	**Student Tools**
Power Presentations	@Home Tutor
EasyPlanner CD-ROM	ClassZone.com
Test Generator CD-ROM	eEdition Online or CD-ROM

En resumen, Repaso de la lección, pp. 127–129

OBJECTIVES
- Review lesson grammar and vocabulary.

STANDARDS
- 1.2 Understand language, Act. 1
- 1.3 Present information, Acts. 2–5
- 4.2 Compare cultures, Act. 5

FOCUS AND MOTIVATE
❏ Review the information in ¡Llegada! by asking: "¿Qué deportes juegan?" "¿Saben jugar al tenis?" "¿Conocen a un atleta famoso?"

TEACH
❏ Quickly go over **jugar, saber, conocer,** the personal **a,** and the vocabulary using the En resumen on p. 127 as a reference.

❏ Activity 1, p. 128. Play the Audio Program, 1B TXT CD 1 track 20 while students do the exercise.

PRACTICE AND APPLY
❏ Have students work in pairs to do Activities 2, 3 and 4, pp. 128–129. Then have them change partners to check their work.

❏ To review cultural information, do Activity 5, p. 129 as a whole-class activity.

IEP modification   Each student draws 5 items of sports equipment. Working in pairs, they show their drawings and ask "¿Qué deporte practico?" The partner replies, "Juegas al (béisbol, etc.)". The first partner then asks, "¿Sabes jugar al (béisbol, etc.)?" and the other answers.

ASSESS AND RETEACH
❏ Homework: Study En resumen, p. 127; *Cuaderno,* pp. 61–72; *Cuaderno para hispanohablantes*, pp. 63–72.

❏ Lesson Test, On-level Assessment, pp. 261–267.

OPTIONAL RESOURCES
Plan
- Best Practices Toolkit
- PE Answers, MSRB, Transp. 75–78
- Workbook Answers, UTB 6, Transp. 32–39
- Absent Student Copymasters, URB 6, p. 100

Present
- Warm-up Transp. 19, UTB 6
- Audio Script, URB 6, pp. 73–77

Practice
- Practice Games, URB 6, p. 38
- Sing-along Audio CD

Assess
- Review Games Online
- Lesson Test, Modified Assessment, pp. 206–212
- Lesson Test, Pre-AP Assessment, pp. 206–212
- Lesson Test, Heritage Learners Assessment, pp. 212–218

TECHNOLOGY TOOLS	
Teacher Tools	**Student Tools**
Power Presentations	@Home Tutor
EasyPlanner CD-ROM	ClassZone.com
Test Generator CD-ROM	eEdition Online or CD-ROM
McDougal Littell Assessment System	

Lesson Opener,
Presentación y práctica de vocabulario, pp. 130–135

OBJECTIVES

- Introduce lesson theme: **La salud.**
- **Culture:** Compare healthy outdoor activities with activities teens do in other parts of the world.
- Present and practice vocabulary: activities to stay healthy, parts of the body.

STANDARDS

- 1.2 Understand language, Act. 1
- 1.3 Present information, Act. 2
- 2.2 Products and perspectives
- 4.2 Compare cultures

FOCUS AND MOTIVATE

❑ Lesson opener, pp. 130–131: Direct students' attention to the photo and ask the ¿Qué ves? questions. Read and discuss the Compara con tu mundo segment on p. 130.

TEACH

❑ Presentación de vocabulario, pp. 132–134: play the Vocabulary Presentation Video, DVD 2.

❑ Review the vocabulary introduced in the video. Have students repeat the bolded words and phrases on pp. 132–134 after you. Assist with pronunciation.

PRACTICE AND APPLY

❑ Play the ¡A responder! activity (1B TXT CD 1, track 21) to assess comprehension.

❑ Do Activities 1–2, p. 135, aloud as a class.

IEP Modification   Ask students what they would rather do to keep their good health. Give them a choice: e.g., "Para tener buena salud: ¿escribes correos electrónicos o montas en bicicleta? ¿descansas o corres? ¿andas en patineta o miras televisión? ¿paseas o hablas por teléfono?"

ASSESS AND RETEACH

❑ Para y piensa, p. 135. Challenge students to do the activity without looking at their textbook.

❑ Vocabulary Recognition Quiz, On-level Assessment, p. 273.

❑ Homework: *Cuaderno*, pp. 73–75; *Cuaderno para hispanohablantes*, pp. 73–76.

OPTIONAL RESOURCES

Plan

- Best Practices Toolkit
- Absent Student Copymasters, URB 6, p. 101
- PE Answers, MSRB, Transp. 79–82
- Workbook Answers, UTB 6, Transp. 40–47

Present

- Warm-up Transp. 20, UTB 6
- Vocabulary Transp. 8–9, UTB 6
- TPRS, pp. 78–84

- Video Script, URB 6, pp. 71–72
- Audio Script, URB 6, pp. 78–82
- Vocabulary Video, DVD 2

Practice

- Practice Games, URB 6, p. 39
- Video Activities, URB 6, pp. 59–60

Assess

- Reteaching Copymasters, URB 6, pp. 13–14

TECHNOLOGY TOOLS	
Teacher Tools	**Student Tools**
Power Presentations	@Home Tutor
EasyPlanner CD-ROM	ClassZone.com
	Cultura interactiva
	eEdition Online or CD-ROM

Vocabulario en contexto, pp. 136–137

OBJECTIVES
- Understand and practice activity vocabulary in context.
- Practice using **doler** to say what hurts.
- **Recycle:** stem-changing o → ue verbs, p. 34

FOCUS AND MOTIVATE
- ❏ Telehistoria escena 1, p. 136: Ask students to look at the two photos and describe what is happening.

TEACH
- ❏ Telehistoria escena 1, p. 136: Strategies. Read the Cuando lees strategy. Have kids listen for and label the body parts mentioned in the scene.
- ❏ Show Telehistoria escena 1, DVD 2.
- ❏ Nota gramatical, p. 137: Briefly review the use of **gustar,** then present the forms of **doler.**

IEP Modification   Point to a few of your body parts (e.g. eyes, nose, knees, arm) and have students identify them. Write them on the board. Then repeat but act as though each part is in pain. Ask students to say what is wrong by forming the sentence "A Ud. le duele(n)...". Write their responses on the board, encouraging self-correction of any errors.

PRACTICE AND APPLY
- ❏ *Comprensión del episodio*, p. 137: Go over the comprehension exercise (use Audio Program TXT CD 6, track 14 if video not shown).
- ❏ Pair students up to do Activity 4.

ASSESS AND RETEACH
- ❏ Para y piensa, p. 137. Have students complete this section orally with the whole class.
- ❏ Vocabulary Production Quiz, On-level Assessment, p. 274.

OPTIONAL RESOURCES

Plan
- Best Practices Toolkit
- PE Answers, MSRB, Transp. 79–82
- Workbook Answers, UTB 6, Transp. 40–47
- Absent Student Copymasters, URB 6, p. 102

Present
- Warm-up Transp. 20, UTB 6
- Audio Script, URB 6, pp. 78–82
- Video Script, URB 6, pp. 71–72

Practice
- Video Activities, URB 6, pp. 61–62
- Practice Games, URB 6, p. 40

Assess
- Reteaching Copymasters, URB 6, pp. 13, 15, 22, 23

| TECHNOLOGY TOOLS ||
Teacher Tools	Student Tools
Power Presentations	@Home Tutor
EasyPlanner CD-ROM	ClassZone.com
Test Generator CD-ROM	eEdition Online or CD-ROM

Presentación y práctica de gramática 1, pp. 138–141

OBJECTIVES

- Present and practice the preterite of regular -ar verbs.
- **Recycle:** telling time, p. 14.
- **Culture:** Discuss how artists reflect their values through their paintings.

STANDARDS

- 1.1 Engage in conversation, Acts. 9–10
- 1.3 Present information, Acts. 5–10, PYP
- 2.2 Products and perspectives, CC
- 4.1 Compare languages
- 4.2 Compare cultures, CC

FOCUS AND MOTIVATE

❑ Presentación de gramática, p. 138. Ask students to brainstorm some activities using -ar verbs that they do frequently. Write the verbs on the board. Point to each verb and tell students whether you did the activity yesterday, e.g. "**Ayer** yo hablé por teléfono." Then ask students if they did the activity yesterday, e.g.: "¿**Ayer** hab**laste** por teléfono, Marcos?"

ALTERNATE: Presentación de gramática, p. 138. Briefly review conjugation of -ar verbs in the present tense, reinforcing that there is a different form for each person. Give examples of when the present tense is used (i.e. habitual or frequent activities).

TEACH

❑ Presentación de gramática, p. 138. Present the conjugation of regular -ar verbs. Point out that the nosotros form is the same in the present and in the preterite, but explain that the tense can usually be inferred from context (as with the use of a time indicator like **ayer** or **anoche**).

❑ Comparación cultural, p. 141. Ask students to describe the painting and how it might reflect elements of life in the Dominican Republic.

IEP Modification Have students make flashcards for 10 subject pronouns and/or names (e.g. yo, tú, tú y yo, Fernando y Luis, etc.) and each verb phrase in Act. 10, plus three more. With a partner, they should pick one card from each pile and make a sentence.

PRACTICE AND APPLY

❑ Práctica de gramática, pp. 139–141. Do Activity 5 as a class to practice **preterite -ar** verbs and to review telling time. Assign Activity 6.

❑ Pair students to do Activity 9. Ask them to form groups to do Activity 10. In both cases, circulate and help with correct grammar and pronunciation.

ASSESS AND RETEACH

❑ Para y piensa, p. 141. Have students use the correct preterite form.

❑ Homework: *Cuaderno*, pp. 76–78; *Cuaderno para hispanohablantes*, pp. 77–79.

OPTIONAL RESOURCES

Plan
- Best Practices Toolkit
- PE Answers, MSRB, Transp. 79–82
- Workbook Answers, UTB 6, Transp. 40–47
- Absent Student Copymasters, URB 6, p. 103
- Easy Planner CD-ROM
- ClassZone.com

Present
- Warm-up Transp. 21, UTB 6
- Grammar Presentation Transp. 12, UTB 6

- Fine Art Activities, URB 6, p. 88
- Fine Art Transp. 4, UTB 6
- Audio Script, URB 6, pp. 78–82

Practice
- Practice Games, URB 6, p. 41

Assess
- Reteaching Copymasters, URB 6, pp. 16, 17, 24

TECHNOLOGY TOOLS	
Teacher Tools	**Student Tools**
Power Presentations	@Home Tutor
EasyPlanner CD-ROM	ClassZone.com
Test Generator CD-ROM	eEdition Online or CD-ROM

Gramática en contexto, pp. 142–143

OBJECTIVES

- Practice using the preterite of regular **-ar** verbs in context.
- Identify lesson vocabulary in context.

STANDARDS

- 1.2 Understand language, Acts. 11–13
- 1.3 Present information, Acts. 12–13, PYP

FOCUS AND MOTIVATE

❏ Telehistoria escena 2, p. 142. Read the Cuando lees strategy.

TEACH

❏ Telehistoria escena 2, p. 142. Direct students' attention to the photo(s) and have them guess what is happening in the scene.

❏ Telehistoria escena 2, p. 142. Have students read the dialogue first silently for comprehension and then out loud for correct pronunciation and intonation.

PRACTICE AND APPLY

❏ **Comprensión del episodio,** Activity 11, p. 143. Listen to the dialogue on TXT CD 6, track 15. Call on students to give the answers.

❏ Have students work in pairs to do Activity 13, p. 143. Write three more questions and the appropriate answers.

IEP Modification Have students list additional activities and expand on them. For example, one student asks a partner: "¿Caminaste en el parque?" and the other must answer with additional information: "Sí, ayer caminé en el parque y ahora me duelen las piernas".

ASSESS AND RETEACH

❏ Para y piensa, p. 143. Have students write the answers in their notebook. Select three students to write them on the board.

❏ Grammar Quiz 1, On-level Assessment, p. 275.

OPTIONAL RESOURCES

Plan

- Best Practices Toolkit
- PE Answers, MSRB, Transp. 79–82
- Workbook Answers, UTB 6, Transp. 40–47
- Absent Student Copymasters, URB 6, p. 104

Present

- Warm-up Transp. 21, UTB 6
- Audio Script, URB 6, pp. 78–82
- Video Script, URB 6, pp. 71–72

Practice

- Practice Games, URB 6, p. 42
- Video Activities, URB 6, pp. 63–64

Assess

- Reteaching Copymasters, URB 6, pp. 16, 18

| TECHNOLOGY TOOLS ||
Teacher Tools	**Student Tools**
Power Presentations	@Home Tutor
EasyPlanner CD-ROM	ClassZone.com
Test Generator CD-ROM	eEdition Online or CD-ROM

Presentación y práctica de gramática 2, pp. 144–147

OBJECTIVES

- Present and practice using the preterite of verbs ending in **-car, -gar, zar.**
- **Culture:** Learn about a merengue festival.

FOCUS AND MOTIVATE

- ❑ Students have already learned the pronunciation of the soft **c** before **e, i** and the hard c before **a, o,** and **u.** They will practice on p. 146 the pronunciation of the soft **g** before **e, i.** Point out that when a hard **g** or **c** sound is required before **e or i,** a spelling change is required. Give examples of contrasting words to demonstrate this, e.g. **canta, quinta;** or **gitana, guitarra.**

STANDARDS

- 1.1 Engage in conversation, Acts. 17–18
- 1.2 Understand language, Act. 16, Pronunciación
- 1.3 Present information, Acts. 14–15, 17–19
- 2.1 Practices and perspectives, Act. 19
- 4.1 Compare languages
- 4.2 Compare cultures, Act. 19

TEACH

- ❑ Presentación de gramática, p. 144. Present the spelling changes in **-car, -gar,** and **-zar** verbs. Note that the spelling change in **-zar** verbs was at one time, but is no longer, a necessity for retaining pronunciation. Explain that there was a pronunciation shift in Spanish several centuries ago, but the language retained the spelling change. Now **z** is almost never used before **z** or **i** (e.g. **feliz** becomes **felices** in the plural).
- ❑ Pronunciación, p. 146 Play TXT CD 6, track 17. Have students repeat the words and sentences using the soft **g.** Point out that as they have just learned, when a hard **g** is required before **e** or **i,** a **u** is inserted (e.g. **jugué, guitarra**).
- ❑ Comparación cultural, p. 147.

IEP Modification Demonstrate that while English is inconsistent in its use of soft **g** with **e** and **i,** Spanish is quite consistent. Offer examples (*give* and *get* vs. *gist* and *gentle;* whereas no exceptions to Spanish rule).

PRACTICE AND APPLY

- ❑ Assign Activity 14, p. 145. Ask students to tell you what happened "a las cuatro el viernes", "a la una el sábado", etc., using the preterite.
- ❑ Activity 16, p. 146. Play 1B TXT CD 1, track 22 while students write down answers to Mario's questions. Then have students write their answers on the board (several at a time). Ask the class to help you correct any errors.
- ❑ Pair students up to do Activity 17, p. 146.
- ❑ Assign Activity 19, p. 147.

ASSESS AND RETEACH

- ❑ Para y piensa, p. 147. Have students spell the verb form in each sentence.
- ❑ Homework: *Cuaderno,* pp. 79–81; *Cuaderno para hispanohablantes,* pp. 80–83.

OPTIONAL RESOURCES

Plan
- Best Practices Toolkit
- PE Answers, MSRB, Transp. 79–82
- Workbook Answers, UTB 6, Transp. 40–47
- Absent Student Copymasters, URB 6, p. 105

Present
- Warm-up Transp. 22, UTB 6
- Grammar Presentation Transp. 13, UTB 6

Practice
- Practice Games, URB 6, p. 43
- Audio Script, URB 6, pp. 78–82

Assess
- Reteaching Copymasters, URB 6, pp. 19, 20

TECHNOLOGY TOOLS	
Teacher Tools	**Student Tools**
	@Home Tutor
Power Presentations	ClassZone.com
EasyPlanner CD-ROM	
Test Generator CD-ROM	eEdition Online or CD-ROM

Todo junto, Juegos y Diversiones, pp. 148–151

OBJECTIVES

- Integrate lesson content.
- Practice using and integrating lesson vocabulary and grammar.
- Review parts of the body by playing a game of Simon Says.

FOCUS AND MOTIVATE

- ❑ Telehistoria, escena 3, p. 148. Have students look at the photos to recap scenes 1 and 2 and to predict what happens in scene 3.

TEACH

- ❑ Telehistoria, escena 3, p. 148: Strategies. Read the Cuando escuchas strategy to focus listening.
- ❑ Video Program DVD 2, Unit 6. Show Telehistoria scenes 1 and 2 as a review before showing scene 3.
- ❑ Telehistoria escena 3, p. 148. After viewing and discussion, have students read the dialogue out loud for correct pronunciation and intonation.

PRACTICE AND APPLY

- ❑ *Comprensión de los episodios*, p. 149. If not viewing the video, play TXT CD 6 tracks 14, 15, and 18 to do Activities 20, 21.
- ❑ Activity 22, p. 149. Pair students together to do the activity. Walk around and help students with vocabulary as needed.
- ❑ Activity 23 Integración, p. 150. Exercise students' reading, writing, listening, and speaking skills.
- ❑ Assign writing Activity 24, p. 150.
- ❑ Have students play Simón dice to review parts of the body.

IEP Modification   For Activity 20, provide answers (scrambled) on a list format, on the board: **...no puede levantarlas con las piernas, ...caminó delante (de la bicicleta) de Mario, ...está herido, ...jugar al fútbol o al béisbol, ...aficionados en el estadio, ...quieren su autógrafo.**

ASSESS AND RETEACH

- ❑ Para y piensa, p. 150. Ask a student to write the answers on the board.
- ❑ Grammar Quiz 2, On-level Assessment, p. 276.
- ❑ Homework: *Cuaderno*, pp. 82–83; *Cuaderno para hispanohablantes*, pp. 84–85.

OPTIONAL RESOURCES

Plan
- Best Practices Toolkit
- PE Answers, MSRB, Transp. 79–82
- Workbook Answers, UTB 6, Transp. 40–47
- Absent Student Copymasters, URB 6, p. 106

Present
- Warm-up Transp. 22, UTB 6
- Audio Script, URB 6, pp. 78–82
- Video Script, URB 6, pp. 71–72

Practice
- Learning Scenarios on Easy Planner
- Conversation cards on Easy Planner and ClassZone
- Video activities, URB 6, pp. 65–66
- Practice Games, URB 6, p. 44

Assess
- Reteaching Copymasters, URB 6, pp. 19, 21

TECHNOLOGY TOOLS	
Teacher Tools	**Student Tools**
Power Presentations	@Home Tutor
EasyPlanner CD-ROM	ClassZone.com
Test Generator CD-ROM	eEdition Online or CD-ROM

Lectura/Proyectos culturales, pp. 152–154

OBJECTIVES

- Read about two world-class athletes representing the Dominican Republic and from Venezuela.
- Compare their careers and achievements.
- **Culture:** Learn about the gestures that are uniquely those of Spanish-speaking countries.

STANDARDS
• 1.2 Understand language
• 1.3 Present information
• 2.1 Practices and perspectives
• 4.1 Compare languages
• 4.2 Compare cultures
• 5.1 Spanish in the community

FOCUS AND MOTIVATE

❑ Lectura cultural, pp. 152–154: Direct students to look at the photos. Ask them to describe who the athletes are and what sport they practice.

❑ Proyectos culturales, p. 156: Discuss the importance of gestures and proverbs in culture and communication.

TEACH

❑ Lectura cultural, «Dos atletas de alta velocidad» pp. 152–153. Have students read along as they listen to Audio Program TXT CD 6, track 21.

❑ Proyectos culturales: Gestos, p. 154. Demonstrate the four gestures and discuss similarities or differences with gestures in the U.S.

❑ Proyectos culturales: Refranes, p. 154. Ask students to read aloud the refranes and think about what they mean.

IEP Modification   Ask English learners about gestures and proverbs from their home country. Can they find similarities? Explain that there are English equivalents for the three Spanish language proverbs (1. Seek and ye shall find; 2. You snooze, you lose; 3. When one door closes, another opens).

PRACTICE AND APPLY

❑ Lectura cultural, «Dos atletas de alta velocidad» pp. 152–153. Have students reread silently and complete the chart presented in the reading strategy. Then discuss.

❑ Proyectos culturales: Gestos y refranes, p. 154, Proyectos 1 and 2. Have students vote on which project they would like to do in class.

ASSESS AND RETEACH

❑ Para y piensa, p. 153. Have students do ¿Comprendiste? orally. Have them work in pairs to do ¿Y tú? and report what their partner said using the preterite.

❑ Culture Quiz, On-level Assessment, p. 277.

OPTIONAL RESOURCES

Plan
- Best Practices Toolkit
- PE Answers, MSRB, Transp. 79–82
- Workbook Answers, UTB 6, Transp. 40–47
- Absent Student Copymasters, URB 6, pp. 107–108

Present
- Warm-up Transp. 23, UTB 6

Practice
- Lecturas para todos, pp. 57–61
- Lecturas para hispanohablantes
- Practice Games, URB 6, p. 45

TECHNOLOGY TOOLS

Teacher Tools	Student Tools
Power Presentations	@Home Tutor
EasyPlanner CD-ROM	ClassZone.com
Test Generator CD-ROM	eEdition Online or CD-ROM

En resumen, Repaso de la lección, pp. 155–157

OBJECTIVES
- Review lesson grammar and vocabulary.

FOCUS AND MOTIVATE
- ❑ En resumen, p. 155: Briefly review vocabulary terms and grammar items.

- ❑ Repaso de la lección, pp. 156–157: Go over items in ¡Llegada! Box and encourage questions.

TEACH
- ❑ En resumen: Assess which vocabulary terms need more practice and encourage students to form sentences with each.

- ❑ Repaso de la lección, Activity 1: Review preterite. Play Audio Program 1B TXT CD 1, track 25.

PRACTICE AND APPLY
- ❑ Repaso de la lección, Activities 2, 3, 4, 5, pp. 156–157. Have students work in pairs to do Activities 2, 3 and 4. Have them change partners to check their work. They should tell you if they do not agree on an answer. Spot–check to make sure they are on task.

IEP Modification   Encourage students to answer the items in Activity 5 in Spanish.

ASSESS AND RETEACH
- ❑ Homework: Study En resumen, p. 155; *Cuaderno*, pp. 84–95; *Cuaderno para hispanohablantes*, pp. 86–95.
- ❑ Lesson Test, On-level Assessment, pp. 278–284.

OPTIONAL RESOURCES

Plan
- Best Practices Toolkit
- PE Answers, MSRB, Transp. 79–82
- Workbook Answers, UTB 6, Transp. 40–47
- Absent Student Copymasters, URB 6, p. 109

Present
- Warm-up Transp. 23, UTB 6
- Audio Script, URB 6, pp. 78–82

Practice
- Practice Games, URB 6, p. 46
- Sing-along Audio CD

Assess
- Review Games Online
- Lesson Test, Modified Assessment, pp. 218–224
- Lesson Test, Pre-AP Assessment, pp. 218–224
- Lesson Test, Heritage Learners Assessment, pp. 224–230

TECHNOLOGY TOOLS

Teacher Tools	Student Tools
Power Presentations	@Home Tutor
EasyPlanner CD-ROM	ClassZone.com
Test Generator CD-ROM	eEdition Online or CD-ROM
McDougal Littell Assessment System	

¡AVANCEMOS!
Unidad 6 Lección 2

Comparación cultural, Repaso inclusivo, pp. 158–161

OBJECTIVES

- Read about the favorite sports of teens from the Dominican Republic, Honduras, and Venezuela.
- Compare their favorite sports with your own.
- Cumulative review.

STANDARDS
- 1.1 Engage in conversation, Acts. 3–5
- 1.2 Understand language, Act. 1
- 1.3 Present information, Acts. 2–6
- 2.1 Practices and perspectives
- 4.2 Compare cultures

FOCUS AND MOTIVATE

❏ Comparación cultural, pp. 158–159: Have students look at the three photos and describe what is happening in each.

TEACH

❏ Comparación cultural, pp. 158–159. Play Audio Program TXT CD 6 track 23 as students follow along. Then call on students to read the descriptions of **the three countries**. Encourage them to note similarities and differences.

❏ Comparación cultural, p. 158. Use the writing strategy to guide students in their own descriptions.

❏ Repaso inclusivo, pp. 160–161: Choose key vocabulary terms and grammar points from units 1–6 that students have had difficulty with for extra review.

PRACTICE AND APPLY

❏ Comparación cultural, p. 158. Assign writing activity. Help students increase their cultural awareness by doing the **Compara con tu mundo** activity.

❏ Repaso inclusivo, pp. 160–161, Activities 1–6. Play Audio Program TXT CD 6 track 24 for students to complete Activity 1.

IEP Modification   Working with a partner, have students research a sports figure from the Dominican Republic and do an interview for a sports network.

ASSESS AND RETEACH

❏ Homework: *Cuaderno*, pp. 96–98; *Cuaderno para hispanohablantes*, pp. 96–98.

❏ Unit Test, On-level Assessment, pp. 290–296.

OPTIONAL RESOURCES

Plan
- Absent Student Copymasters, URB 6, pp. 110–111

Present
- Audio Script, URB 6, pp. 78–82

Practice
- Situational Transp. and Copymasters, UTB 6, Transp. 14–15, pp. 1–2
- Family Involvement Activity, URB 6, p. 92
- ¡AvanzaCómics! SuperBruno y Nati, Episodio 2

Assess
- Unit Test, Modified Assessment, pp. 230–236
- Unit Test, Pre-AP Assessment, pp. 230–236
- Unit Test, Heritage Learners Assessment, pp. 236–242

TECHNOLOGY TOOLS

Teacher Tools	Student Tools
EasyPlanner CD-ROM	@Home Tutor
Test Generator CD-ROM	ClassZone.com
McDougal Littell Assessment System	eEdition Online or CD-ROM

Unit and Lesson Opener,
Presentación y práctica de vocabulario, pp. 162–169

OBJECTIVES

- Introduce lesson theme: **En el cibercafé.**
- Present and practice vocabulary: technology-related activities, parts of a computer.
- Present sequence words.

STANDARDS

- 1.2 Understand language, Act. 1
- 1.3 Present information, Act. 2, PYP
- 4.2 Compare cultures

FOCUS AND MOTIVATE

❏ Introduce students to the culture of Argentina and the lesson theme of talking about technology, pp. 162–165.

TEACH

❏ Presentación de vocabulario, pp. 166–168, paragraphs A–C. Read the paragraphs.

❏ Video Program DVD 2, Unit 7. Show the Vocabulary Presentation video.

❏ Audio Program TXT CD 7, track 1. Play the Vocabulary Presentation audio.

IEP Modification   Have students draw a picture of a computer, labeling as many parts as they can.

PRACTICE AND APPLY

❏ Lesson 1 Opener, pp. 164–165. Read Comparación cultural. Have students view the photographs and respond to the ¿Qué ves? questions.

❏ Listen to 1B TXT CD 2 track 1 to do ¡A responder! activity, p. 168.

ASSESS AND RETEACH

❏ Para y piensa, p. 169. Have students name things related to computers and the Internet.

❏ Vocabulary Recognition Quiz, On-level Assessment, p. 302.

❏ Homework: *Cuaderno*, pp. 99–101; *Cuaderno para hispanohablantes*, pp. 99–102.

OPTIONAL RESOURCES

Plan
- family letter, urb 7, p. 91
- Family letters in Haitian Creole and Spanish on ClassZone.com
- Best Practices Toolkit
- Absent Student Copymasters, URB 7, p. 93
- PE Answers, MSRB, Transp. 83–86
- Workbook Answers, UTB 7, Transp. 32–39

Present
- Warm-up Transp. 16, UTB 7
- Atlas Map, UTB 1, Transp. 5
- Map Transp. 1, UTB 7
- Map-Culture Activities, URB 7, pp. 83–84
- Música del mundo hispano

- Fine Art Activities, URB 7, pp. 87, 89
- Fine Art Transp. 3, 5, UTB 7
- Vocabulary Transp. 6–7, UTB 7
- TPRS, pp. 85–91
- Video Script, URB 7, pp. 69–70
- Audio Script, URB 7, pp. 73–77
- Vocabulary Video, DVD 2

Practice
- Practice Games, URB 7, p. 31
- Video Activities, URB 7, pp. 51–52

Assess
- Reteaching Copymasters, URB 7, pp. 1–2

TECHNOLOGY TOOLS	
Teacher Tools	**Student Tools**
Power Presentations	@Home Tutor
EasyPlanner CD-ROM	ClassZone.com
	Cultura interactiva
	eEdition Online or CD-ROM

¡AVANCEMOS!
Unidad 7 Lección 1

Vocabulario en contexto, pp. 170–171

OBJECTIVES
- Understand and practice activity vocabulary in context.
- **Recycle:** Affirmative **tú** commands, p. 82.

STANDARDS
- 1.1 Engage in conversation, Act. 5
- 1.2 Understand language, Acts. 3–4, PYP
- 1.3 Present information, Act. 5

FOCUS AND MOTIVATE
- ❑ Telehistoria escena 1, p. 170. Read the Cuando lees strategy.

TEACH
- ❑ Telehistoria escena 1, p. 170. Direct students' attention to the photo(s) and have them guess what is happening in the scene.
- ❑ Video Program DVD 2, Unit 7. Show the video for scene 1.
- ❑ Audio Program TXT CD 7, track 3. Play the audio for scene 1.

PRACTICE AND APPLY
- ❑ Comprensión del episodio, Activity 3, p. 171. Play TXT CD 7 track 4. Call on students to give the answers.
- ❑ Activity 4, p. 171. Play 1B TXT CD 2, track 2.
- ❑ Activity 5, p. 171. Recycle: Affirmative **tú** commands p. 82.

IEP Modification   Remind students to take notes as the description in Activity 4 is being read.

ASSESS AND RETEACH
- ❑ Para y piensa, p. 171. Have students arrange the sentences in the activity.
- ❑ Vocabulary Production Quiz, On-level Assessment, p. 303.

OPTIONAL RESOURCES
Plan
- Best Practices Toolkit
- PE Answers, MSRB, Transp. 83–86
- Workbook Answers, UTB 7, Transp. 32–39
- Absent Student Copymasters, URB 7, p. 94

Present
- Warm-up Transp. 16, UTB 7
- Audio Script, URB 7, pp. 73–77
- Video Script, URB 7, pp. 69–70

Practice
- Video Activities, URB 7, pp. 53–54
- Practice Games, URB 7, p. 32

Assess
- Reteaching Copymasters, URB 7, pp. 1, 3, 10

TECHNOLOGY TOOLS	
Teacher Tools	**Student Tools**
Power Presentations	@Home Tutor
EasyPlanner CD-ROM	ClassZone.com
Test Generator CD-ROM	eEdition Online or CD-ROM

Presentación y práctica de gramática 1, pp. 172–175

OBJECTIVES

- Present and practice using the preterite of regular -**er** and -**ir** verbs.
- **Recycle:** telling time, p. 14; foods and beverages, pp. 2, 20, 29.
- **Culture:** Find out how slang words develop.

FOCUS AND MOTIVATE

❑ Presentación de gramática, p. 172. Introduce the preterite of -**er** and -**ir** verbs. Remind students that the preterite tense tells that an action was completed at a definite time in the past.

TEACH

❑ Presentación de gramática, p. 172. Explain that all regular -**er** and -**ir** verbs have the same endings. Have them repeat the forms after you.

❑ Comparación cultural, p. 173. Play part of a tango by Gardel, and have them listen to the lyrics. Ask them to talk about the music they listen to, and if they can think of any English slang terms that have originated in music.

❑ Pronunciación, p. 174. Play TXT CD 7, track 5. Direct students to compare the Spanish and English pronunciation of this letter combination.

IEP Modification   Ask students to name other letter combinations they know, in Spansh and English (ch, ph, ll, etc.)

PRACTICE AND APPLY

❑ Activity 6, p. 173. Recycle: Review telling time, p. 14.

❑ Activity 10, p. 175. Recycle: Review foods and beverages, pp. 2, 20, 29.

ASSESS AND RETEACH

❑ Para y piensa, p. 175. Have students fill in the correct preterite form. Talk about why the forms are correct or incorrect.

❑ Homework: *Cuaderno*, pp. 102–104; *Cuaderno para hispanohablantes*, pp. 103–105.

OPTIONAL RESOURCES

Plan
- Best Practices Toolkit
- PE Answers, MSRB, Transp. 83–86
- Workbook Answers, UTB 7, Transp. 32–39
- Absent Student Copymasters, URB 7, p. 95
- Easy Planner CD-ROM
- ClassZone.com

Present
- Warm-up Transp. 17, UTB 7
- Grammar Presentation Transp. 10, UTB 7
- Audio Script, URB 7, pp. 73–77

Practice
- Practice Games, URB 7, p. 33

Assess
- Reteaching Copymasters, URB 7, pp. 4, 5, 11

TECHNOLOGY TOOLS	
Teacher Tools	**Student Tools**
Power Presentations	@Home Tutor
EasyPlanner CD-ROM	ClassZone.com
Test Generator CD-ROM	eEdition Online or CD-ROM

¡AVANCEMOS!
Unidad 7 Lección 1

Gramática en contexto, pp. 176–177

OBJECTIVES
- Identify preterite forms of regular -ar verbs in context.
- Identify lesson vocabulary in context.

STANDARDS
- 1.2 Understand language, Act. 12
- 1.3 Present information, Act. 13, PYP

FOCUS AND MOTIVATE
❑ Telehistoria escena 2, p. 176. Read the Cuando escuchas strategy.

TEACH
❑ Telehistoria escena 2, p. 176. Audio Program TXT CD 7, track 6. Play the audio for scene 2. Have students make a list of the preterite forms of -er and -ir that they hear.

❑ Video Program DVD 2, Unit 7. Show the video for scene 2.

❑ Have students read the dialogue aloud for correct pronunciation and intonation.

PRACTICE AND APPLY
❑ Comprensión del episodio, Activity 12, p. 177. Play TXT CD 7, track 6. Call on students to give the answers.

IEP Modification   For Activity 13, have students answer the questions in full sentences in their notebooks, using the answers they have selected.

ASSESS AND RETEACH
❑ Para y piensa, p. 177. Have students complete sentences with the preterite form of the verbs **salir, compartir,** or **recibir.**

❑ Grammar Quiz 1, On-level Assessment, p. 304.

OPTIONAL RESOURCES

Plan
- Best Practices Toolkit
- PE Answers, MSRB, Transp. 83–86
- Workbook Answers, UTB 7, Transp. 32–39
- Absent Student Copymasters, URB 7, p. 96

Present
- Warm-up Transp. 17, UTB 7
- Audio Script, URB 7, pp. 73–77
- Video Script, URB 7, pp. 69–70

Practice
- Practice Games, URB 7, p. 34
- Video Activities, URB 7, pp. 55–56

Assess
- Reteaching Copymasters, URB 7, pp. 4, 6

TECHNOLOGY TOOLS

Teacher Tools	Student Tools
Power Presentations	@Home Tutor
EasyPlanner CD-ROM	ClassZone.com
Test Generator CD-ROM	eEdition Online or CD-ROM

¡AVANCEMOS!
Unidad 7 Lección 1

Presentación y práctica de gramática 2, pp. 178–181

OBJECTIVES
- Present and practice affirmative and negative words.
- Explain the negative form **ningunos(as).**
- **Recycle:** Preterite of regular **-ar** verbs, p. 138.

STANDARDS
- 1.1 Engage in conversation, Acts. 16–18
- 1.3 Present information, Acts. 14–19, PYP
- 2.1 Practices and perspectives, Act. 18
- 4.1 Compare languages
- 4.2 Compare cultures, Act, 18

FOCUS AND MOTIVATE
- ❑ Presentación de gramática, p. 178. Introduce affirmative and negative words. Remind students that they have already learned several of the words (**siempre, nunca,** and **también**).

TEACH
- ❑ Presentación de gramática, p. 178. Emphasize that each word or construction has an opposite meaning (**siempre / nunca, alguien / nadie,** etc.).
- ❑ Not a gramatical, p. 180. Explain the limited use of **ningunos(as).**
- ❑ Comparación cultural, p. 181. Ask students to describe the beach activities in the painting by Daniel Kaplan. Remind them that summer in this area is in December.

IEP Modification   Practice when a double negative is used. Ask students to create three example sentences where a negative word is used before the verb, and three sentences where no is needed.

PRACTICE AND APPLY
- ❑ Activity 17, p. 180. Recycle: Review preterite of regular **-ar** verbs, p. 331. Ask students to answer the questions in their notebooks, then compare their answers with classmates in groups of four. Each student should read his or her answers aloud.

ASSESS AND RETEACH
- ❑ Para y piensa, p. 181. Have students write sentences using affirmative and negative words.
- ❑ Homework: *Cuaderno,* pp. 105–107; *Cuaderno para hispanohablantes,* pp. 106–109.

OPTIONAL RESOURCES
Plan
- Best Practices Toolkit
- PE Answers, MSRB, Transp. 83–86
- Workbook Answers, UTB 7, Transp. 32–39
- Absent Student Copymasters, URB 7, p. 97

Present
- Warm-up Transp. 18, UTB 7
- Fine Art Activities, URB 7, p. 86

- Fine Art Transp. 2, UTB 7
- Grammar Presentation Transp. 11, UTB 7

Practice
- Practice Games, URB 7, p. 35

Assess
- Reteaching Copymasters, URB 7, pp. 7, 8, 12

TECHNOLOGY TOOLS	
Teacher Tools	**Student Tools**
Power Presentations	@Home Tutor
EasyPlanner CD-ROM	ClassZone.com
Test Generator CD-ROM	eEdition Online or CD-ROM

Todo junto, Juegos y Diversiones, pp. 182–185

OBJECTIVES

- Integrate lesson content.
- Practice using and integrating lesson vocabulary and grammar.
- Review vocabulary by playing a game.

STANDARDS

- 1.1 Engage in conversation, Acts. 22–23
- 1.2 Understand language, Acts. 20–21, 23
- 1.3 Present information, Acts. 22–24, PYP
- 5.2 Life-long learners, Juegos y diversiones

FOCUS AND MOTIVATE

❑ Todo junto, p. 182. Do the reading or listening strategies prior to reading the dialogue, listening to the audio CD, or watching the DVD.

TEACH

❑ Telehistoria escena 3, p. 182. Video Program DVD 2, Unit 7. Show Telehistoria scenes 1 and 2 as a review before showing scene 3.

❑ Audio Program TXT CD 7 tracks 3 and 6. Play Telehistoria scenes 1 and 2 as a review before playing scene 3 (TXT CD 7 track 7).

❑ Have students read the dialogue aloud for correct pronunciation and intonation.

IEP Modification   Have students work on Activities 20 and 21 in pairs.

PRACTICE AND APPLY

❑ Comprensión de los episodios, p. 183. Play TXT CD 7 tracks 3, 6, and 7 to do Activities 20 and 21.

❑ Activity 23, p. 184. Practice using reading, writing, listening, and speaking skills. Audio program: 1B TXT CD 2 tracks 3, 4.

❑ Activity 24, p. 184. Writing practice.

❑ Have students play ¿Qué letra? to review vocabulary.

ASSESS AND RETEACH

❑ Para y piensa, p. 184. Have students answer the questions, and translate their answers.

❑ Grammar Quiz 2, On-level Assessment, p. 305.

❑ Homework: *Cuaderno,* pp. 108–109; *Cuaderno para hispanohablantes,* pp. 110–111.

OPTIONAL RESOURCES

Plan
- Best Practices Toolkit
- PE Answers, MSRB, Transp. 83–86
- Workbook Answers, UTB 7, Transp. 32–39
- Absent Student Copymasters, URB 7, p. 98

Present
- Warm-up Transp. 18, UTB 7
- Audio Script, URB 7, pp. 73–77
- Video Script, URB 7, pp. 69–70

Practice
- Learning Scenarios on Easy Planner
- Conversation cards on Easy Planner and ClassZone
- Video activities, URB 7, pp. 57–58
- Practice Games, URB 7, p. 36

Assess
- Reteaching Copymasters, URB 7, pp. 7, 9

TECHNOLOGY TOOLS

Teacher Tools	Student Tools
Power Presentations	@Home Tutor
EasyPlanner CD-ROM	ClassZone.com
Test Generator CD-ROM	eEdition Online or CD-ROM

Lectura/Conexiones, pp. 186–188

OBJECTIVES

- Read about how to protect a computer from viruses.
- Take a virus-protection questionnaire.
- Read about a language game played by children in Argentina.

STANDARDS
- 1.2 Understand language
- 1.3 Present information
- 3.1 Knowledge of other disciplines
- 3.2 Acquire information

FOCUS AND MOTIVATE

☐ Lectura, Un cuestionario sobre las computadoras, pp. 186–187. Ask students what they think this reading selection will be about. Ask them what other questionnaires they have taken.

TEACH

☐ Lectura, Un cuestionario sobre las computadoras, pp. 186–187. Play Audio Program TXT CD 7, track 10. Make a list of computer technology terms from the questionnaire. Have students take turns defining the words.

☐ Conexiones, p. 188. Ask them if they ever played language games when they were young children.

PRACTICE AND APPLY

☐ Lectura, Un cuestionario sobre las computadoras, pp. 186–187. Have each group present their cause and effect chart to the class.

☐ Conexiones, p. 188. Assign each Proyecto to a group of students. Have the groups present what they have learned to the class.

IEP Modification Prepare a paragraph that is translated into **jeringozo,** and have the students translate it back to Spanish.

ASSESS AND RETEACH

☐ Para y piensa, p. 187. Have students answer questions in complete sentences.

☐ Culture Quiz, On-level Assessment, p. 306.

OPTIONAL RESOURCES

Plan
- Best Practices Toolkit
- PE Answers, MSRB, Transp. 83–86
- Workbook Answers, UTB 7, Transp. 32–39
- Absent Student Copymasters, URB 7, p. 99

Present
- Warm-up Transp. 19, UTB 7

Practice
- Lecturas para todos, pp. 62–66
- Lecturas para hispanohablantes
- Practice Games, URB 7, p. 37

TECHNOLOGY TOOLS	
Teacher Tools	**Student Tools**
Power Presentations	@Home Tutor
EasyPlanner CD-ROM	ClassZone.com
Test Generator CD-ROM	eEdition Online or CD-ROM

¡AVANCEMOS!
Unidad 7 Lección 1

En resumen, Repaso de la lección, pp. 189–191

OBJECTIVES
- Review lesson grammar and vocabulary.

FOCUS AND MOTIVATE
- ❏ En resumen, p. 189. Review all vocabulary terms and grammar items.
- ❏ Repaso de la lección, pp. 190–191. Review the information in ¡Llegada! Do a quick oral review of preterite of regular **-er** and **-ir** verbs, affirmative and negative words, and vocabulary.

TEACH
- ❏ En resumen, p. 189. Assess which vocabulary terms need more practice and encourage students to form sentences with each.
- ❏ Repaso de la lección, pp. 190–191. Point out the pages students can review before doing each activity.

PRACTICE AND APPLY
- ❏ Repaso de la lección, Activity 1, p. 190. Play Audio Program 1B TXT CD 2 track 5 while they do Activity 1.
- ❏ Complete activities 2–5, pp. 190–191.

IEP Modification   Instruct students to answer the items in Activity 5 in Spanish.

ASSESS AND RETEACH
- ❏ Homework: Study En resumen, p. 189; *Cuaderno*, pp. 110–121; *Cuaderno para hispanohablantes,* pp. 112–121.
- ❏ Lesson Test, On-level Assessment, pp. 307–313.

OPTIONAL RESOURCES

Plan
- Best Practices Toolkit
- PE Answers, MSRB, Transp. 83–86
- Workbook Answers, UTB 7, Transp. 32–39
- Absent Student Copymasters, URB 7, p. 100

Present
- Warm-up Transp. 19, UTB 7
- Audio Script, URB 7, pp. 73–77

Practice
- Practice Games, URB 7, p. 38
- Sing-along Audio CD

Assess
- Review Games Online
- Lesson Test, Modified Assessment, pp. 242–248
- Lesson Test, Pre-AP Assessment, pp. 242–248
- Lesson Test, Heritage Learners Assessment, pp. 248–254

TECHNOLOGY TOOLS	
Teacher Tools	**Student Tools**
Power Presentations	@Home Tutor
EasyPlanner CD-ROM	ClassZone.com
Test Generator CD-ROM	eEdition Online or CD-ROM
McDougal Littell Assessment System	

¡AVANCEMOS!
Unidad 7 Lección 1

Lesson Opener,
Presentación y práctica de vocabulario, pp. 192–197

OBJECTIVES

- Introduce lesson theme: **Uni dia en el parque de diversiones.**
- Present and practice vocabulary: amusement parks, places of interest and special events, extending and declining invitations, talking on the phone.

FOCUS AND MOTIVATE

❏ Introduce students to the culture of Argentina and the lesson theme of how to talk on the phone and extend invitations, and talking about what you did on the weekend and how it was, pp. 192–193.

TEACH

❏ Presentación de vocabulario, pp. 194–196, paragraphs A–D. Read the paragraphs.
❏ Video Program DVD 2, Unit 7. Show the Vocabulary Presentation video.
❏ Audio Program TXT CD 7, track 12. Play the Vocabulary Presentation audio.

IEP Modification   The vocabulary word for answering the phone is **¿Aló?** Ask students what words they use when answering the phone in Spanish.

PRACTICE AND APPLY

❏ Lesson 1 Opener, pp. 192–193. Read Comparación cultural. Have students view the photographs and respond to the ¿Qué ves? questions.
❏ Play 1B TXT CD 2 track 6 to do ¡A responder! activity, p. 196.

ASSESS AND RETEACH

❏ Para y piensa, p. 197. Have students name amusement park rides and places that require tickets.
❏ Vocabulary Recognition Quiz, On-level Assessment, p. 319.
❏ Homework: *Cuaderno*, pp. 122–124; Cuaderno para hispanohablantes, pp. 122–125.

OPTIONAL RESOURCES

Plan
- Best Practices Toolkit
- Absent Student Copymasters, URB 7, p. 101
- PE Answers, MSRB, Transp. 87–90
- Workbook Answers, UTB 7, Transp. 40–47

Present
- Warm-up Transp. 20, UTB 7
- Vocabulary Transp. 8–9, UTB 7
- TPRS, pp. 92–98

- Video Script, URB 7, pp. 71–72
- Audio Script, URB 7, pp. 78–82
- Vocabulary Video, DVD 2

Practice
- Practice Games, URB 7, p. 39
- Video Activities, URB 7, pp. 59–60

Assess
- Reteaching Copymasters, URB 7, pp. 13–14

TECHNOLOGY TOOLS	
Teacher Tools	**Student Tools**
Power Presentations	@Home Tutor
EasyPlanner CD-ROM	ClassZone.com
	Cultura interactiva
	eEdition Online or CD-ROM

Vocabulario en contexto, pp. 198–199

OBJECTIVES
- Understand and practice activity vocabulary in context.
- **Recycle:** noun/adjective agreement, p. 7.

STANDARDS
- 1.1 Engage in conversation, Act. 4
- 1.2 Understand language, Acts. 3–4, PYP
- 1.3 Present information, PYP

FOCUS AND MOTIVATE
- ❑ Telehistoria escena 1, p. 198. Read the Cuando lees strategy.

TEACH
- ❑ Telehistoria escena 1, p. 198. Direct students' attention to the photos and have them guess what is happening in the scene.
- ❑ Video Program DVD 2, Unit 7. Show the video for scene 1.
- ❑ Audio Program TXT CD 7, track 14. Play the audio for scene 1.
- ❑ Nota gramatical, p. 199. Emphasize the **¡Qué** + adjective! constructions that are part of this lesson's vocabulary.

PRACTICE AND APPLY
- ❑ Comprensión del episodio, Activity 3, p. 199. Play TXT CD 7 track 14. Call on students to give the answers.
- ❑ Activity 4, p. 199. Have students make a list of all of the adjectives they could use in this activity.

IEP Modification   Give students examples of situations, and ask them to react using **¡Qué** + adjective! Allow them to use varied vocabulary, and adjectives as well as nouns.

ASSESS AND RETEACH
- ❑ Para y piensa, p. 199. Have students practice the structure **Qué** + an adjective.
- ❑ Vocabulary Production Quiz, On-level Assessment, p. 320.

OPTIONAL RESOURCES

Plan
- Best Practices Toolkit
- PE Answers, MSRB, Transp. 87–90
- Workbook Answers, UTB 7, Transp. 40–47
- Absent Student Copymasters, URB 7, p. 102

Present
- Warm-up Transp. 20, UTB 7
- Audio Script, URB 7, pp. 78–82
- Video Script, URB 7, pp. 71–72

Practice
- Video Activities, URB 7, pp. 61–62
- Practice Games, URB 7, p. 40

Assess
- Reteaching Copymasters, URB 7, pp. 13, 15, 22

TECHNOLOGY TOOLS	
Teacher Tools	**Student Tools**
Power Presentations	@Home Tutor
EasyPlanner CD-ROM	ClassZone.com
Test Generator CD-ROM	eEdition Online or CD-ROM

¡AVANCEMOS!
Unidad 7 Lección 2

Presentación y práctica de gramática 1, pp. 200–203

OBJECTIVES
- Identify preterite forms of **ir, ser** and **hacer** in context.
- Identify lesson vocabulary in context.

STANDARDS
- 1.1 Engage in conversation, Acts. 6, 8–9
- 1.2 Understand language, Act. 7
- 1.3 Present information, Acts. 5–10, PYP
- 2.1 Practices and perspectives, CC
- 4.1 Compare languages
- 4.2 Compare cultures, CC

FOCUS AND MOTIVATE
- ❏ Presentación de gramática, p. 200. Introduce the preterite of **ir, ser,** and **hacer.** Remind students what it means to use the preterite tense.

TEACH
- ❏ Presentación de gramática, p. 200. Explain that **ir** and **ser** have the same conjugations in the preterite, and how students will be able to tell which verb is being used.
- ❏ Comparación cultural, p. 203. Talk about why port cities may be different from cities that are not close to a large body of water.

IEP Modification Talk about other verbs in Spanish that are irregular, and any special ways the students remember their conjugations.

PRACTICE AND APPLY
- ❏ Activity 7, p. 201. Play 1B TXT CD 2, track 7.

ASSESS AND RETEACH
- ❏ Para y piensa, p. 203. Have students complete sentences with the preterite form of **hacer, ir,** or **ser.** Ask them whether they used **ir** or **ser.**
- ❏ Homework: *Cuaderno,* pp. 125–127; *Cuaderno para hispanohablantes,* pp. 126–128.

OPTIONAL RESOURCES
Plan
- Best Practices Toolkit
- PE Answers, MSRB, Transp. 87–90
- Workbook Answers, UTB 7, Transp. 40–47
- Absent Student Copymasters, URB 7, p. 103
- Easy Planner CD-ROM
- ClassZone.com

Present
- Warm-up Transp. 21, UTB 7
- Grammar Presentation Transp. 12, UTB 7

- Fine Art Activities, URB 7, p. 88
- Fine Art Transp. 4, UTB 7
- Audio Script, URB 7, pp. 78–82

Practice
- Practice Games, URB 7, p. 41

Assess
- Reteaching Copymasters, URB 7, pp. 16–17

TECHNOLOGY TOOLS	
Teacher Tools	**Student Tools**
Power Presentations	@Home Tutor
EasyPlanner CD-ROM	ClassZone.com
Test Generator CD-ROM	eEdition Online or CD-ROM

Gramática en contexto, pp. 204–205

OBJECTIVES

- Identify preterite forms of **ir, ser** and **hacer.**
- Identify lesson vocabulary in context.
- **Recycle:** Places around town, p. 29.

> ### STANDARDS
> - 1.1 Engage in conversation, Act. 12, PYP
> - 1.2 Understand language, Act. 11
> - 4.1 Compare languages, Pronunciación

FOCUS AND MOTIVATE

☐ Telehistoria escena 2, p. 204. Read the Cuando escuchas strategy.

TEACH

☐ Telehistoria escena 2, p. 204. Video Program DVD 2, Unit 7. Show the video for scene 2.

☐ Audio Program TXT CD 7, track 16. Play the audio for scene 2.

☐ Have students read the dialogue aloud for correct pronunciation and intonation.

☐ Pronunciación, p. 205. Play TXT CD 7, track 17.

PRACTICE AND APPLY

☐ Comprensión del episodio, Activity 11, p. 205. Play TXT CD 7 track 16. Call on students to give the answers.

IEP Modification   Ask Spanish speakers if they have heard **ll** and **y** pronounced differently from what they heard on the recording.

ASSESS AND RETEACH

☐ Para y piensa, p. 205. Have students form questions using **ir, ser,** and **hacer.**

☐ Grammar Quiz 1, On-level Assessment, p. 321.

OPTIONAL RESOURCES

Plan
- Best Practices Toolkit
- PE Answers, MSRB, Transparencies 87–90
- Workbook Answers, UTB 7, Transparencies 40–47
- Absent Student Copymasters, URB 7, p. 104

Present
- Warm-up Transp. 21, UTB 7
- Audio Script, URB 7, pp. 78–82
- Video Script, URB 7, pp. 71–72

Practice
- Practice Games, URB 7, p. 42
- Video Activities, URB 7, pp. 63–64

Assess
- Reteaching Copymasters, URB 7, pp. 16, 18, 23

TECHNOLOGY TOOLS	
Teacher Tools	**Student Tools**
Power Presentations	@Home Tutor
EasyPlanner CD-ROM	ClassZone.com
Test Generator CD-ROM	eEdition Online or CD-ROM

¡AVANCEMOS!
Unidad 7 Lección 2

Copyright © by McDougal Littell, a division of Houghton Mifflin Company.

¡Avancemos!
Level 1B Unidad 7

148

Lección 2

Presentación y práctica de gramática 2, pp. 206–209

OBJECTIVES

- Present and practice using pronouns after prepositions.
- **Culture:** Learn about food from Argentina.
- **Recycle:** stem-changing verbs: e → i, p. 35.

STANDARDS
- 1.1 Engage in conversation, Acts. 15, 18
- 1.3 Present information, Acts. 13–18, PYP
- 4.2 Compare cultures, Act. 17
- 4.1 Compare languages

FOCUS AND MOTIVATE

- ❑ Presentación de gramática, p. 206. Introduce pronouns after prepositions. Remind students of the different prepositions they already know (**a, con, de, para**).

TEACH

- ❑ Presentación de gramática, p. 206. Show that the pronouns used after prepositions are the same pronouns used with verbs like **gustar** or **doler.**
- ❑ Comparación cultural, p. 209. Talk about the students' own diets and how they compare to what people from Argentina eat.

IEP Modification Have students list prepositions and accompanying pronouns in English, and then think of their Spanish equivalents.

PRACTICE AND APPLY

- ❑ Activity 14, p. 207. Stress to students that not only must they change the verb when answering questions, but they must also frequently change the prepositional pronoun as well. Go over the model in this exercise, explaining that **nosotros** must be changed to **ustedes.**
- ❑ Activity 17, p. 209. Recycle: Review stem-changing verbs e → ie, p. 35.

ASSESS AND RETEACH

- ❑ Para y piensa, p. 209. Have students complete sentences with the correct pronouns.
- ❑ Homework: *Cuaderno*, pp. 128–130; *Cuaderno para hispanohablantes*, pp. 129–132.

OPTIONAL RESOURCES

Plan
- Best Practices Toolkit
- PE Answers, MSRB, Transp. 87–90
- Workbook Answers, UTB 7, Transp. 40–47
- Absent Student Copymasters, URB 7, p. 105

Present
- Warm-up Transp. 22, UTB 7
- Grammar Presentation Transp. 13, UTB 7

Practice
- Practice Games, URB 7, p. 43

Assess
- Reteaching Copymasters, URB 7, pp. 19, 20, 24

TECHNOLOGY TOOLS	
Teacher Tools	**Student Tools**
Power Presentations	@Home Tutor
EasyPlanner CD-ROM	ClassZone.com
Test Generator CD-ROM	eEdition Online or CD-ROM

¡AVANCEMOS!
Unidad 7 Lección 2

Todo junto, Juegos y diversiones, pp. 210–213

OBJECTIVES

- Integrate lesson content.
- Practice using and integrating lesson vocabulary and grammar.
- Review vocabulary by playing a game.

STANDARDS

- 1.1 Engage in conversation, Acts. 21–22
- 1.2 Understand language, Acts. 19–20, 22
- 1.3 Present information, Acts. 20–23, PYP
- 5.2 Life-long learners, Juegos y diversiones

FOCUS AND MOTIVATE

- ❑ Todo junto, p. 210. Do the reading or listening strategies prior to reading the dialogue, listening to the audio CD, or watching the DVD.

TEACH

- ❑ Telehistoria escena 3, p. 210. Video Program DVD 2, Unit 7. Show Telehistoria scenes 1 and 2 as a review before showing scene 3.
- ❑ Audio Program TXT CD 7 tracks 14 and 16. Play Telehistoria scenes 1 and 2 as a review before playing scene 3 (TXT CD 7 track 18).
- ❑ Have students read the dialogue aloud for correct pronunciation and intonation.

IEP Modification Have students write a summary, or **resumen,** for scene 3. Have them use the summaries on p. 210 of scenes 1 and 2 as examples.

PRACTICE AND APPLY

- ❑ Comprensión de los episodios, p. 211. Play TXT CD 7 tracks 14, 16, and 18 to do Activities 19 and 20.
- ❑ Activity 22, p. 212. Audio: 1B TXT CD 2, Tracks 8, 9. Have students practice reading, listening, speaking, and writing skills.
- ❑ Activity 23, p. 212.
- ❑ Have students play Categorías to review vocabulary.

ASSESS AND RETEACH

- ❑ Para y piensa, p. 212. Have students create sentences in the preterite with pronouns after prepositions.
- ❑ Grammar Quiz 2, On-level Assessment, p. 322.
- ❑ Homework: *Cuaderno,* pp. 131–132; *Cuaderno para hispanohablantes,* pp. 133–134.

OPTIONAL RESOURCES

Plan

- Best Practices Toolkit
- PE Answers, MSRB, Transp. 87–90
- Workbook Answers, UTB 7, Transp. 40–47
- Absent Student Copymasters, URB 7, p. 106

Present

- Warm-up Transp. 22, UTB 7
- Audio Script, URB 7, pp. 78–82
- Video Script, URB 7, pp. 71–72

Practice

- Learning Scenarios on Easy Planner
- Conversation cards on Easy Planner and ClassZone
- Video activities, URB 7, pp. 65–66
- Practice Games, URB 7, p. 44

Assess

Reteaching Copymasters, URB 7, pp. 19, 21

TECHNOLOGY TOOLS	
Teacher Tools	**Student Tools**
Power Presentations	@Home Tutor
EasyPlanner CD-ROM	ClassZone.com
Test Generator CD-ROM	eEdition Online or CD-ROM

Lectura/Proyectos culturales, pp. 214–216

OBJECTIVES

- **Culture:** Read about two unusual museums in Argentina and Bolivia.
- Compare the two museums in terms of name, location, focus, and exhibits.
- Read about how names are inherited in Spanish-speaking countries.

FOCUS AND MOTIVATE

❏ Lectura cultural, Museos excepcionales, pp. 214–215. Ask students to tell you what museums they have visited, and put their reponses on the board. Also have students read the Leer strategy and complete the chart when they have finished.

TEACH

❏ Lectura cultural, Museos excepcionales, pp. 214–215. Play Audio Program TXT CD 7, track 21. Have students read the Leer strategy and complete the chart when they have finished.

❏ Proyectos culturales, p. 216. Use the picture provided to explain the progression of names.

PRACTICE AND APPLY

❏ Lectura cultural, Museos excepcionales, pp. 214–215. Have students answer the ¿Y tú? questions in pairs.

❏ Proyectos culturales, p. 216. Have students tell the class about the family tree they created.

IEP Modification   Discuss with students that although in English-speaking countries people usually have one last name, there are exceptions. What are some exceptions in these countries, Spanish-speaking countries, and their own or their parents' countries of origin?

ASSESS AND RETEACH

❏ Para y piensa, p. 215. Have students answer the questions in the activity with complete sentences.

❏ Culture Quiz, On-level Assessment, p. 323.

OPTIONAL RESOURCES

Plan
- Best Practices Toolkit
- PE Answers, MSRB, Transp. 87–90
- Workbook Answers, UTB 7, Transp. 40–47
- Absent Student Copymasters, URB 7, pp. 107–108

Present
- Warm-up Transp. 23, UTB 7

Practice
- Lecturas para todos, pp. 67–71
- Lecturas para hispanohablantes
- Practice Games, URB 7, p. 45

TECHNOLOGY TOOLS	
Teacher Tools	**Student Tools**
Power Presentations	@Home Tutor
EasyPlanner CD-ROM	ClassZone.com
Test Generator CD-ROM	eEdition Online or CD-ROM

¡AVANCEMOS!
Unidad 7 Lección 2

En resumen, Repaso de la lección, pp. 217–219

OBJECTIVES
- Review lesson grammar and vocabulary.

STANDARDS
• 1.2 Understand language, Act. 1
• 1.3 Present information, Acts. 2–4
• 4.2 Compare cultures, Act. 5

FOCUS AND MOTIVATE
- ❏ En resumen, p. 217. Review all vocabulary terms and grammar items.
- ❏ Repaso de la lección, pp. 218–219. Review the information in ¡Llegada! Do a quick oral review of preterite of regular **ir, ser,** and **hacer,** pronouns after prepositions, and vocabulary.

TEACH
- ❏ En resumen, p. 217. Assess which vocabulary terms need more practice and encourage students to form sentences with each.
- ❏ Repaso de la lección, pp. 218–219. Point out the pages students can review before doing each activity.

PRACTICE AND APPLY
- ❏ Repaso de la lección, Activity 1, p. 218. Listen to Audio Program 1B TXT CD 2 track 10 while they do Activity 1.
- ❏ Complete activities 2–5, pp. 218–219.

IEP Modification   Instruct students to answer the items in Activity 5 in Spanish.

ASSESS AND RETEACH
- ❏ Homework: Study En resumen, p. 217; *Cuaderno,* pp. 133–144; *Cuaderno para hispanohablantes,* pp. 135–144.
- ❏ Lesson Test, On-level Assessment, pp. 324–330.

OPTIONAL RESOURCES

Plan
- Best Practices Toolkit
- PE Answers, MSRB, Transp. 87–90
- Workbook Answers, UTB 7, Transp. 40–47
- Absent Student Copymasters, URB 7, p. 109

Present
- Warm-up Transp. 23, UTB 7
- Audio Script, URB 7, pp. 78–82

Practice
- Practice Games, URB 7, p. 46
- Sing-along Audio CD

Assess
- Review Games Online
- Lesson Test, Modified Assessment, pp. 254–260
- Lesson Test, Pre-AP Assessment, pp. 254–260
- Lesson Test, Heritage Learners Assessment, pp. 260–266

TECHNOLOGY TOOLS	
Teacher Tools	**Student Tools**
Power Presentations	@Home Tutor
EasyPlanner CD-ROM	ClassZone.com
Test Generator CD-ROM	eEdition Online or CD-ROM
McDougal Littell Assessment System	

¡AVANCEMOS!
Unidad 7 Lección 2

Comparación cultural, Repaso inclusivo, pp. 220–223

OBJECTIVES

- Read about places where teens like to go to have fun.
- Compare favorite places of teens in Bolivia, Argentina, and Nicaragua with favorite places of teens in the U.S.
- Write about a place you visited recently.
- Cumulative review.

STANDARDS
- 1.1 Engage in conversation, Acts. 3, 5–6
- 1.2 Understand language, Act. 1
- 1.3 Present information, Acts. 2–6
- 2.1 Practices and perspectives
- 4.2 Compare cultures

FOCUS AND MOTIVATE

- ❏ Comparación cultural, ¿Conoces un lugar divertido?, pp. 220–221. Have students read about places where teens can go to have fun in Bolivia, Argentina, and Nicaragua.
- ❏ Repaso inclusivo, pp. 222–223. Choose certain activities for your students to complete.

TEACH

- ❏ Comparación cultural, ¿Conoces un lugar divertido?, pp. 220–221. Call on students to read the descriptions of Luis, Liliana, and Eva. Encourage them to note similarities between the three in language and theme.
- ❏ Audio Program TXT CD 7 track 23. Listen to Luis, Liliana, and Eva.
- ❏ Repaso inclusivo, pp. 222–223. Review the En resumen pages in Units 1–7 to prepare students for Activities 1–6.

PRACTICE AND APPLY

- ❏ Comparación cultural, ¿Conoces un lugar divertido?, pp. 220–221. Help students increase their cultural awareness by doing the **Compara con tu mundo** activity.
- ❏ Repaso inclusivo, p. 222. Play Audio Program TXT CD 7 track 24 to complete Activity 1.
- ❏ Repaso inclusivo, pp. 222–223. Complete Activities 2–6.

IEP Modification   Have students take notes during the recorded phone conversation in Activity 1.

ASSESS AND RETEACH

- ❏ Homework: *Cuaderno*, pp. 145–147; *Cuaderno para hispanohablantes*, pp. 145–147.
- ❏ Unit Test, On-level Assessment, pp. 336–342.

OPTIONAL RESOURCES

Plan
- Absent Student Copymasters, URB 7, pp. 110–111

Present
- Audio Script, URB 7, pp. 78–82

Practice
- Situational Transp. and Copymasters, UTB 7, Transp. 14–15, pp. 1–2
- Family Involvement Activity, URB 7, p. 92
- ¡AvanzaCómics! SuperBruno y Nati, Episodio 3

Assess
- Unit Test, Modified Assessment, pp. 266–272
- Unit Test, Pre-AP Assessment, pp. 266–272
- Unit Test, Heritage Learners Assessment, pp. 272–278

TECHNOLOGY TOOLS	
Teacher Tools	**Student Tools**
EasyPlanner CD-ROM	ClassZone.com
Test Generator CD-ROM	Cultura interactiva
McDougal Littell Assessment System	eEdition Online or CD-ROM

¡AVANCEMOS!
Unidad 7 Lección 2

Unit and Lesson Opener,
Presentación y práctica de vocabulario, pp. 224–231

OBJECTIVES

- Introduce lesson theme: **Pensando en last vacaciones.**
- Present and practice vocabulary: daily routine, personal-care items, vacation destinations, ways to travel.
- **Recycle:** preterite of **hacer,** p. 200.

FOCUS AND MOTIVATE

- ❑ Unit Opener, pp. 224–225: Introduce students to the lesson theme of "a different routine," and ask students to comment on the photos of Costa Rica.
- ❑ Lesson Opener, pp. 226–227: Have students look at the photo and answer ¿Qué ves? and Compara con tu mundo questions.

TEACH

- ❑ Read A–D, pp. 228–230. Have students repeat the reflexive verbs after you while acting them out with simple gestures.
- ❑ View Vocabulary Presentation video.

PRACTICE AND APPLY

- ❑ Use the ¡A responder! Activity (1B TXT CD 2, Track 11) on p. 230 to check recognition of new vocabulary.
- ❑ Assign Activities 1 and 2 on p. 231 to practice new vocabulary.

IEP Modification Write the vocabulary words on pieces of paper. Divide students into teams and have students draw the objects, actions, or places on the chalkboard for their teammates to guess.

ASSESS AND RETEACH

- ❑ Para y piensa, p. 231. Have students name activities from their daily routine and ways to travel.
- ❑ Vocabulary Recognition Quiz, On-level Assessment, p. 348.
- ❑ Homework: *Cuaderno*, pp. 148–150; *Cuaderno para hispanohablantes*, pp. 148–151.

OPTIONAL RESOURCES

Plan
- Family Letter, URB 8, p. 91
- Family letters in Haitian Creole and Spanish on ClassZone.com
- Best Practices Toolkit
- Absent Student Copymasters, URB 8, p. 93
- PE Answers, MSRB, Transp. 91–94
- Workbook Answers, UTB 8, Transp. 32–39

Present
- Warm-up Transp. 16, UTB 8
- Atlas Map, UTB 1, Transp. 3
- Map Transp. 1, UTB 8
- Map-Culture Activities, URB 8, pp. 83–84
- Música del mundo hispano

- Fine Art Activities, URB 8, pp. 87, 89
- Fine Art Transp. 3, 5, UTB 8
- Vocabulary Transp. 6–7, UTB 8
- TPRS, pp. 99–105
- Video Script, URB 8, pp. 69–70
- Audio Script, URB 8, pp. 73–77
- Vocabulary Video, DVD 2

Practice
- Practice Games, URB 8, p. 31
- Video Activities, URB 8, pp. 51–52

Assess
- Reteaching Copymasters, URB 8, pp. 1, 2, 10

TECHNOLOGY TOOLS	
Teacher Tools	**Student Tools**
Power Presentations	@Home Tutor
EasyPlanner CD-ROM	ClassZone.com
	Cultura interactiva
	eEdition Online or CD-ROM

Vocabulario en contexto, pp. 232–233

OBJECTIVES

- Understand and practice activity vocabulary in context.
- **Recycle:** Direct object pronouns, p. 32.

STANDARDS
- 1.1 Engage in conversation, Act. 4
- 1.2 Understand language, Act. 3
- 1.3 Present information, Act. 4, PYP

FOCUS AND MOTIVATE

❑ Telehistoria escena 1, p. 232. Prepare studentsto watch the video by looking at the photoand predicting what will happen.

TEACH

❑ Telehistoria escena 1, p. 232: Strategies. Have students do the reading strategy prior to listening to the audio or viewing the DVD.

❑ Show Telehistoria escena 1, Video program, DVD 2. Ask students to summarize what happens between the characters Susana and Jorge.

PRACTICE AND APPLY

❑ *Comprensión del episodio*, p. 233: Do Activity 3 with TXT CD 8, Track 3 (if video not shown).

❑ Have students review direct object pronouns on p. 32 before doing Activity 4, p. 233.

IEP Modification   Have students write down each item pictured in Activity 4 before they pair up with a partner.

ASSESS AND RETEACH

❑ Para y piensa, p. 233. Have students complete the sentences.

❑ Vocabulary Production Quiz, On-level Assessment, p. 349.

OPTIONAL RESOURCES

Plan
- Best Practices Toolkit
- PE Answers, MSRB, Transp. 91–94
- Workbook Answers, UTB 8, Transp. 32–39
- Absent Student Copymasters, URB 8, p. 94

Present
- Warm-up Transp. 16, UTB 8
- Audio Script, URB 8, pp. 73–77
- Video Script, URB 8, pp. 69–70

Practice
- Video Activities, URB 8, pp. 53–54
- Practice Games, URB 8, p. 32

Assess
- Reteaching Copymasters, URB 8, pp. 1, 3, 11

TECHNOLOGY TOOLS	
Teacher Tools	**Student Tools**
Power Presentations	@Home Tutor
EasyPlanner CD-ROM	ClassZone.com
Test Generator CD-ROM	eEdition Online or CD-ROM

Presentación y práctica de gramática 1, pp. 234–237

OBJECTIVES
- Present and practice reflexive pronouns and reflexive verbs.
- **Recycle:** parts of the body, p. 133.
- **Culture:** Learn about the Costa Rican landscape through the art of Manuel de la Cruz González.

STANDARDS
- 1.1 Engage in conversation, Act. 9
- 1.3 Present information, Acts. 5–10
- 2.2 Products and perspectives, CC
- 4.1 Compare languages
- 4.2 Compare cultures, CC

FOCUS AND MOTIVATE
❑ Presentación de gramática, p. 415. Ask students what they notice about verbs such as **lavarse, acostarse,** and **vestirse.** How are they different from other infinitives they have learned?

TEACH
❑ Use student volunteers to present reflexive verbs (p. 234). Give one student some dishes to "wash," while another student acts out washing his/her face. Ask students to listen for differences as you point to each student and say: **Lava los platos, Se lava la cara.**

❑ Comparación cultural, p. 237. Use the fine art transparency to present *Paisaje.* Ask students: **¿Qué colores hay en la pintura?, ¿Qué tiempo hace?**

IEP Modification Have students label index cards with the reflexive pronouns: **me, te, se, nos,** and parts of the conjugated verb **lavar: lav, o, as, a, amos, an.** Have them practice forming the correct conjugations using the cards.

PRACTICE AND APPLY
❑ Have students review parts of the body on p. 133 before doing Activity 5 on p. 235.
❑ Have students do Activities 6, 7, 8, and 10 individually and Activity 9 in groups (pp. 235–237).

ASSESS AND RETEACH
❑ Para y piensa, p. 237. Have students create sentences with the information provided, using reflexive pronouns when necessary.
❑ Homework: *Cuaderno,* pp. 151–153; *Cuaderno para hispanohablantes,* pp. 152–154.

OPTIONAL RESOURCES
Plan
- Best Practices Toolkit
- PE Answers, MSRB, Transp. 91–94
- Workbook Answers, UTB 8, Transp. 32–39
- Absent Student Copymasters, URB 8, p. 95
- Easy Planner CD-ROM
- ClassZone.com

Present
- Warm-up Transp. 17, UTB 8
- Grammar Presentation Transp. 10, UTB 8

- Fine Art Activities, URB 8, p. 86
- Fine Art Transp. 2, UTB 8

Practice
- Practice Games, URB 8, p. 33

Assess
- Reteaching Copymasters, URB 8, pp. 4, 5, 12

TECHNOLOGY TOOLS

Teacher Tools	Student Tools
Power Presentations	@Home Tutor
EasyPlanner CD-ROM	ClassZone.com
Test Generator CD-ROM	eEdition Online or CD-ROM

¡AVANCEMOS!
Unidad 8 Lección 1

Gramática en contexto, pp. 238–239

OBJECTIVES

- Identify preterite lesson vocabulary and reflexive verbs in context.
- Learn about and practice the pronunciation of dipthongs in Spanish.

STANDARDS

- 1.2 Understand language, Acts. 11–12, Pronunciación
- 1.3 Present information, Acts. 11–12

FOCUS AND MOTIVATE

☐ Telehistoria escena 2, p. 238. Have students look at the photo and answer the following warm-up questions: **¿Qué hace la familia? ¿Qué hay en la mesa?**

TEACH

☐ Show Telehistoria escena 2, Video Program, DVD 2. Ask students to listen for reflexive verbs and then write a list of the words they hear on the board.

☐ Present Pronunciación, p. 239. Use TXT CD 8, Track 6 to practice diphthongs.

PRACTICE AND APPLY

☐ Go over Activity 11 on p. 239. Have students complete the activity individually and then review answers as a class. Use TXT CD 8, tracks 4 and 5 if video not shown.

☐ Have students complete Activity 12 while playing the audio, 1B TXT CD 2 Track 12.

IEP Modification   Play the audio two or three times to give students the chance to hear and understand the whole sequence and write down the letters in order. Pause between each statement if necessary.

ASSESS AND RETEACH

☐ Para y piensa, p. 239. Have students practice the verbs **acostarse** and **levantarse.**

☐ Grammar Quiz 1, On-level Assessment, p. 350.

OPTIONAL RESOURCES

Plan
- Best Practices Toolkit
- PE Answers, MSRB, Transp. 88–91
- Workbook Answers, UTB 8, Transp. 32–39
- Absent Student Copymasters, URB 8, p. 96

Present
- Warm-up Transp. 17, UTB 8
- Audio Script, URB 8, pp. 73–77
- Video Script, URB 8, pp. 69–70

Practice
- Practice Games, URB 8, p. 34
- Video Activities, URB 8, pp. 55–56

Assess
- Reteaching Copymasters, URB 8, pp. 4, 6

TECHNOLOGY TOOLS	
Teacher Tools	**Student Tools**
Power Presentations	@Home Tutor
EasyPlanner CD-ROM	ClassZone.com
Test Generator CD-ROM	eEdition Online or CD-ROM

¡AVANCEMOS!
Unidad 8 Lección 1

158
¡Avancemos!
Level 1B Unidad 8

Lección 1

Presentación y práctica de gramática 2, pp. 240–243

OBJECTIVES
- Present and practice the present progressive tense.
- **Recycle:** Chores, p. 70; parts of a house, p. 42
- **Culture:** Learn about and practice the use of **usted, tú,** and **vos.**

STANDARDS
- 1.1 Engage in conversation, Acts. 16–17
- 1.3 Present information, Acts. 13–18, PYP
- 2.1 Practices and perspectives, Act. 17
- 4.1 Compare languages
- 4.2 Compare cultures, Act. 17

FOCUS AND MOTIVATE
- ❑ Presentación de gramática, p. 240. Review the present tense conjugation of **estar** with students before introducing the present progressive tense.

TEACH
- ❑ Introduce the present progressive tense, p. 240. Point out to students that the present progressive tense has two parts, a present tense form of **estar** and the participle.
- ❑ Comparación cultural, p. 243. Have student volunteers read the parts of the superhero and the assistant in the comic strip. Ask if they notice a difference in how the two address each other.

IEP Modification Stress the direct correlation with English. In English, we conjugate *be* and add *-ing* to the verb that represents the action.

PRACTICE AND APPLY
- ❑ Review vocabulary related to chores (p. 70) and houses (p. 42) to prepare students for Activities 13 and 16 (pp. 421–422).
- ❑ Before students pair up for Activity 17, have them brainstorm topics they might talk about with a sibling, such as homework, parents, or after-school activities. Encourage students to use these ideas, as well as the present progressive tense, during their conversation.

ASSESS AND RETEACH
- ❑ Para y piensa, p. 243. Have students complete sentences with the present progressive form of verbs.
- ❑ Homework: *Cuaderno,* pp. 154–156; *Cuaderno para hispanohablantes,* pp. 155–158.

OPTIONAL RESOURCES

Plan
- Best Practices Toolkit
- PE Answers, MSRB, Transp. 88–91
- Workbook Answers, UTB 8, Transp. 32–39
- Absent Student Copymasters, URB 8, p. 97

Present
- Warm-up Transp. 18, UTB 8
- Grammar Presentation Transp. 11, UTB 8

Practice
- Practice Games, URB 8, p. 35

Assess
- Reteaching Copymasters, URB 8, pp. 7, 8

TECHNOLOGY TOOLS	
Teacher Tools	**Student Tools**
Power Presentations	@Home Tutor
EasyPlanner CD-ROM	ClassZone.com
Test Generator CD-ROM	eEdition Online or CD-ROM

Todo junto, Juegos y diversiones, pp. 244–247

OBJECTIVES

- Integrate lesson content.
- Practice using and integrating lesson vocabulary and grammar.
- Review vocabulary by playing a game.

STANDARDS

- 1.1 Engage in conversation, Acts. 21–22
- 1.2 Understand language, Acts. 19–20, 22
- 1.3 Present information, Acts. 20–23, PYP
- 5.2 Life-long learners, Juegos y diversiones

FOCUS AND MOTIVATE

❑ Telehistoria completa, p. 244. Have students look at the photos and ask them: **¿Dónde están los chicos?, ¿Qué está haciendo Jorge?**

TEACH

❑ Read the Resumen sections for Telehistoria escenas 1 and 2 on p. 244.

❑ Show Telehistoria escena 3, Video program, DVD 2. Ask students to raise their hand each time they hear the present progressive tense.

❑ Play scenes 1, 2, and 3 all together.

PRACTICE AND APPLY

❑ If not showing the videos, play the audio TXT CD tracks 3, 4, and 7 for Activities 19 and 20 on p. 245.

❑ Have students review telling time on p. 14 and then complete the strategy on p. 244 before pairing up with a partner for Activity 21.

❑ Play the audio 1B TXT CD 2 tracks 13, 14 for students to do Activity 22, p. 246.

❑ Assign Activity 23, p. 246.

❑ Have students play Tu rutina diaria to review vocabulary.

IEP Modification Before writing in Activity 23, students can create a quick outline. In it they can organize their thoughts and work out details. Where are they going on vacation? What types of activities can one do there? What would constitute a typical routine? What might the student be doing while he/she is writing in his/her diary?

ASSESS AND RETEACH

❑ Para y piensa, p. 246. Have students practice the present progressive.

❑ Grammar Quiz 2, On-level Assessment, p. 351.

❑ Homework: *Cuaderno*, pp. 157–158; *Cuaderno para hispanohablantes*, pp. 159–160.

OPTIONAL RESOURCES

Plan
- Best Practices Toolkit
- PE Answers, MSRB, Transp. 88–91
- Workbook Answers, UTB 8, Transp. 32–39
- Absent Student Copymasters, URB 8, p. 98

Present
- Warm-up Transp. 18, UTB 8
- Audio Script, URB 8, pp. 73–77
- Video Script, URB 8, pp. 69–70

Practice
- Learning Scenarios on Easy Planner
- Conversation cards on Easy Planner and ClassZone
- Video activities, URB 8, pp. 57–58
- Practice Games, URB 8, p. 36

Assess
- Reteaching Copymasters, URB 8, pp. 7, 9

TECHNOLOGY TOOLS	
Teacher Tools	**Student Tools**
Power Presentations	@Home Tutor
EasyPlanner CD-ROM	ClassZone.com
Test Generator CD-ROM	eEdition Online or CD-ROM

Lectura/Conexiones, pp. 248–250

OBJECTIVES

- Read about a vacation to Costa Rica.
- **Culture:** Learn about Monteverde, a nature reserve in Costa Rica.
- Read about a natural science museum in Costa Rica, its sections and exhibits.

FOCUS AND MOTIVATE

❏ Lectura, pp. 248–249. Have student look over the photos and ask if anyone has seen any similar places or done any similar activities.

TEACH

❏ Lectura, «Mi viaje a Costa Rica», pp. 248–249. Play the audio TXT CD 8 Track 10 as students follow along.

❏ Conexiones, p. 250. Have students look at the poster and ask them what they would expect to find in the museum.

IEP Modification To set students up for comprehension, ask them to scan the photos before reading and describe where they were taken and what they see in each.

PRACTICE AND APPLY

❏ Lectura, «Mi viaje a Costa Rica», pp. 248–249. Have students do the reading strategy as they read the scrapbook.

❏ Conexiones, p. 250, Proyectos 1, 2, 3. Allow students to choose the project that interests them most.

ASSESS AND RETEACH

❏ Para y piensa, p. 249. Have students answer the questions with complete sentences.

❏ Culture Quiz, On-level Assessment, p. 352.

STANDARDS

- 1.2 Understand language
- 1.3 Present information
- 2.1 Practices and perspectives
- 3.1 Knowledge of other disciplines
- 3.2 Acquire information

OPTIONAL RESOURCES

Plan
- Best Practices Toolkit
- PE Answers, MSRB, Transp. 88–91
- Workbook Answers, UTB 8, Transp. 32–39
- Absent Student Copymasters, URB 8, p. 99

Present
- Warm-up Transp. 19, UTB 8

Practice
- Lecturas para todos, pp. 178–182
- Lecturas para hispanohablantes
- Practice Games, URB 8, p. 37

TECHNOLOGY TOOLS

Teacher Tools	Student Tools
Power Presentations	@Home Tutor
EasyPlanner CD-ROM	ClassZone.com
Test Generator CD-ROM	eEdition Online or CD-ROM

En resumen, Repaso de la lección, pp. 251–253

OBJECTIVES

- Review lesson grammar and vocabulary.

FOCUS AND MOTIVATE

- ☐ Do a quick review of the vocabulary and grammar in the En Resumen on p. 251.
- ☐ Review the information in the ¡Llegada! box on p. 252.

TEACH

- ☐ Activity 1, p. 252. Play Audio 1B TXT CD 2, track 15 while students match the items with the people who need them. Ask students to explain their answers aloud using the present progressive of the appropriate reflexive verbs.

IEP Modification   Before playing the audio in Activity 1, have students write down the reflexive verbs that would logically go with each item.

ASSESS AND RETEACH

- ☐ Homework: Study En resumen, p. 251; *Cuaderno*, pp. 159–170; *Cuaderno para hispanohablantes*, pp. 161–170.
- ☐ Lesson Test, On-level Assessment, pp. 353–359.

STANDARDS

- 1.2 Understand language, Act. 1
- 1.3 Present information, Acts. 2–4
- 4.2 Compare cultures, Act. 5

OPTIONAL RESOURCES

Plan

- Best Practices Toolkit
- PE Answers, MSRB, Transp. 88–91
- Workbook Answers, UTB 8, Transp. 32–39
- Absent Student Copymasters, URB 8, p. 100

Present

- Warm-up Transp. 19, UTB 8
- Audio Script, URB 8, pp. 73–77

Practice

- Practice Games, URB 8, p. 38
- Sing-along Audio CD

Assess

- Review Games Online
- Lesson Test, Modified Assessment, pp. 278–284
- Lesson Test, Pre-AP Assessment, pp. 278–284
- Lesson Test, Heritage Learners Assessment, pp. 284–290

TECHNOLOGY TOOLS	
Teacher Tools	**Student Tools**
Power Presentations	@Home Tutor
EasyPlanner CD-ROM	ClassZone.com
Test Generator CD-ROM	eEdition Online or CD-ROM
McDougal Littell Assessment System	

162

¡Avancemos!
Level 1B Unidad 8

¡AVANCEMOS!
Unidad 8 Lección 1

Lección 1

Lesson Opener,
Presentación y práctica de vocabulario, pp. 254–259

OBJECTIVES

- Introduce lesson theme: **Vamos de vacaciones.**
- Present and practice vocabulary: vacation activities, handicrafts, jewelry, bargaining expressions.

STANDARDS
- 1.2 Understand language
- 1.3 Present information, Acts. 1–2
- 2.2 Products and perspectives
- 4.2 Compare cultures, CC

FOCUS AND MOTIVATE

❑ Lesson Opener, pp. 254–255: Have students preview the information in the ¡Vamos de vacaciones! and Comparación cultural boxes.

❑ Ask students to look at the photo and describe where the kids are and what they see there.

TEACH

❑ Presentación de vocabulario, pp. 256–259. Read A–D . Have students repeat the labeled vocabulary after you.

❑ Show Vocabulary Presentation video, DVD 2.

❑ Review using **gustar** with an infinitive by posing questions to individual students about the various activities presented.

❑ Play 1B TXT CD 2, Track 16, while students do ¡A responder! activity, p. 258.

IEP Modification   In advance, write each activity on a piece of paper, and include the artesanía vocabulary by adding a verb (e.g. **ponerse un arete, hacer cerámica**). Divide the class into two teams and play charades.

PRACTICE AND APPLY

❑ Práctica de vocabulario, p. 259. Have students do Activity 1 to tell what items are available in the souvenir store.

❑ Práctica de vocabulario, p. 259. Pair up students to work to do Activity 2, then invite volunteers to present the conversation aloud.

ASSESS AND RETEACH

❑ Para y piensa, p. 259. Have students do the activity on to check their comprehension of the new vocabulary.

❑ Vocabulary Recognition Quiz, On-level Assessment, p. 365.

❑ Homework: *Cuaderno*, pp. 171–173; *Cuaderno para hispanohablantes*, pp. 171–174.

OPTIONAL RESOURCES

Plan
- Best Practices Toolkit
- Absent Student Copymasters, URB 8, p. 101
- PE Answers, MSRB, Transp. 92–95
- Workbook Answers, UTB 8, Transp. 40–47

Present
- Warm-up Transp. 20, UTB 8
- Vocabulary Transp. 8–9, UTB 8
- TPRS, pp. 106–112

- Video Script, URB 8, pp. 71–72
- Audio Script, URB 8, pp. 78–82
- Vocabulary Video, DVD 2

Practice
- Practice Games, URB 8, p. 39
- Video Activities, URB 8, pp. 59–60

Assess
- Reteaching Copymasters, URB 8, pp. 13–14

TECHNOLOGY TOOLS	
Teacher Tools	**Student Tools**
Power Presentations	@Home Tutor
EasyPlanner CD-ROM	ClassZone.com
	Cultura interactiva
	eEdition Online or CD-ROM

¡AVANCEMOS!
Unidad 8 Lección 2

Vocabulario en contexto, pp. 260–261

OBJECTIVES

- Understand and practice activity vocabulary in context.

> **STANDARDS**
> - 1.1 Engage in conversation, Act. 4
> - 1.2 Understand language, Act. 3
> - 1.3 Present information, Act. 4, PYP

FOCUS AND MOTIVATE

- ❏ Telehistoria escena 1, p. 260. Have students answer warm–up questions by looking at the photos and using their imagination.

TEACH

- ❏ Telehistoria escena 1, p. 260. Read the listening strategy.
- ❏ Show Telehistoria escena 1, DVD 2.
- ❏ Ask students questions based on the dialogue.

IEP Modification   Before listening, go over the reading strategy and read the dialogue. Break it up into sections based on where the stage directions occur. Ask comprehension questions for each section, and see if students get Susana's line about the blue car and the saleswoman's line about bargaining.

PRACTICE AND APPLY

- ❏ Vocabulario en contexto, pp. 260–261. Do Activity 3 with TXT CD 8, track 14.
- ❏ Have students do Activity 4 in small groups.
- ❏ Encourage students to do the Expansión activity by telling how often they do certain activities.

ASSESS AND RETEACH

- ❏ Para y piensa, p. 261. Have students choose the correct word to create logical sentences. Allow them to look back at the dialogue on p. 260 if necessary.
- ❏ Vocabulary Production Quiz, On-level Assessment, p. 366.

OPTIONAL RESOURCES

Plan
- Best Practices Toolkit
- PE Answers, MSRB, Transp. 92–95
- Workbook Answers, UTB 8, Transp. 40–47
- Absent Student Copymasters, URB 8, p. 102

Present
- Warm-up Transp. 20, UTB 8
- Audio Script, URB 8, pp. 78–82
- Video Script, URB 8, pp. 71–72

Practice
- Video Activities, URB 8, pp. 61–62
- Practice Games, URB 8, p. 40

Assess
- Reteaching Copymasters, URB 8, pp. 13, 15

TECHNOLOGY TOOLS	
Teacher Tools	**Student Tools**
Power Presentations	@Home Tutor
EasyPlanner CD-ROM	ClassZone.com
Test Generator CD-ROM	eEdition Online or CD-ROM

Presentación y práctica de gramática 1, pp. 262–265

OBJECTIVES

- Present and practice indirect object pronouns.
- **Culture:** Discuss means of transportation in different countries.
- **Recycle:** family members, p. 21; numbers from 200 to 1,000,000, p. 21.

STANDARDS
- 1.1 Engage in conversation, Acts. 9–10
- 1.3 Present information, Acts. 5–11, PYP
- 2.2 Products and perspectives, CC
- 4.1 Compare languages
- 4.2 Compare cultures, CC

FOCUS AND MOTIVATE

❏ Presentación de gramática, p. 262. Quickly review **gustar** to practice the different indirect pronouns that students have already learned lexically.

❏ Presentación de gramática, p. 262. Review the vocabulary for family members by asking questions about the people in their families.

TEACH

❏ Presentación de gramática, p. 262. Review the English Grammar Connection note and the example.

❏ Presentación de gramática, p. 262. Present the indirect object pronouns by going over the chart on p. 262.

❏ Comparación cultural: El transporte, p. 264. Have a volunteer read aloud the information about transportation in Costa Rica. Then ask for examples of how transportation in their area compares to that of Costa Rica.

PRACTICE AND APPLY

❏ Práctica de gramática, p. 263. Have students do Activities 5, 6, and 7.

❏ Práctica de gramática, pp. 264–265. Have students do Activities 8 and 11 independently.

❏ Práctica de gramática, p. 265. Pair students together to do Activities 9 and 10 verbally.

IEP Modification   Pair a slower-paced learner with a more advanced learner for peer support in Activity 9.

ASSESS AND RETEACH

❏ Para y piensa, p. 265. Have students give the correct indirect object pronoun for each sentence.

❏ Homework: *Cuaderno*, pp. 174–176; *Cuaderno para hispanohablantes*, pp. 175–177.

OPTIONAL RESOURCES

Plan
- Best Practices Toolkit
- PE Answers, MSRB, Transp. 92–95
- Workbook Answers, UTB 8, Transp. 40–47
- Absent Student Copymasters, URB 8, p. 103
- Easy Planner CD-ROM
- ClassZone.com

Present
- Warm-up Transp. 21, UTB 8
- Grammar Presentation Transp. 12, UTB 8

Practice
- Practice Games, URB 8, p. 41

Assess
- Reteaching Copymasters, URB 8, pp. 16, 17, 22, 23

TECHNOLOGY TOOLS	
Teacher Tools	**Student Tools**
Power Presentations	@Home Tutor
EasyPlanner CD-ROM	ClassZone.com
Test Generator CD-ROM	eEdition Online or CD-ROM

¡AVANCEMOS!
Unidad 8 Lección 2

Gramática en contexto, pp. 266–267

OBJECTIVES

- Identify lesson vocabulary and indirect object pronouns in context.
- **Recycle: gustar** with an infinitive, p. 8.
- Pronunciation: Linking words in Spanish.

FOCUS AND MOTIVATE

- ❑ Telehistoria escena 2, p. 442. Have students answer warm–up questions by looking at the photo and using their imagination.

TEACH

- ❑ Show Telehistoria escena 2, DVD 2. Direct students to notice the common shopping expressions as outlined in the Cuando lees strategy.
- ❑ Telehistoria escena 2, p. 266. Have students read and repeat the dialogue after you for correct pronunciation and intonation.
- ❑ Review with students the information given in the También se dice note.
- ❑ Pronunciación, p. 267. Play TXT CD 8, track 14 and have students repeat the sentences. Note that elision occurs markedly when the same sound occurs at the end of one word and the beginning of the next (e.g. **mi hija** sounds like **mija**).

IEP Modification   Give additional examples of elision to students who have trouble with listening skills. Point to examples in the Telehistoria (vendedor's third line, "¿**A u**sted le gusta..."; Susana's last line, "¿qué te pas**a a** ti?"). Have students repeat the phrases quickly.

PRACTICE AND APPLY

- ❑ Comprensión del episodio, p. 266. Listen to TXT CD 8, Track 15, Activity 9 if video not shown. Then have students indicate which statements were true and how they corrected those that were false.
- ❑ Work in pairs to do Activity 13, p. 267.

ASSESS AND RETEACH

- ❑ Para y piensa, p. 267. Have students complete each sentence with the correct indirect object pronoun, based on the Telehistoria.
- ❑ Grammar Quiz 1, On-level Assessment, p. 367.

OPTIONAL RESOURCES

Plan
- Best Practices Toolkit
- PE Answers, MSRB, Transp. 92–95
- Workbook Answers, UTB 8, Transp. 40–47
- Absent Student Copymasters, URB 8, p. 104

Present
- Warm-up Transp. 21, UTB 8
- Audio Script, URB 8, pp. 78–82
- Video Script, URB 8, pp. 71–72

Practice
- Practice Games, URB 8, p. 42
- Video Activities, URB 8, pp. 63–64

Assess
- Reteaching Copymasters, URB 8, pp. 16, 18

| TECHNOLOGY TOOLS ||
Teacher Tools	Student Tools
Power Presentations	@Home Tutor
EasyPlanner CD-ROM	ClassZone.com
Test Generator CD-ROM	eEdition Online or CD-ROM

Presentación y práctica de gramática 2, pp. 268–271

OBJECTIVES
- Present and practice demonstrative adjectives.
- **Recycle:** the present progressive, p. 240; classroom objects, p. 12.
- **Culture:** Discuss how artists depict important industries of their country.

STANDARDS
- 1.1 Engage in conversation, Acts. 16–19
- 1.2 Understand language, Act. 15
- 1.3 Present information, Acts. 14–19, PYP
- 2.1 Products and perspectives, Act. 18
- 4.1 Compare languages, Pronunciación
- 4.2 Compare cultures, Act. 18

FOCUS AND MOTIVATE
- ❏ Review with students the information in the English Grammar Connection note on p. 268.

TEACH
- ❏ Presentación de gramática, p. 268. Begin with a quick review of the concept of gender and number agreement. Emphasize how the articles modify the nouns in gender and number.
- ❏ Begin with the masculine, singular examples in the chart on p. 444 to explain that demonstrative adjectives must also agree in gender and number with the nouns they modify. Continue your presentation of demonstrative adjectives by working through the remaining examples and sentences on the chart.
- ❏ Comparación Cultural: El café, p. 271. Ask students to describe the painting *Midiendo café* and then discuss the paragraph about coffee in Costa Rica.

IEP Modification   Use three similar objects (e.g. three copies of *¡Avancemos!*), one placed directly in front of you, one in front of a student, and one all the way across the classroom, to visually demonstrate the concept of **ese, este,** and **aquel.** Use exaggerated gestures.

PRACTICE AND APPLY
- ❏ Práctica de gramática, p. 269. Have students do Activity 14.
- ❏ Play 1B TXT CD 2 Track 17 and have students complete Activity 15, p. 269.
- ❏ Comparación Cultural: El café, p. 271. Pair students off to do Activity 18.
- ❏ Have students work in pairs on Activity 19, p. 271.

ASSESS AND RETEACH
- ❏ Para y piensa, p. 271. Check students' understanding of the grammar skill by having them complete each sentence with the correct demonstrative adjective.
- ❏ Homework: *Cuaderno,* pp. 177–179; *Cuaderno para hispanohablantes,* pp. 178–181.

OPTIONAL RESOURCES

Plan
- Best Practices Toolkit
- PE Answers, MSRB, Transp. 92–95
- Workbook Answers, UTB 8, Transp. 40–47
- Absent Student Copymasters, URB 8, p. 105

Present
- Warm-up Transp. 22, UTB 8
- Fine Art Activities, URB 8, p. 88
- Fine Art Transp. 4, UTB 8
- Grammar Presentation Transp. 13, UTB 8

Practice
- Practice Games, URB 8, p. 43

Assess
- Reteaching Copymasters, URB 8, pp. 19, 20, 24

TECHNOLOGY TOOLS	
Teacher Tools	**Student Tools**
Power Presentations	@Home Tutor
EasyPlanner CD-ROM	ClassZone.com
Test Generator CD-ROM	eEdition Online or CD-ROM

Todo junto, Juegos y diversiones, pp. 272–275

OBJECTIVES

- Integrate lesson content.
- Practice using and integrating lesson vocabulary and grammar.
- Review vocabulary by playing a game.

FOCUS AND MOTIVATE

❑ Todo junto, p. 272. Refer to particular students and point to objects in the classroom to ask warm–up questions.

TEACH

❑ Telehistoria completa, p. 272. Read the Resumen sections for Escenas 1 and 2.

❑ Ask students to look at the photo on p. 272 and predict what is going to happen in the final scene.

❑ Go over the Cuando escuchas strategy on p. 272, then show Telehistoria completa, DVD 2. To review, show all three scenes together.

IEP Modification To prepare students for this scene, ask them to recall or review what happened at the end of the Telehistoria completa in Lesson 1, p. 244 (Jorge forgets Alicia's t-shirt). Ask students why they think Jorge needs to bring the t-shirt with him.

PRACTICE AND APPLY

❑ Have students complete Activities 20 and 21 (Audio TXT CD 8, tracks 14, 15, and 18, if video not shown). Invite a volunteer to tell the class in which order he/she put the sentences.

❑ Activity 22, p. 273. Assign students to work in pairs and barter back and forth.

❑ Activity 23, p. 274. Play Audio 1B TXT CD 8, tracks 18, 19. Have students read the guide and listen to the ad. Then call on volunteers to share what they would like to do at Playa Tamarindo and tell what they are going to buy for whom.

❑ Have students play El mercado to review vocabulary.

ASSESS AND RETEACH

❑ Para y piensa, p. 274. Have students complete the sentences to demonstrate their ability to use indirect object pronouns and demonstrative adjectives correctly.

❑ Grammar Quiz 2, On-level Assessment, p. 368.

❑ Homework: *Cuaderno*, pp. 180–181; *Cuaderno para hispanohablantes*, pp. 182–183.

OPTIONAL RESOURCES

Plan
- Best Practices Toolkit
- PE Answers, MSRB, Transp. 92–95
- Workbook Answers, UTB 8, Transp. 40–47
- Absent Student Copymasters, URB 8, p. 106

Present
- Warm-up Transp. 22, UTB 8
- Audio Script, URB 8, pp. 78–82
- Video Script, URB 8, pp. 71–72

Practice
- Learning Scenarios on Easy Planner
- Conversation cards on Easy Planner and ClassZone
- Video activities, URB 8, pp. 65–66
- Practice Games, URB 8, p. 44

Assess
- Reteaching Copymasters, URB 8, pp. 19, 21

TECHNOLOGY TOOLS	
Teacher Tools	**Student Tools**
Power Presentations	@Home Tutor
EasyPlanner CD-ROM	ClassZone.com
Test Generator CD-ROM	eEdition Online or CD-ROM

¡AVANCEMOS!
Unidad 8 Lección 2

¡Avancemos!
Level 1B Unidad 8

168

Lección 2

Lectura/Proyectos culturales, pp. 276–278

OBJECTIVES

- **Culture:** Read about markets in Costa Rica and Uruguay.
- Learn what these markets sell and why people go there.
- Read about traditional desserts from Costa Rica and Uruguay.

STANDARDS
- 1.1 Engage in conversation
- 1.2 Understand language
- 2.1 Practices and perspectives
- 3.1 Knowledge of other disciplines
- 4.2 Compare cultures
- 5.1 Spanish in the community

FOCUS AND MOTIVATE

- ❏ Lectura cultural, p. 276–277. Preview the reading strategy. Have students prepare a three-circle Venn diagram on a sheet of paper before listening and/or reading.
- ❏ Proyectos culturales, p. 278. Ask students what kind of snacks they know how to cook at home.

TEACH

- ❏ Lectura cultural: «Mercados en Costa Rica y Uruguay, 276–277». Play TXT CD 8 Track 21. Students should listen and follow along, then reread silently. Check students' understanding of the passage.
- ❏ Proyectos culturales: Present the information on desserts in Costa Rica and Uruguay. Choose one of the two recipes ahead of time to have the items ready for the class to prepare.

IEP Modification Break the reading down into three paragraphs. After each paragraph, ask comprehension questions and clarify any vocabulary issues.

PRACTICE AND APPLY

- ❏ Lectura cultural, pp. 276–277. As they read, have students fill in their Venn diagrams with information about markets in Costa Rica and Uruguay. Ask them to think about markets and bargaining in the United States and add this information to the third circle of their Venn diagram.
- ❏ Proyectos culturales, p. 278. Have students read the recipe and reiterate the instructions. Have them work in groups to prepare the chosen recipe.

ASSESS AND RETEACH

- ❏ Para y piensa, p. 277. Have students answer the questions with complete sentences.
- ❏ Culture Quiz, On-level Assessment, p. 369.

OPTIONAL RESOURCES

Plan
- Best Practices Toolkit
- PE Answers, MSRB, Transp. 92–95
- Workbook Answers, UTB 8, Transp. 40–47
- Absent Student Copymasters, URB 8, pp. 107–108

Present
- Warm-up Transp. 23, UTB 8

Practice
- Lecturas para todos, pp. 183–187
- Lecturas para hispanohablantes
- Practice Games, URB 8, p. 45

TECHNOLOGY TOOLS	
Teacher Tools	**Student Tools**
Power Presentations	@Home Tutor
EasyPlanner CD-ROM	ClassZone.com
Test Generator CD-ROM	eEdition Online or CD-ROM

En resumen, Repaso de la lección, pp. 279–281

OBJECTIVES
- Review lesson grammar and vocabulary.

STANDARDS
- 1.2 Understand language, Act. 1
- 1.3 Present information, Acts. 2–4
- 4.2 Compare cultures, Act. 5

FOCUS AND MOTIVATE
- ❑ Do a quick review of lesson vocabulary and grammar by asking questions and scanning the En resumen on p. 279.
- ❑ Repaso de la lección, p. 280. Review the information in the ¡Llegada! box.

TEACH
- ❑ Repaso de la lección, pp. 280–281. Play 1B TXT CD 2 Track 20 while students complete Activity 1, p. 280. For a review of indirect object pronouns or demonstrative adjectives, return to p. 262 or 268.

PRACTICE AND APPLY
- ❑ Activity 2, p. 280. Have students work in pairs or small groups to complete the conversation.
- ❑ Activity 3, p. 281. Have students complete the activity to check their ability to use demonstrative adjectives correctly while talking about vacation activities.
- ❑ Comparación cultural, p. 281. Have students answer questions 1–4.

IEP Modification Encourage students to consult the En resumen or flip back to the referenced pages if they are having trouble.

ASSESS AND RETEACH
- ❑ Homework: Study En resumen, p. 279; *Cuaderno*, pp. 182–193; *Cuaderno para hispanohablantes*, pp. 184–193.
- ❑ Lesson Test, On-level Assessment, pp. 370–376.

OPTIONAL RESOURCES

Plan
- Best Practices Toolkit
- PE Answers, MSRB, Transp. 92–95
- Workbook Answers, UTB 8, Transp. 40–47
- Absent Student Copymasters, URB 8, p. 109

Present
- Warm-up Transp. 23, UTB 8
- Audio Script, URB 8, pp. 78–82

Practice
- Practice Games, URB 8, p. 46
- Sing-along Audio CD

Assess
- Review Games Online
- Lesson Test, Modified Assessment, pp. 290–296
- Lesson Test, Pre-AP Assessment, pp. 290–296
- Lesson Test, Heritage Learners Assessment, pp. 296–302

TECHNOLOGY TOOLS	
Teacher Tools	**Student Tools**
Power Presentations	@Home Tutor
EasyPlanner CD-ROM	ClassZone.com
Test Generator CD-ROM	eEdition Online or CD-ROM
McDougal Littell Assessment System	

**¡AVANCEMOS!
Unidad 8 Lección 2**

Comparación cultural, Repaso inclusivo, pp. 282–285

OBJECTIVES
- Read about travel destinations in Uruguay, Ecuador and Costa Rica.
- Compare favorite vacation spots of teens in Uruguay, Ecuador and Costa Rica, and the U.S.
- Cumulative review.

> **STANDARDS**
> - 1.1 Engage in conversation, Acts. 2–3, 5
> - 1.2 Understand language, Act. 1
> - 1.3 Present information, Acts. 2–6
> - 2.1 Practices and perspectives
> - 4.2 Compare cultures

FOCUS AND MOTIVATE
- ❑ Comparación Cultural, pp. 282–283. Have students describe what they see in the three photos on pp. 282–283.

TEACH
- ❑ Comparación Cultural, pp. 282–283. Play Audio program TXT CD 8 Track 23 as students follow along. Then call on students to read the descriptions of the three countries. Encourage them to note similarities and differences.
- ❑ Comparación cultural. Use the writing strategy to guide students in their own descriptions.
- ❑ Repaso inclusivo, pp. 284–285: Choose for extra review key vocabulary terms and grammar points from units 1–8 that students have had difficulty with.

PRACTICE AND APPLY
- ❑ Comparación Cultural, pp. 282–283. Assign the writing activity. Help students increase their cultural awareness by doing the **Compara con tu mundo** activity.
- ❑ Repaso inclusivo, pp. 284–285. Activities 1–6. Play Audio Program TXT CD 8 track 24 for students to complete Activity 1.

IEP Modification   For Activity 6, have students first brainstorm a list of possible questions to ask. Assist students with any grammar or vocabulary issues.

ASSESS AND RETEACH
- ❑ Homework: *Cuaderno*, pp. 194–196; *Cuaderno para hispanohablantes*, pp. 194–196.
- ❑ Unit Test, On-level Assessment, pp. 382–388.

OPTIONAL RESOURCES

Plan
- Absent Student Copymasters, URB 8, pp. 110–111

Present
- Audio Script, URB 8, pp. 78–82

Practice
- Situational Transp. and Copymasters, UTB 8, Transp. 14–15, pp. 1–2
- Family Involvement Activity, URB 8, p. 92
- ¡AvanzaCómics! SuperBruno y Nati, Episodio 3

Assess
- Unit Test, Modified Assessment, pp. 302–308
- Unit Test, Pre-AP Assessment, pp. 302–308
- Unit Test, Heritage Learners Assessment, pp. 308–314

TECHNOLOGY TOOLS	
Teacher Tools	**Student Tools**
EasyPlanner CD-ROM	ClassZone.com
Test Generator CD-ROM	Cultura interactiva
McDougal Littell Assessment System	eEdition Online or CD-ROM

Instructional Modifications for At-Risk Language Learners

Name of Student _____ Class _____

Week Starting _____

The following modifications have been made for this student:

Make Classroom Accommodations

Accommodation	✔
Provide a simple study guide for the day's activities.	
Present major points orally and on overheads simultaneously.	
Provide guided pair work activities to practice / reinforce a concept, pair stronger / weaker language learners.	
Task-analyze the concept to be learned and talk students through the sequence of steps needed to master the concept (especially important in teaching grammar concepts). Have written samples to show.	
Require students to keep a notebook and help them organize it.	
Speak slowly and with clear pronunciation, using same phrases repeatedly. Print out the material and distribute it so students can follow along by pointing at each word as you speak.	
Provide daily structured written reviews of material covered that day.	
Use verbal / visual (pictorial) mnemonic devices to assist in memory; let students design their own mnemonic devices and discuss value of this strategy.	
Write vocabulary words on the board as you say them slowly sound by sound and / or syllable by syllable; students repeat each word slowly three times, and write each word in their notebooks.	
Develop a routine where the class slowly repeats a new multisyllabic vocabulary word after you say it and then says the word slowly syllable by syllable as they tap out each syllable.	
Use color coding to illustrate grammar rules (e.g., pair blue verb stems with red endings); ask students to explain the grammar rule as they practice matching verb stems with endings.	
Provide a list with explanations of "Key Words" or "Clue Words" (such as *completa*, *habla*, *escucha*, *imagínate*, *describe*, *explícale*, etc.) as a tool to decode direction lines.	
Use the *modelos* for each activity so that students have a clear understanding of what they are expected to do.	
Confirm students' understanding of the task by having them repeat directions orally.	
Have a peer restate the directions to a task so that students have another discrete delivery and greater chance of correctly internalizing the directions.	
Use the bookmarks in the back of the *Cuaderno* and *Cuaderno para hispanohablantes* as a study guide.	
Use devices such as games, movement, music, mnemonic devices, jingles, and stories for review and practice so that students have a variety of sensory memory aids. **(Total Physical Response Storytelling, Sing-Along Audio CD)** .	
Other:	

Copyright © by McDougal Littell, a division of Houghton Mifflin Company.

	Other:	
	Other:	

Customize Materials

Skill focus:	**L** = Listening	**R** = Reading	**O** = Organization
	S = Speaking	**W** = Writing	

Skill focus		✔
L	Provide **Audio CD** so student can replay as often as he / she needs.	
L, R	Provide printed **Audioscript** so student can follow along during listening activities.	
L	Provide **DVD** so student can replay as often as he / she needs.	
L, R	Provide student with **Videoscript** so he / she can follow along during viewing activities.	
L, S	Administer **Vocabulary Quizzes** orally.	
L, S	Administer **Grammar Quizzes** orally.	
R, W	Assign *Cuaderno*, Level A activities.	
L, R, W	Assign **@HomeTutor** Level A activities (on CD-ROM or online).	
R	Use *Lecturas para todos* for reading comprehension support.	
R	Project the **Power Presentations CD-ROM**.	
R	Use **Grammar Presentation Transparencies**.	
L	Play **Sing-Along Audio CD**.	
R	Allow flashcards to practice and review so students have visual reminders of key information. Students can make their won or use the Vocabulary flashcards on **Classzone.com**.	
L	Establish a listening goal and work with the student to help him or her choose how to achieve that goal. Choices may include: **DVD** and accompanying Video Activities in the **Unit Resource Book, Audio CD,** *Escuchar* activities in the **Pupil Edition,** *Cuaderno, Cuaderno para hispanohablantes,* and **@HomeTutor.**	
S	Establish a speaking goal and work with the student to help him or her choose how to achieve that goal. Choices may include: **Conversation Cards** or **Learning Scenarios** on **Classzone.com**, and projects in the **Teacher Edition**.	
R	Establish a reading goal and work with the student to help him or her choose how to achieve that goal. Choices may include: *Lectura* or *Lectura cultural* in the **Pupil Edition** or *Lectura para todos*, *Lectura* activities on the **@HomeTutor**, or Reading A, B, or C in *Cuaderno*.	
W	Establish a writing goal and work with the student to help him or her choose how to achieve that goal. Choices may include: *Comparación cultural* in the **Pupil Edition**, or **WebQuests** on **Classzone.com**.	

L, S, R, W	Establish a vocabulary practice goal and work with the student to help him or her choose how to achieve that goal. Choices may include *Vocabulario* A, B, or C in *Cuaderno*, *Flashcards* on **Classzone.com**, activities in the **Pupil Edition**, the **@HomeTutor**, or vocabulary songs on the **Sing-Along Audio CD**.	
L, S, R, W	Establish a grammar practice goal and work with the student to help him or her choose how to achieve that goal. Choices may include: *Gramática* A, B, or C in *Cuaderno*, *Gramática* on the **@HomeTutor**, activities in the **Pupil Edition**, **Grammar Presentation Transparencies**, grammar songs on the **Sing-Along Audio CD**, or **Power Presentations CD-ROM**.	
	Other:	
	Other:	
	Other:	

Manage behavior

	✔
Set up explicit class routines and schedules and alert students in advance of any change so that expectations are clear and students are not unduly surprised or frustrated by changes.	
Use **Absent Student Copymasters** to provide a checklist of materials needed in class so students will have help remembering and be able to focus on the essentials of any lesson or activity. These can also function as short-term contracts so that students are more likely to maintain focus and remain motivated. Use short-term contracts so that students have frequent opportunities to confirm successful learning and behaviors.	
Use the **Warm Up Transparencies** at the beginning of class to help students focus and make the transition to their Spanish class.	
Pair students with good role models in pair work so that they can learn by peer example.	
Build frequent breaks or movement into the class periods so that students maintain interest and energy.	
Give active students roles such as handing out and collecting materials, rearranging chairs, and running errands. This way they learn the importance of responsible contributions to the classroom as a whole and are less restless.	
Teach students polite code words or phrases that they can use so that they can signal when they may not have seen or heard important information. Demonstrate when and how to use these signals effectively.	
Provide a clear view of and close proximity to speakers so that students see and hear everything they need in order to participate successfully in class.	
Give students private space for independent study when appropriate so they are not distracted by other classroom activities. The **@HomeTutor** works well for independent study.	
Have frequent one-on-one conferences so that students know that learning is an ongoing process and that their performance will be evaluated consistently.	
Explain all evaluation and grading requirements and procedures clearly so that students can learn to respect reliability and know what to work for. Provide students with the grading rubrics beforehand.	
Send daily and / or weekly progress notes home. Use the **Family Letters** and **Family Involvement Activities** in the **Unit Resource Book** so that the reinforcement process consistently involves the parents as well.	

Increase frequency of feedback so that students are not discouraged or frustrated by delay between the time they complete a task and the time they are evaluated. The **@HomeTutor** provides students with immediate feedback.	
Have students complete the *Para y piensa* review at the end of each section so that they can see that they have achieved the section objectives and celebrate their accomplishments.	
Provide reading, writing, listening, and speaking activities for each lesson so that students have opportunities for multiple input / output of information.	
Other:	
Other:	
Other:	

Alter assignments

	✔
Allow students to demonstrate understanding by providing oral response in addition to written completion of assignments.	
Use fill-in-the-blank rather than written-answer practice and review questions for students who have difficulty writing, so they have adequate opportunity to concentrate on essential information and perform successfully.	
Allow students to start an assignment earlier or finish it later as needed, so they have added opportunities to succeed and demonstrate understanding.	
Special projects in lieu of assignments:	
Reduced assignments:	
Other:	
Other:	
Other:	

Assessment

	✔
Use short, frequent quizzes such as the **Vocabulary** and **Grammar Quizzes** so that students can maintain better focus and concentration and have frequent opportunities to experience success.	
Use the **Test Generator** or **McDougal Littell Assessment System** to group questions into smaller sections, for example, three instead of five or five instead of ten, and use separate directions for each group of questions so that students more easily maintain focus and more authentically express their acquired knowledge.	
Group similar types of questions together. For example, all questions that ask students to "define" something should be grouped together, so that students get comfortable with one question type before being expected to change to another.	

Allow students to use computer test programs such as **McDougal Littell Assessment System** or word processing for assessment purposes so that students who have difficulty writing have appropriate opportunities to succeed and demonstrate content mastery.	
Provide a "mini-word bank" under the blank or provide a word bank for each test section so that students have clear and easy-to-access choices.	
Use the **Audioscript** to read the Listening Comprehension portions of the test at a slower speed.	
Provide enlarged copies of tests to students with vision problems.	
Allow students with hearing problems to do listening portions of tests using headphones so they can adjust the volume to suit their hearing.	
Provide large blanks for fill-in-the-blank questions so that students with sight and / or motor-control problems have adequate and appropriate opportunities to enter or mark answers legibly.	
Modify your standard test by circling targeted items that the student must answer to demonstrate mastery of core content.	
Permit breaks during tests so that students can more easily maintain concentration and do not become frustrated by the test-taking situation.	
Allow untimed testing so that a sense of being rushed does not interfere with an authentic representation of knowledge. Allow students to start earlier or finish later as needed so they have appropriate opportunities to demonstrate authentic content mastery.	
Other:	
Other:	

Instructional Modifications for At-Risk Language Learners

Name of Student _____ Class _____
Week Starting _____

The following modifications have been made for this student:

Accommodations:	
Customize Materials:	
Manage Behavior:	
Alter Assignments:	
Assessment:	